Foreword

Why is this book important and worth your reading? Simply, it captures a bit of life in the Bitterroot Valley deep in the Rocky Mountains of western Montana. *Son of Montana* is a family story of an eldest son's experiences.

Readers born in the 1940s will find they share many of the same experiences. Readers of the 1950s and 1960s can relate to the ending of this age and the beginning of a new one. Still younger readers will find it easier relating to your grandparents, parents and older siblings. When you see the photo of the old telephone ask them if they had the Kellogg Switchboard and Supply Company's wall telephone too. Share this book with them and learn where it leads in your family history. Listen to their stories before it is too late!

The nation's agriculture shifted away from family farms and local production became nonexistence. As a result young people lost job opportunities and valuable learning experiences. Farming neighborhoods changed to hobby ranches and the owners worked in town at other occupations. This story was the same for many young men and women in communities across the nation during a changing time.

As for my part of the Wax family, I was the youngest son and I walked in my brothers' footsteps. I too experienced the labor intensive farm and lumber mill work and learned a certain work ethic which benefitted me throughout my life.

I thank and appreciate my brother Donald Wax for putting his personal story into this book. It is my story too! It is your story! You will not be disappointed in *Son of Montana*.

Gordon Wax - Stevensville, Montana

Donald R Wax

DEDICATION

I dedicate this book to Bill and Helen Wax (my parents), and to all those that came before me.

Son of Montana

Describes growing up during mid-twentieth century in the Bitterroot Valley of western Montana

Volume I

Donald R Wax

Cover Photos

The front cover photo is in the fall of 1959 looking southeast toward the dry land wheat fields in the foothills of the Sapphire Mountains. Note rock pile and uniform wheat field in the east half of the 50.

The back cover photo is also from 1959 overlooking the Willoughby Creek area off the south side of the Sunset Bench. It is the view we saw when catching the school bus each morning.

CONTENTS

CONTENTS

ACKNOWLEDGMENTS

Curiosity led me to contact the Darold D. Wax family living in Wenatchee, WA, my current home. Wax is a not a common name; we can't prove that we are related. We can trace our respective families back to central Pennsylvania in the early1800s. Our two Wax families also followed similar migration paths westward. Darold is a retired history professor from Oregon State University and as we became better acquainted I felt secure enough to mention what I was doing and asked him to read what I had written. He agreed.

Darold read, edited, offered suggestions and encouragement. The relationship proved most fortunate for me because I was looking for a reviewer about my age.

My sincere thanks to Darold for the many hours he spent assisting me with my project, and for the friendship of Darold and his wife, Mary Ellen.

I also want to thank my wife, Svetlana Rudstein. She encouraged me often, read what I wrote, offered suggestions and helped me find the time to complete this project.

Thank You,

Donald R Wax

INTRODUCTION

Objectives

I want to tell about a place and time in which I was a part: to do a brain dump, a recording of the memories living with my parents in western Montana from 1939 to 1959. It will be necessary to expand a little before and a little after this period to establish a beginning and to provide an ending.

Why would I want to write a memoir? One of the reasons was to help me better understand myself and to get my arms around the larger picture, why I always had a feeling that there was something different about those who were second and third generation Montanans. Why I always felt I was living on the edge of society and needed acceptance.

My audience is another reason. I want my siblings, my children and grandchildren, to be able to experience this period through my eyes. I also want to acknowledge the influence that those I mention had on my life. Your friends, your neighbors and even your enemies provide the limits and guidelines that shape your life.

Methods

I divided my thinking into segments around a group, thing or event. Then I used old photos to prod my brain to recall a more complete picture of this group, thing or event. I often left markers in my descriptions of the photos to help me fit the pieces together. These markers may not mean anything to you.

When addressing each segment I tried to do so chronologically. You will see that this was not always followed and sometimes you will find that I have repeated some things in different segments but with different details. A first reading may not allow fitting all the pieces together easily.

Lastly, I read several books about life in the Montana territory, its history and place as one of 48 states (later 50), and viewed photographs of Montana settlers and wild life during the early 20th century. I also transcribed my mother's diary and Dad's letters before their marriage. All of this will be the chaff I use to help me recall these stories, the foundation for my discussion of this Montanan.

I will use the real names of people in my stories. Most of those mentioned that were my parents age and older are now dead, many my age and younger are still living. I tried not to embarrass anyone and hope that everyone will take what I have written in the same spirit as I wrote it. I am not a negative person and tried not to say negative things about anyone. My goal was to paint as real a picture as possible to contrast with life today.

I also want the stories to move quickly and provide a sense of involvement. Do you feel what I felt? Do you see what I saw? Do you understand what I learned? Do you now think about things differently?

Occasionally I offered some speculation and analysis, and sometimes a look back from where I am today. I feel able to do this after sifting through a lifetime of memories and the experience of knowing other countries and cultures. It is not my intention to argue these points; you can do your own speculation, analysis and looking back.

Son Of Montana

Process

I began collecting family photos after I retired in 1999. There was a large increase in volume after my parents died (2001, 2006) and again after my cousin passed in 2012. As I sorted through the photos and papers I realized many would not survive much longer, and I made a plan to scan and store them in digital form. This turned out to be a major project which required a new computer and scanner.

I bought the equipment in January 2013 and got to work. It was repetitive and boring so I began to recall my life from the period reflected in the photo. Soon the memories became more important than the scanning and I began to write what I remembered. These stories were scattered and disconnected, but seemed interesting enough for me to try to organize them into a more complete history.

I needed a process to do this. I could not organize chronologically without major research because time (day, month and even year) was not important during my youth. I simply could not remember what came first, second, etc. So I began organizing into segments (chapters). I reviewed photos and story snippets to help me remember which allowed me to add detail to each chapter.

Location

Stevensville is located south of Missoula in the Bitterroot Valley in western Montana (Ravalli County). I won't provide any of the history of Stevensville except to say that it was first settled by whites in 1841. You can find information on the internet or at a library if you want to learn more about the history of this area. Search for Stevensville or Ravalli County, Montana.

The Bitterroot Valley is oriented north and south with the Bitterroot mountain range to the west and the Sapphire mountain range to the east. The Bitterroot Mountains rise sharp and bold on the west and the Sapphire Mountains are set back some 5-8 miles to the east from the valley floor. This set back is occupied by several fingers of raised land which separates creek bottom lands of varying width, all connected by rolling foothills to the forested mountains beyond.

One of these fingers of raised land southeast of Stevensville is called the Sunset Bench. This bench up rise begins about two miles east of the Bitterroot River with scrub jack pine and sage brush and continues a gentle upward slope to wider, flatter and more fertile lands. The Sunset Bench occupies this flat area about a mile wide and about four miles long bounded by Burnt Fork Creek to the north and Willoughby Creek to the south. Our home was located here, five miles southeast of Stevensville. Google maps can be used to locate this area.

Go to "896 Pine Hollow Road, Stevensville, MT" on Google Maps, click on the street view and see the driveway to the Wax farm.

I'm always impressed with the view from the Wax farm each time I visit. It is possible to see much of the Bitterroot Valley from Hamilton (south) to Lolo (north) and unobstructed views of the mountain ranges to the east and west. The lights of Victor are visible across the valley. The nighttime glows of Hamilton and Missoula are visible at each end of the valley. We could see storm clouds approaching, forest fires burning, changing fall colors and the descending snow line clearly. It is one of nature's beautiful sights, and it was our home.

People

The people you will learn the most about (other than me) are my parents Bill and Helen Wax, and mentioned often without introduction are my siblings: Norman, Patsy, Dolores, Gordon and Lavon. My brother Norman is one year and one day younger than me. He was closest to me in every respect. We fought and cooperated, worked and played together, friends and companions. Patsy (Patricia, now Pat) is four years younger, Gordon 10 years younger and Lavon 12 years younger.

Others mentioned are relatives, friends, neighbors, classmates and employers.

Photo 1-01 is of: Norman (30), Pat (27), Don (31), Gordon (21) and Lavon (19) in the summer of 1970 in our dining room.

photo 1-02

This photo 1-02 is of Norman, Dad, Pasty and me with Case tractor in the summer of 1946, 24 years earlier than photo 1-01.

Enjoy,

Don Wax

The Beginning

Moving west and a wedding delayed.

To begin The Beginning was not easy; I had a lot of questions and very few answers. My initial thought was simply to say that the Wax family (my grandparents Walter and Carrie, daughter Doris, son Bill and grandson Marion) moved to the Bitterroot Valley in 1936. I was told the reason for leaving the Wax homestead in eastern Montana (Garfield County) was the drought and depression, but that seemed too simple.

My mother and father (Bill Wax) never discussed the move in any depth, and there always seemed to be a certain level of discomfort when responding to questions. I have gone over comments and body language I heard and saw while living at home, and have come to think that the reason for relocating was more complex and involved my Aunt Doris.

When I discovered documents 2-01 and 2-02 among other legal papers I began to draw some conclusions. These are speculative conclusions, but permit me the leeway to state what is on my mind. I may find a different conclusion is more reasonable in the future.

NO. 7—BILL OF SALE

Know All Men By These Presents:

THAT

Walter M. Wax of Cohagen, Garfield County, Montana.

the part...y...... of the first part, for and in consideration of the sum of...........................

....................One and no/loo .... DOLLARS

Lawful money...........of the United States of America, to...... him

in hand paid by............M. William...Wax....of Cohagen, Montana,.

the part...y...of the second part, the receipt whereof is hereby acknowledged, does....by these pres-

ents grant, bargain, sell and convey unto the part...y....of the second part............his

executors, administrators and assigns....all of the following described

Personal property. to wit :-

Twenty head of horses Branded 8X— right shoulder

Twenty-Three head of cattle Branded 8X— right rib

One Hundred Fifty head of sheep branded with a red B

Also all farm machinery such as Drill, Disc, 2 cultivators,

Hay -rake, 3 plows, wagon, Household Furniture , Harness,

Together with the increase from the aforementioned cattle,

Horses , Sheep and all personal property belonging to the party

of the first part and now located upon the East half of

Section Twenty, Township Sixteen north, Range Forty East

of the Montana principal meridian.

document 2-01

Why was there a need for such a bill of sale? Notice that all the livestock conveyed was branded with Dad's brand (reverse B X bar). Normally that would be enough to signify ownership.

According to this bill-of-sale Bill Wax (my father) now owned all the personal property on the my grandfather's homestead.

My father had been farming in partnership with his father since graduating from high school in 1930. The bill-of-sale maybe was to establish a more formal relationship between father and son. Bill Wax owned a nice start for a 22 year old farmer in 1935.

Note document 2-02 (continuation of document 2-01) was

TO HAVE AND TO HOLD the same, to the said part...Y....of the second part,....his.......executors, administrators and assigns, FOREVER; and ....he does do..........., for himself executors, and administrators, covenant and agree to and with said part...Y...of the second part, ...his......executors, administrators and assigns, to warrant and defend the sale of the said property, goods and chattels hereby made, unto the said part...y.... of the second part,......his.......... executors, administrators and assigns, against all and every person and persons whomsoever, lawfully claiming or to claim the same.

IN WITNESS WHEREOF, ...I....have hereunto set........my.... ....hand.........and seal the....4th...........day of...December.......in the year of our Lord one thousand nine hundred...Thirty...Five..........................

Signed, Sealed and delivered in the Presence of

document 2-02

witnessed by R. B. McWilliams (Ray, ex-father-in-law of Doris Wax McWilliams) and Hugh Weimer, a local official (school board, maybe banker?) mentioned in Mom's diary.

This bill-of-sale seems to suggest that there was some kind of money problem and that it was necessary to protect the remaining assets. Aunt Doris is well liked and very outgoing, but had recently (1935?) divorced her first husband, so Doris and her ex-husband (Elton R. McWilliams) may have been involved. I'm going to add Aunt Doris to the list of reasons why the Waxes moved in 1936.

I remember on several occasions Mom talked about Aunt Doris as though she thought that Doris received special treatment and that she had too much influence in the Wax family.

The Wax family (my grandparents Walter and Carrie, daughter Doris, son Bill and grandson Marion) had moved to the Sunset Bench in the spring of 1936. Dad told about pulling a wagon load with the car from Cohagen to Stevensville; it took two days. They must have moved some things by train, too. They occupied the Webster property on the Sunset Bench with house and buildings located on lot 20 (see Maps in the Appendix).

They would later lose this property due to lack of payment, but it is not clear who exactly undertook the obligation, or to whom. The best I can tell it was between Dad and the Federal Land Bank of Spokane, and was just a 'take over the payments' type of agreement.

photo 2-01

Photo 2-01 is from the summer of 1936 just after moving to the Sunset Bench. I think those trees are in the coulee west of our farm where I used to play.

Son Of Montana

Let me back up a little and try to start again after having set the scene as it existed in the summer of 1936 (my father Bill Wax is in Stevensville and Helen Zimmerman (Mom) is still living in Garfield county and teaching school).

My parents were both born in 1913. Their families both homesteaded in Garfield County, Montana. Their formative years were spent in the crucible of the last great frontier tradition of sod busting homesteaders on the prairie of empty eastern Montana. They received most of their schooling between the end of WWI and the beginning of the Great Depression (1918-1930) with little intervention from newspapers or radio connected to the outside world. Both were children of "do without" homesteaders and developed an appreciation for cash during the hard knock years of the 1930s.

Mom and Dad went to high school together and knew each other socially. They had some early affection for each other and may even have courted in the traditional sense of the word. They were very well acquainted and appreciated each other's company, though they had some disagreements later during their married life. I want to fast forward from their early days in eastern Montana to their arrival in western Montana.

The Wax family was well enough established on the Sunset Bench that my mother came with her sister (Aunt Pearl) to visit them in 1937. The Waxes were busy haying the Webster property and perhaps some other land, too.

Photo 2-02 is of Mom on July 4th, 1937 at the Burnt Fork Creek. Dad liked to go fishing in the Burnt Fork when I was young. He cleaned, Mom fried and we ate his catch of Rainbow trout. The Burnt Fork creek was where all irrigation water came from for the Sunset bench.

photo 2-02

Dad's letters to Mom in 1938 (see appendix) tell us more about life for the Wax family during those first years on the Sunset Bench. These photos along with the letters tell us that Mom and Dad were making plans for the future.

Photo 2-03 is dated July 4, 1937. I assume that this is the time that Dad proposed marriage and Mom accepted. It would only be a matter of setting the time and place.

photo 2-03

A few of Dad's letters have survived; I did not find any of Mom's letters, only her diary. I transcribed Dad's letters to digital format and they are in the Appendix.

During the summer of 1938 Mom was taking classes at the State Normal School in Billings (now Montana State University-Billings, MSUB) and Dad was busy haying on the Sunset Bench, so their plan was to get married on Saturday, July 2nd. Dad would travel Thursday afternoon to Billings, pick up Mom on Friday morning, do some shopping and go on to her parent's house near Jordan, Montana. Saturday morning the preacher was scheduled to arrive for the wedding followed by a short honeymoon Saturday night, Sunday and Monday before Mom returned to school on Tuesday. That was the plan, but it didn't work out that way.

They were married not on Saturday but on Sunday, July 3, 1938. Why the change? The lane to Grandpa Zimmerman's house is a

mile in length and crossed the Big Dry Creek. There was a heavy rain Friday night and by Saturday

photo 2-04

morning the creek was flooded. The preacher couldn't cross. He would return the next day to try again. In the meantime the Zimmerman men (Grandpa and Uncle Don) and Dad organized horses and a wagon, and selected a place to ferry across if necessary.

Photo 2-04 is of the Big Dry Creek on that Saturday morning. Two cars are visible on the far shore, photo 2-05. Normally this creek

would have only a few inches to a foot of water flowing in it, when it ran water. It was called the Big Dry Creek because most of the time it didn't have

photo 2-05

Donald R Wax

flowing water.

On Sunday morning (July 3rd) the creek was still high, so the preacher was ferried over to the house in a wagon. I remember seeing a photo of the wagon with the preacher standing in it being ferried across the flooded creek. A quick wash up, a change of clothes and everybody was ready for the ceremony. A short time later Mom and Dad were Mr. and Mrs. Bill Wax.

As far as I know there were no guests at the wedding, only the

photo 2-06

preacher. All of Mom's family was there: Grandpa and Grandma Zimmerman, Uncle Don, Aunts Florence and Pearl. The flooded creek prevented other guests from attending.

Photo 2-06 is their wedding photo with the preacher. Notice how tanned Dad's hands are, and how large. They were a handsome couple in their time.

Now their honeymoon was even shorter, only Sunday night and Monday so Mom could be back in school on Tuesday. Dad returned to the Sunset Bench to continue haying. Mom finished school on the 11th of August, 1938 and soon they were together again. I was born on May 11, 1939. They lived in the hired-help house during their first year or so of marriage.

Photo 2-07 is me in the summer of 1939 (Donald Robert Wax), named after my two uncles (Donald Zimmerman and Robert Wax). This was probably along the west side of the hired-help house.

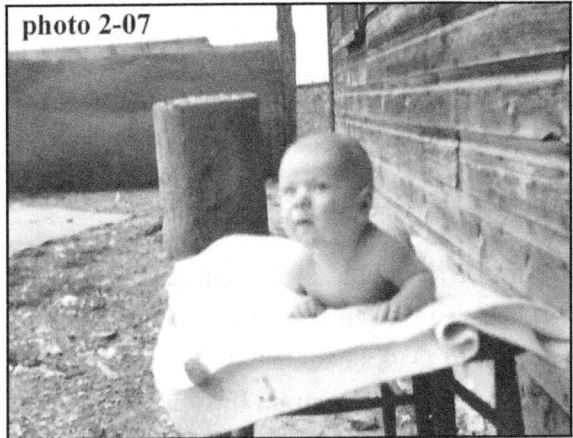

photo 2-07

Grandpa and Grandma Wax and Aunt Doris with cousin Marion moved to Missoula in the spring of 1940. Norman was born on May 12, 1940. I cannot be sure where my parents lived when he was born, but by the fall of 1940 they had a home of their own.

We are now getting close to the end of The Beginning. The late 1930s is the starting point for what follows with an ending at the close of the 1950s.

I will on occasion add my own look back with the experience and wisdom of my seventy-five plus years, giving me the time to review and rehash a life time of memories.

photo 2-08

Photo 2-08 is of Dad with chickens and lambs on the Webster property. The white chickens appear to be new. The dark hen to the right has several chicks in tow. We are looking east southeast in the late afternoon. Note Dad's hat cocked at an angle. The box to Dad's back is laying nests for the eggs. The field in the back is planted to grain in the spring of 1939, just after I was born. Will this be the stubble field I was once lost in?

photo 2-09

Photo 2-09 is my Dad moving hay in 1937 on property across the road from the Wax farm. I believe we are looking west-northwest, and the trees in the background are in the coulee west of our house where we once looked for a mountain lion.

The Land

A short history, purchases, making it produce.

The area where the Wax farm was located first came to private ownership on December 9, 1887 when the General Land Office issued a patent to Milton Baker and John Baker. The Bakers filed for water rights from the Burnt Fork Creek and began the distribution network that provided irrigation water for most of the Sunset Bench lands. Today, one of the distribution ditches of the Sunset Irrigation District is called the Baker ditch. These lands were divided, sold and mortgaged a number of times to/from several Bakers.

By the early 1900s the Smith and Whitesitt families had bought and sold smaller tracts. In 1909 the Sunset Orchard Land Company (SOLC) began to acquire this land and to develop 10 acre orchard lots (see Maps in Appendix). SOLC was a Montana company created by investors from Minneapolis, Minnesota.

The Minneapolis investors via SOLC had already sold, mortgaged and foreclosed on these orchards lots several different times when Frank Webster and wife bought lots 18-20 from Emil Hayek in December 1919, subject to a mortgage of $2000.00 from the Federal Land Bank of Spokane.

It appears that the Websters tried to acquire additional lots and perhaps did hold some type of claim to lots 9-13, 21 and 23 (total of 100 acres) at the time of his death in 1932. The road in front of the Webster farm was called Webster Lane.

When Frank Webster died his will left the estate to his wife and daughter. Mrs. Webster was named executrix and believed the estate contained 100 acres plus machinery and animals, valued at about $3700. Appraisers found lots 13, 18-20, 21 and 23 (only 60 acres) worth $3000 in September, 1932. No further action occurred until June, 1935 when it was noted that taxes from 1931 to 1935 were delinquent, a total of $530.

The Federal Land Bank of Spokane foreclosed on the $2000 mortgage of Emil Hayek in November, 1935, and all subsequent owners of lots 18-20. Ben and Evelyn Magini were added to the list of owners in January, 1936.

The Federal Land Bank filings indicated that the first 25 semi-annual payments were made which would bring us up to the death of Frank Webster. The remaining balance plus interest was now $2369.96. A Sheriff's sale happened June 12, 1936 and resulted in the property being returned to the Federal Land Bank of Spokane.

The Frank Webster estate was lost to back taxes and foreclosures. A Marian Pugh foreclosed on the Webster estate and gained control of lot 13 before 1936.

The preceding is a summary of the Abstract of Title records for lots 9-13 and 21-23, which was prepared for Dad in 1950.

How do we determine what agreements were made and by whom in 1936 when my grandparents Wax arrived on the Sunset Bench with their son Bill, daughter Doris and grandson Marion? My conclusion now is that Bill Wax (in cooperation with his parents) simply agreed to take over the payments on the Webster property, perhaps from Ben and Evelyn Magini who probably agreed to take over the payments from somebody else, perhaps the Webster estate.

It was during the Great Depression and no one had any money; the Federal Land Bank just wanted to receive the payments. There are no court records to indicate any formal agreements such as deeds, claims, or mortgages. The court records always referred to lots 18-20 as the Webster property.

Photo 3-01 is of Dad and Aunt Doris at their Sunset Bench home in 1937.

There were 60 acres on the Webster property, and maybe more available that could have been farmed because some lots appear to have been abandoned and unoccupied.

Photo 3-02 is probably from 1937 and is looking west down the driveway of the Webster farm. That is a boom type hay stacker, and is located across the road in what was known to me as the Dayton property. Dad mentions haying the 150 acres across the road in one of his letters. I don't know who owned the property when this photo was taken.

We used this type of stacker until 1949, maybe even this exact one. It was home-made from lodge pole pine, blacksmith constructed iron bands with store bought cable and pulleys. I drove the 1945 Case tractor to pull loads of hay up with this stacker in the summers of 1946, 47 and 48.

photo 3-03

Photo 3-03 is of my grandparents Wax in the shade of a tree in 1937. This house burned down in the early 1940s, when it was unoccupied. The house was not large and was of the craftsman type popular in the early 1920s. Besides the house, there was a cow barn for milking and hay storage, a chicken house, a granary and a small house for the hired help. There was also a concrete cistern beside the ditch at the east end of this lot that fed water to a trough at the barn for the cows and horses. Dad makes reference to this cistern in one of his letters.

photo 3-04

Mom and Dad lived in this small house for less than two years (photo 3-04), and then moved into the main house after Grandpa Wax and family moved to Missoula in the spring of 1940.

The Waxes (Dad in partnership with Grandpa) gave up this place due to non-payment. It seems now that it probably was the correct decision considering the amount of the outstanding debt, approximately $2900 of loan, interest and back taxes.

The transactions that would eventually comprise Mom and Dad's farm began April 10, 1937 when Grandma Wax received via Quit Claim Deed lot 13 from a Marian Pugh which was transferred to Dad on September 29, 1941. Dad signed a contract for lots 9 and 21 on June 13, 1939; Grandpa Wax took a contract on Lot 10 on the same day. Mom signed a contract for lot 22 on October 2, 1939. Dad signed a contract for lot 11 on September 3, 1940 and a contract for lot 12 and 23 on June 17, 1941. See maps in the Appendix.

Mom and Dad had contracts on 70 acres (lots 9, 11-13 and 21-23); Grandpa Wax had a contract on lot 10 (all contracts were for five years). The county owned these lots because of non-payment of taxes. Mom and Dad were farming 80 acres of their own by the fall of 1941.

They made all the payments on their various contracts for 7 lots; Grandpa Wax did the same. They borrowed money to buy the Case tractors in 1945 and 1948, and a Chevrolet car in 1948. Loans for the tractors and car were paid off and in 1950 they needed to get a proper mortgage on their farm which they thought was 80 acres.

Somehow they forgot that Grandpa Wax had the title to lot 10. Aunt Doris got involved and soon it became a big disagreement about who owned lot 10. As I remember, Mom and Dad did pay some additional money to get a clear title to lot 10. Dad immediately hired a land attorney to build an Abstract of Title for the 80 acres. Each time he bought additional land after that he also bought an Abstract of Title. It was interesting to search through those abstracts.

The next land to be farmed was 20 acres on a share crop basis from

Oscar Enebo, an insurance agent in Stevensville. Dad share cropped this land from about the mid-1940s to the early 1970s. There was an Enebo girl (Millie) a few years ahead of me in school.

The term 'share crop' comes from the method of renting land in which the crop is divided between the land owner and the farmer. On the Sunset Bench the division was a 40-60, 50-50 or 60-40 arrangement depending on the crop type and the condition of the soil and improvements. If the land was to be converted from pasture to grain the farmer usually got 60% for the first year, 50% for the following years of grain, 50% for alfalfa or clover crops and 40% if it was just a grass hay crop. The land owner could take his share of the crop, or the farmer paid the owner cash.

In 1950 Dad bought lot 17 from Jack Prather who had a dairy farm down on Burnt Fork Creek near Stevensville. I went to school with several Prather children: Ross, David and Marcia (a local doctor today). Prather sold because it was just too far from his dairy. Dad was farming 110 acres in the fall of 1958 when I joined the Army.

In 1964 Dad purchased 45 acres from Leonard and Shirley Smith at the corner of Drift In Lane and Pine Hollow Road, and then he added lot 18 and half of lot 19 from the remains of the Murray estate in 1971.

That same year (1971) my bother Gordon bought lots 24-26 from the remains of the Potter estate, which Dad share cropped. In 1975 I bought the 40 acres between the Enebo 20 and Dad's 45 from Wayne Dayton, which Dad share cropped. When Dad retired in 1980, he was farming 220 acres, 150 of his own and 70 he share cropped from his sons.

The following is from the Abstract of Title for lots 18 and south half of 19 (18+S ½19). This was the more interesting Abstract of

Title notes because these people were neighbors and well known in the Stevensville area.

Marvin (Buzz) Murray and wife bought the Webster property (lots 18-20) in July, 1950 from the Federal Land Bank of Spokane. Buzz Murray died in January 1965 and his new wife lost control of the estate through court actions to Myrtle Pope Potter, Buzz's oldest sister. A claim of $18,500 against the estate was brought by Buzz's former wife in June, 1968. The property was divided in half to protect the interest of the claimant. The court took action to remove Myrtle Potter as Administratrix because of inaction. Soon after, Myrtle died on October 1, 1970. In 1971 Buzz's other sisters (Mae, Martha, Minnie) gained control of their half of the property (18+S ½19). Mom and Dad signed an agreement to purchase this property in January, 1971.

The estates of Buzz Murray and Myrtle Potter were now combined, and it was quiet large with an initial appraisal of $365,656. Buzz owned the bar where he spent so much time during the years he lived on the Webster property, plus additional property in Stevensville. Myrtle owned a number of rental properties and her house in Stevensville plus lots 24-26. In July, 1971 the heirs petitioned the court to distribute the remainder of the estate valued at $241,726.

Buzz Murray owned the Webster property from 1950 until he died. Myrtle and her sister-in-law (Mavis Potter) also lived on the Sunset Bench for several years in the 1940s. We were not close to Buzz Murray, Myrtle and Mavis Potter, although they visited on occasion and were neighborly. Mavis Potter lived with Myrtle for many years and was granted a share of the estate. Myrtle had a checkered reputation and Dad often make unkind remarks about her.

To make the land productive again Dad broke up the sod on any new acreage and planted a grain crop: oats, barley or wheat. After three or four crops of grain he seeded it back to clover or alfalfa. This crop rotation allowed the soil to recover and continue producing a good yield for each crop.

Dad broke the sod with a John Deere chisel point cultivator (we called a 'quack machine') by going over the field three or four times, first on the compass lines and then on the diagonal, each time digging a little deeper. The soil was now loose and broken up and then he would plow and harrow. The soil was now fine and ready for the leveler, usually once each on the diagonals followed by the drill (planting seed) and packer (compact and smooth).

photo 3-05

Irrigating was an activity new to those from eastern Montana; Dad appears to be in rubber boots (photo 3-05) probably in 1938. The granary is over his left shoulder. He is standing at the northwest corner of the house in photo 3-03.

Between planting and the first irrigation he would eyeball the lay of the field and make a mental note of all the ridges and hollows, then map a set of lateral ditches in his head.

Dad built a survey rig from a straight grained board of 16ft. He attached a leg on each end, one leg an inch or so longer than the other. In the center of the board he attached a carpenter's level and with the longer leg in the direction he wanted the water to run, he marked the ground with his shovel when the level indicated level. Then he used a single bottom plow to make laterals to redistribute the water to maintain an even flow over the entire field. He used horses to pull the plow until the horses were replaced by the 1948 Case tractor. Guess who was recruited to drive the tractor?

I was once on the tractor and Dad was on the plow handles. He wanted to make a lateral in the pasture in the back half of lot 22. But he did not mark it with the survey board as he did in the grain field, just telling me to go left or right to follow the path that was in his head. We went over that path several times while he yelled louder and louder each time and I tried to get the tractor on the right path. Finally I got off the tractor and began to cry (couldn't please father). I was only about 10 years old. That was the last time I remember crying. I decided that I was not going to be hurt like that or cry again.

Dad did work very hard and was somewhat of a perfectionist. He walked the fields in the soft dirt and mud to make sure that every inch of the field received an even soaking of water. I remember when Norman and I had our bed on the porch; Dad would pull on his boots and leave the house at first light to check on his irrigation water. It woke us up! His grain crops were so even in growth (no dry spots) that the neighbors made comments about how pretty they looked. And it paid off. Dad's grain crops gave some of the highest yields on the Sunset Bench.

Maybe I need to add a few words of explanation about this method of irrigating, called flood irrigation. Two or three canvas dams are used to empty the water from a supply ditch onto the field in a manner that causes the water to spread evenly. The water flows downhill drifting to one side or the other depending on the lay of the land. Laterals will interrupt the drift and redistribute the water evenly again. In this manner the water flowed evenly across the entire field allowing for an even soaking of the soil. When the water flowed out of the end of the field it was time to move the dams downstream and repeat the process.

Over the years Dad learned how to best irrigate each piece of land that he farmed. After Dad died in 2006 we rented the land to a neighbor, Mark McFadgen. Mark is the third generation of his family to live on the Sunset Bench (he understands irrigating) and he told me that Dad's land was very easy to irrigate.

One chore related to irrigating that we enjoyed doing was burning the dead grass from the ditches in the spring. Each spring when the dead grass was dry enough Norman and I helped Dad burn it. Dad started a fire in the grass and we made little torches from bunches of grass spreading the fire down the ditch. Sometimes Dad used an oil soaked rag for a torch. Rolled up and stuck on a fork, it was used to set the fire. Norman and I ran up and down the ditch bank with the fork setting the grass on fire. Fun for boys!

The last chore in the spring to get ready for irrigation was to clean the sod from the sides of the ditch. This allowed the water to flow free in the ditch. Before 1948 Dad did the cleaning by hand. He sharpened a shovel to a knife edge and chopped the sod from the banks. He carried a file in his pocket and stopped to sharpen again after hitting rocks. Norman and I ran ahead to lift big rocks out of the ditch.

Beginning in1949 we had a manual ditcher blade that we pulled behind the tractor for this job. I drove the tractor and Dad handled the ditcher with two blades fastened in a "V" shape, one blade slid on the ditch bottom while Dad guided the other cutting sod from the ditch bank. The first year or two, Dad positioned the tractor for me to drive. Later I was able to get the tractor astraddle the ditch without his help and the job moved along more quickly.

Breaking up the sod created another chore unfamiliar to those from the eastern Montana dry land; the buried rocks were pulled to the surface. Many rocks on the surface had been picked up over the years and thrown into piles in the field. The eastern half of the 50 had one of those big piles right in the middle of the field. The rocks and the rock piles always irritated Dad. After the field was plowed and planted we picked the rocks and threw them onto the piles.

One spring weekend we were picking rocks - Dad and us four children. Patsy was about 10, Gordon about four, Norman and I were 13 and 14. Dad drove the tractor and wagon to the area to be picked and then Patsy drove the tractor in a straight line across the field. Dad worked one side of the wagon and Norman and I worked the other side. We could really pick a lot of rocks this way compared to Dad picking alone.

There was a washed-out spot in the Baker ditch at the east end of lot 23 where Dad wanted to dump a load of rocks. We drove to the ditch, dumped the load and started back to the field. On the way back Patsy was driving while Dad stood on the draw bar behind the seat helping her cross an irrigation ditch. Gordon was riding on the wagon tongue as if he were riding a horse. It all seemed innocent enough until the tractor wheels dropped into the ditch. As the wagon tongue tipped downward, Gordon tipped forward, grabbed the tongue to steady himself and one of his hands touched the draw bar. His middle finger got caught between the draw bar and the tongue iron, and pinched off the end joint of his finger. That ended the rock picking and instead resulted in a trip to the doctor to stitch up the finger.

I remember doing some of the sod busting in the spring 1952 when Dad broke up the grass hay field on the east side of the 50. I was old enough to run the tractor with the quack machine. The quack machine had two mechanical clutches for raising and lowering half of the cultivator points. Dad attached a rope to each clutch lever and the other end to the tractor seat. He could grab the ropes and trip the clutches at the same time when turning at the end of the field.

I was not strong enough to trip both clutches at the same time. Instead I used both hands to trip one and then the other, quickly turning to reduce the throttle and turn the tractor to start a new row. I tripped one clutch at a time to lower the points, and returned the throttle to full speed. My head lands were always about twice the size of Dad's. A head land is the space at the end of the field where the turns are made.

The front halves of lots 21 and 23 and the back half of 22 were also farmed in the same manner. The land that always remained in pasture was the back half of lots 21 and 23. Dad used this same method to farm the 45 acres, lot 18+S ½19, Gordon's 30 acres and my 40 acres

In the 1940s Dad divided the 50 acres (lots 9-13) into eastern and western halves with an irrigation ditch. The entire west half was planted in grain in the spring of 1945. He and Grandpa Wax cut the grain with a grain binder. This half of the 50 acres was farmed the most often because the east half was rocky and the soil was shallow.

photo 3-06

Photo 3-06 is of Dad on his new tractor in the fall of 1945. You can see how high the grain is and how much straw will be in those bundles. All the hard work preparing the land paid off.

During the war years Grandpa Wax lived in Missoula and worked for the railroad, but came to help when he could. Dad was busy with the farm activities, milking, feeding and tending the animals, breaking up the sod and planting the crops.

In 1964 he hired a Caterpillar tractor to dig holes to bury the rock piles on the 50 and the 45. When he retired in 1980 he had 220 acres of very fine hay, grain and pasture land, all under flood irrigation.

Dad was a good steward of the land; perhaps the best in the Sunset Bench. The land is a farmer's biggest capital investment. It is what sustains him. Dad developed a strong attachment to the soil, an attachment I shared.

Donald R Wax

Document 3-01 is a copy of one of the purchase contracts.

CONTRACT OF SALE

This agreement, made and entered into this ____3rd____ day of ____September____ 19__40_, between the County of Ravalli, of the State of Montana, hereinafter called the Vendor, and ____W.W. Wax____ _____ of ____Stevensville____

hereinafter called the Purchaser, witnesseth:

That whereas, the Board of County Commissioners of Ravalli county, Montana, by an order entered upon the minutes of its proceedings on the ____3rd____ day of ____May____, 19__39__, ordered sold at public auction at the front door of the court house the property hereinafter described; and,

Whereas, 20 days' notice of sale was given by the Board of County Commissioners as required by law by publication thereof in a newspaper printed in the county and by posting copies of such notices in at least five public places in the county, and which notice among other things stated the fair market value of said property to be $__50.00__ as determined and fixed by the Board of County Commissioners at the time of making said order for sale; and,

Whereas, there were no bidders for said property on date of sale and now comes ~~become the highest bidder for said property and bid the sum hereinafter set out;~~ W.W. Wax and offers to purchase said property for 90% of the appraised value;

Now, therefore, it is hereby mutually agreed that the Vendor, in consideration of the payment, covenants and agreements on the part of the purchaser, hereinafter contained, agrees to sell and convey unto the Purchaser (and the Purchaser agrees to buy), all of that certain lot and parcel of land situated in the City of _____ County of Ravalli, and State of Montana bounded and described as follows, to-wit:

Lot Eleven (11) block Two (2) Sunset Orchards, according to the official plat

of the survey thereof on file and of record in the office of the County Clerk and

Recorder of Ravalli County, Montana.

For the sum of ____Forty five and No/100 - - - - -____ Dollars, ($__45.00__) in lawful money of the United States of America; and the said Purchaser, in consideration of the premises, agrees to pay to said Vendor the sum of ____Forty five and No/100____

Dollars ($__45.00__) in such lawful money, as follows, to-wit:

____Nine and No/100 - - - - -____ Dollars ($__9.00__) on the execution of this contract;
____Seven and 20/100____ Dollars ($__7.20__) on the __3rd__ day of ____September____ 19__41_;
____Seven and 20/100____ Dollars ($__7.20__) on the __3rd__ day of ____September____ 19__42_;
____Seven and 20/100____ Dollars ($__7.20__) on the __3rd__ day of ____September____ 19__43_;
____Seven and 20/100____ Dollars ($__7.20__) on the __3rd__ day of ____September____ 19__44_;
____Seven and 20/100____ Dollars ($__7.20__) on the __3rd__ day of ____September____ 19__45_;

and the balance, _____ Dollars ($_____), on the _____ day of_____ 19____; together with interest at the rate of ____Four____ per cent (__4__%) per annum from this date on all deferred payments, which interest shall be due and paid annually thereon on the __3rd__ day of ____September____ 19__41_ of each year hereafter during the life of this contract.

document 3-01

Our House

Expansion and rearrangement

The Wax family farm house was built over many years as more space was needed. As the family grew, the house grew, providing a home for the seven of us. I will try to recall as best I can the history of our house from the time of my first memories until the time I left home. This story is not augmented with formal research and I did not collaborate with anyone else. My siblings may remember things differently.

This account should probably start with Mom and the $600 she saved during her six years of teaching school in eastern Montana. She taught from 1932 to 1938 in one room schools on the prairie of Garfield County in eastern Montana. She kept photos of her classes (students in grades 1-8), which ranged in size from about 6 to 16. She then had the money to sign the contract for lot 22 (see document 4-01) which had the apple house, and probably buy the construction materials to build their first home. She occasionally mentioned that the home place was her contribution to the farm, usually when discussions between Mom and Dad were somewhat tense.

Dad built the main part of the house sometime during the fall of 1940, and they began to live there on a permanent basis by the end of 1940. The main part of the house was 18x20ft. The original plan was for it to become the garage when a new permanent house was built later, which explains the size.

I made several drawings which show the floor plans of the house

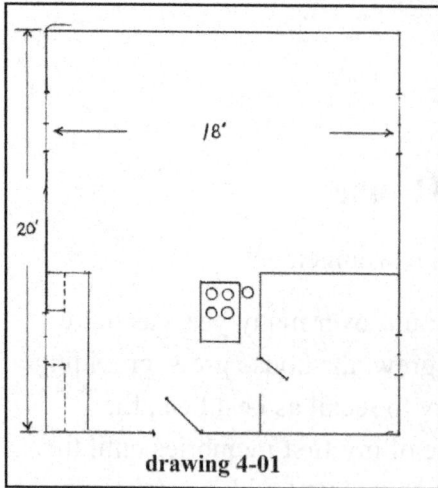

drawing 4-01

and placed them near the descriptions of each expansion. I hope these will make it easier to visualize the size and shape of our house.

Photo 4-01 is of Norman, me and cousin Wayne Burchett taken in the late fall of 1940. This shows the west side with the first layer of boards before the tongue & groove siding was added.

This initial construction was built on a block and rock foundation. It was positioned on the compass lines with the door facing south and was divided into three parts: a kitchen in the southwest corner with cook stove toward the center of the house, a room to the

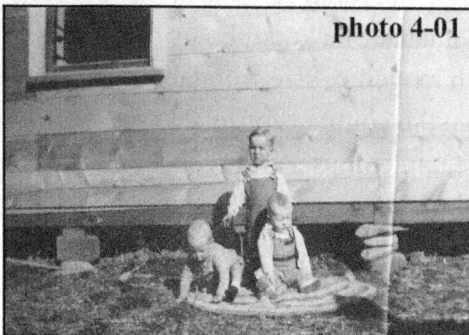

photo 4-01

southeast corner behind the stove, and living room to the north end of the house. I assume that my brother (one year younger) and I slept in the room behind the stove as this would have been the warmest room.

The original entrance was just a set of wooden steps up to the door, which was positioned more or less in the center of the kitchen. There was a small window in the kitchen facing west, a small window in the room behind the stove facing east, two large windows on the opposite (east-west) walls of the living room. This was the house we lived in for the first couple of years after moving to Mom's lot 22.

Photo 4-02 is of Norman, Mom, Dad and me in front of our new house. Some details to note: Dad holding his felt

photo 4-02

Stetson hat, Mom in an apron, kerosene lantern at the upper right edge of photo hanging on the wall, leather strap on Dad's belt to watch pocket holding the Hamilton watch and that wide belt, and the hat line between Dad's forehead and face.

There is one detail I want to describe for you now, the cabinetry. Dad built the kitchen cupboards and a corner cupboard for the living area. The corner cupboard was first located in the northwest corner (upper left); it was moved to the southeast corner (lower right) after the last expansion when this room became our dining room.

Dad purchased a load of number two fir flooring which he used to construct the grain bins in the apple house. From this load he selected the best pieces to make the cabinets. Dad had only basic hand tools for woodworking: saws, square, plane, chisel, hammer, rasp, brace and bits. He was not a professional woodworker, but he was skilled enough to build functional and durable cabinets for our house.

Dad had learned some woodworking skills in high school shop class where he built a chest of drawers. I always thought the chest of drawers that we boys used for our shirts, socks, sweaters and underwear was factory made until one day he told me where it came from. It always surprised me what he could do with basic hand tools.

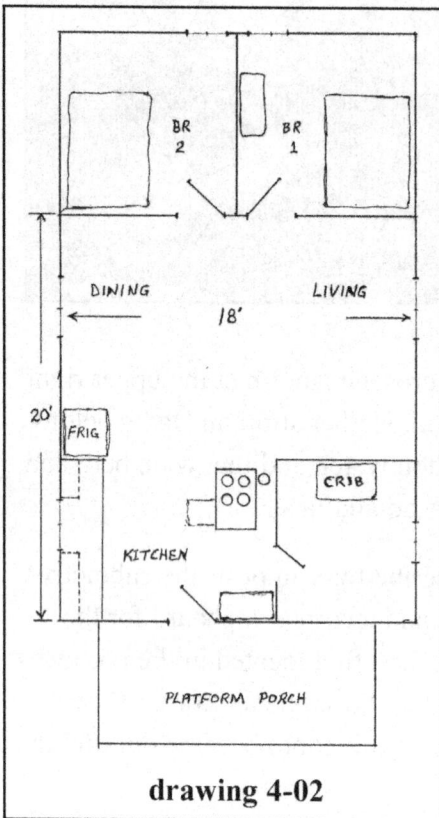

A 9x18ft expansion to the north end of the house added two bedrooms. I don't know when this addition was built, maybe in the fall of 1943 after my sister Patsy was born. I believe that is when the fir tongue and groove siding was installed. A concrete foundation was poured and the house was now nine feet longer.

There were two windows next to the dividing wall near the center of the north wall, and two doors next to each other near the center of the wall to the living room. This was to provide flow through ventilation and allow room along the outside walls for the beds.

drawing 4-02

Mom and Dad slept in bedroom one and my brother and I slept in bedroom two. Baby sister Patricia slept in the room behind the kitchen stove for the next year or so.

A clay pipe and brick chimney was built from about chest high up through the ceiling and roof to the outside. The cook stove stovepipe entered the chimney up near the ceiling. A wood heater was added beside the stove with its stovepipe attached to the same chimney. This heater was one of those black tin metal types of the most inexpensive kind and was not very friendly to young fingers, but we learned quickly.

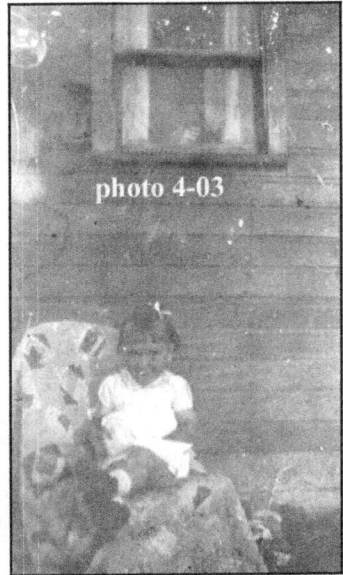

photo 4-03

Photo 4-03 is of my sister Patsy, probably in fall 1944. You can see the tongue & groove siding is now installed, but not yet painted. You can see the nail heads on the unpainted boards. I am convinced that this photo is a reverse of the negative as you can see the electric meter in the upper left corner. It should be to the right of the kitchen window, and Patsy should be facing southwest for best light.

The last addition during the war years was an open wooden porch to the south. This provided additional living space during the summer months and work space all year round. I remember falling asleep on this porch in the summer sun when I was five years old. It felt so nice and warm.

There was a storage box for fire wood, space to store the water cans, some hooks for clothing, space for a washing machine and a place to brush off before entering the house. A pair of water cans (10 gallon milk cans) were filled at the well and carried in a wheel barrow special built to carry two cans. It was where the washing was done, often by hand with tub and washboard.

Our first washing machine was made of wood and operated by a lever that attached to a flywheel connected to the washing mechanism. A hand crank operated the wringer mechanism. It may have been a 1930s Maytag which at one time was powered by a small gasoline engine. This machine was replaced with a new electric motor-driven all metal washer before any more changes were made to the house. The clothes line was a few steps to the east of the porch.

I don't know if Dad had help doing all this construction. I remember that Grandpa Wax was often here helping for a few days or a week at critical times. I always enjoyed the time when Grandpa Wax was here because you could really see the progress. They worked well together, a father and son team.

photo 4-04

Photo 4-04 is during the spring of 1945 and shows Patsy, Mom and Norman beside our freshly painted house. You can see on the porch a wood box, wash tub, bucket, broom and water can behind the tub. Also visible are the incoming power lines to the left and continuing to the apple house on the right. On the far right side you see a tall thin pole which supported the radio antenna (more about the antenna in The Outbuildings). Just to the right of the living room window at the top you can see the ceramic insulator for the telephone wire. The telephone was on the wall just inside, a hand crank wall model. About a dozen neighbors shared this line (a one wire system), so the calling ring was rather complex. Ours was three long rings followed by five short rings. We always paid close attention when the phone rang to be sure we counted off the correct number of rings.

This is the way the house looked when the excavation began for the basement: a four room house with fir tongue and groove siding painted light gray with dark green trim and a green cedar shingle roof with open front porch. It was a nice home for the five of us. During the war years building materials were difficult to buy, but somehow Dad was able to build this house during those years.

In the summer of 1945 more building materials became available, so a new basement was planned and built during the fall of 1945. The porch was moved off to the side. The house was raised up using a hydraulic jack and supported by wood blocks and posts.

My brother and I were now five and six years old and full of energy. We were often scolded and told not to run inside the house because we might cause it to fall off the posts. I was in the first grade and Norman not yet in school. Our baby sister Patsy was two plus. Can you imagine a family of five living in an 18x29ft house raised three feet above ground supported by posts?

Dad excavated the basement area by hand using a pick and shovel, and a horse drawn dirt scoop. The basement area was only under the 18x20ft section - the bedroom addition would have only a concrete foundation. Dad filled the dirt scoop, sometimes on his knees, then pulled the scoop with the horses and dumped the dirt around the perimeter of the apple house. Grandpa Wax was here to help on his free days. He worked for the railroad at the time.

The gravel needed for the concrete was hauled from a gravel pit more than two miles away on the western edges of the Sunset Bench. Dad built a wooden box for the wagon which sat inside the wagon bolsters; the floor was of loose planks which were twisted upright to dump the load. It was a rather long, narrow and shallow box which provided for fairly even distribution of the load. The gravel for the well casing was probably hauled in the same wagon and with the same team of horses.

Dad told about the horses pulling the load up the Kester Hill, a short steep hill which began immediately after a 90 degree right corner. Dad had two teams of horses, a smaller well matched team of beige/grey mares (Cap and Daisy according to Norman) and a larger ill-matched pair named Tony and Prince. He used the smaller team because they worked well together and were very dependable. He told how they stretched out and threw themselves into the load until their stomachs almost touched the ground. He said he would jump off the wagon and go to the rear to help push, urging the team on verbally and with grunts and groans. Making it up this hill was a "do or die" situation. If they should stop there was no way they could start again and would be drawn down the hill backwards and out of control.

He hauled gravel for the basement and a driveway to the main road about 100 feet to the west. Dad built the forms for the first layer of wall. The cement was delivered, and concrete prepared in an electric-motor driven hand-mixer one wheel barrow full at a time. The footer was poured first, and then the walls were poured in eighteen inch increments to a height of about seven feet. The floor was poured next sloping toward the southwest corner for drainage. Last, a set of concrete steps were poured out the southeast corner going south then turning west at the midway point. The house was then set down on the new concrete walls, and the outside was backfilled with excavated dirt.

The basement walls were never sealed against water; when irrigation water ran near the house it would leak into the basement. This never created a big problem because Dad had made a small channel in the concrete floor near the wall to carry the water to the drain at the southwest corner. The main floor area of the basement remained free of water.

The war was over, materials and products were available, farmers were making money, and the Wax family was growing.

The open porch area was enclosed and made permanent. A concrete foundation was poured and the porch completed adding 9x18ft to the south. It was built with a hip roof so it always appeared to be a porch, not an extension of the house. It covered the basement steps providing a weather protected entrance to the basement.

A wood storage box was built to the right of the kitchen door, clothes hooks were added above the wood box, and a small shelf and gun rack were above the clothes hooks. Over the deep part of the basement steps was an elevated shelf for storage. Hundred pound bags of sugar and flour were stored here as well as other supplies. There were three windows, one on the west wall, and one on each side of the door. These were horizontal slider windows which would later be changed to vertical double hung windows.

On this new porch to the left of the kitchen door was space for a bed, where my brother and I slept (he by the wall, I on the aisle side) when the bathroom was completed. My two sisters Patsy and Dolores (born March 8, 1946) slept in bedroom two and Mom and Dad in the bedroom one.

The room behind the stove was converted into a bathroom. A tub was installed along the north wall, a toilet in the southeast corner and a wash basin in the southwest corner. A door was installed and

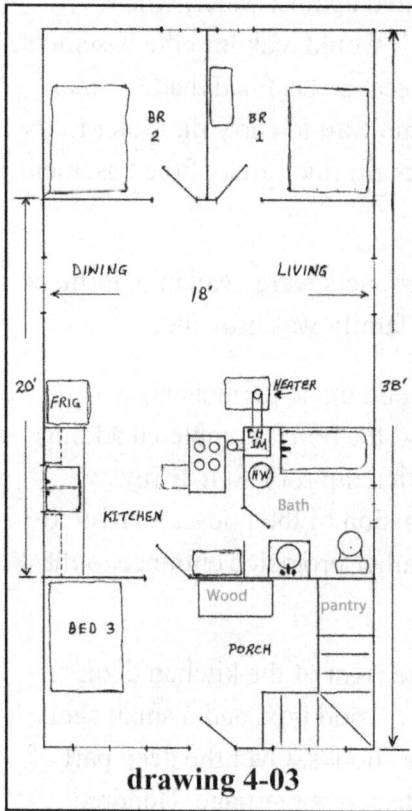

a hot water tank was placed at the head of the tub. Water was plumbed to the tank, tub, toilet, basin, kitchen sink and basement. The hot water was heated in a water jacket (manifold) on the side of the fire box of the kitchen stove. The tank held 40 gallons, and the water could vary tremendously from cold to hot depending on usage and how long the stove was burning.

Cast iron sewer pipe was installed in the basement to drain the bathroom and kitchen. Dad had to cut out a hole in the floor of the porch to install the sewer pipes. He dug under the porch foundation to the bottom of the basement foundation to connect the sewer pipe and drain pipe to the septic tank. He dug under the driveway too, as it was only a few feet from the front steps of the porch, and the space for the septic tank which drained from an open pipe into the coulee about 75' south of the house. It was far enough away that the odor seldom reached the house.

The trench was so deep near the house that the bank was well above Dad's head. Norman and I were scolded many times for playing on the excavated dirt and knocking dirt back into the trench. One time we knocked a rock back into the trench and broke a sewer pipe made of clay pottery. We were punished with a few quick lashes by his belt. It was not the only time that he would

drawing 4-03

have to remove his belt.

Dad dug a trench from the well to the house (about 70 feet) to connect the water. A new pump system was installed in the pump house which supplied constant water pressure. When it was all finished we had running water in the house, indoor toilet, plenty of hot water and a bath tub. No more heating enough water in a bucket on the stove to take the chill off the galvanized tub in the middle of the kitchen floor to bathe, or bathing after those smaller or less dirty than you.

Dad, my brother and I (the men) were still to use the outside and outhouse for our business. The outhouse was located in the northeast corner of the back yard. The men didn't go to the outhouse except for a number two; we managed a number one to the east of the house or the outhouse. Don't know if anybody was looking! The men gradually began to use the indoor toilet four or five years later, and after about ten years we were regularly using the indoor toilet when it was free

The basement was now part of the house. The washing machine was moved into the basement and food storage was moved from the apple house basement. The canned food was stored on shelves along parts of the west and north walls. The washing was done in the southwest corner near the floor drain. Potatoes and carrots were stored along the east wall. The center area was used as needed, sometimes with table for cutting and processing meat, or with a bed or cot.

photo 4-05

Photo 4-05 is of Norman and me in 1947. You can see the outhouse to right. In the right foreground there are several planks used to contain gravel for making concrete. It appears as though the clothes lines were removed (or moved) during construction as they are not visible in this photo. A board is missing on the bottom left of the porch wall.

This was a big improvement over the way the house was before the basement. Mom could wash clothes inside, not outside on the open porch. Food preparation was more convenient because all food and fuel was stored just a few steps from the kitchen. A trip to the toilet for Mom and my sisters was quicker and much more comfortable. It gave us room for expansion on special occasions when extra space was needed, and for drying clothes in cold or wet weather.

I remember taking a pair of jeans from the clothes line that was frozen stiff as a board, then trying to dry them next to that black tin heater before going to school one morning. They were still damp on the way to the bus.

Photo 4-06 is of Grandma and Grandpa Zimmerman with me, Norman, Dolores, plus Ronnie and Verna Schmidt (my cousins). It

was probably taken in fall 1947. To the right side of photo you can see the newly added porch

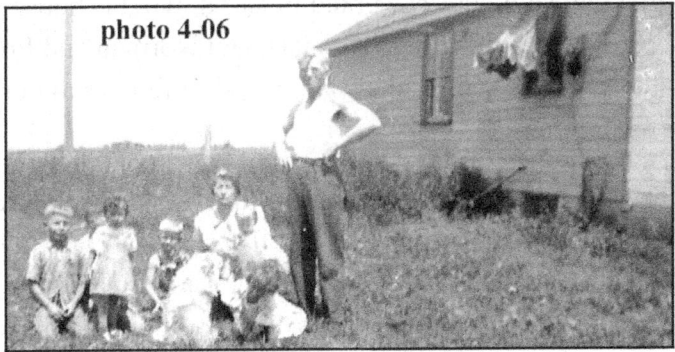

photo 4-06

and an awning over the kitchen window. Below the kitchen window you can see the window to the basement.

Also notice the overgrown grass and the potato fork handle leaning against the wall just to the left of the basement window. Norman and I were supposed to cut the grass with the push mower. Then we raked the clippings with the potato fork using it like a dump rake. The mower was not easy to push which is why we didn't quite finish the job.

I don't recall that we had any way to cool the house on hot summer days except for east breezes after sunset. The kitchen sink was behind that west-facing awning where mother spent many hours preparing food and washing dishes.

The next major change to the premises began in the winter and spring of 1950. Dad built a garage and wood shed south of the back yard. My brother and I were moved to the northeast corner of the garage for sleeping (more about sleeping in the garage in The Outbuildings).

Gene Magini had recently purchased some additional property in Pine Hollow and to the north which had an old farm house off the road in the hollow. Dad bought the old house with the understanding that he would move it off the property. During spare time that summer we worked to tear down this house board by board; Dad pulled the boards off, and Norman and I pulled the nails out. We soon had a wagon load of lumber to build an addition on our house.

There were two pieces of the old farm house that were moved to our property intact. The floor of the main part was divided into equal halves and moved by horse and wagon about two miles up Pine Hollow road to our place. Dad had purchased his bigger tractor by this time, but used the team when working alone and needing to guide or adjust the load. Each piece was 12x18ft. This floor became the floor of the last addition to our house.

The kitchen of the old farm house was an addition and kind of separate. It was also moved intact, walls and roof minus the floor, about a 10x16ft shell. This kitchen would become a machine shop and garage. Serious work on the addition started in the fall.

A concrete foundation was poured to match the size of the salvaged floor (joists and flooring) which did not line up well with the west side of our house. The new addition extended two feet beyond the north wall of the existing house and south to the middle of the kitchen/living room. Dad moved the floor sections into place using a team of horses (Tony and Prince). The smaller team of mares was gone by this time; perhaps they even belonged to Grandpa Wax. They originally came from eastern Montana.

Tony and Prince were not the right team to do exacting work like this. Tony was shorter than Prince, but broader and heavy built. He was steady and even tempered, with movements deliberate and purposeful. Prince was like a spoiled child; he could stay with Tony pound for pound on a pull, but was just as likely to baulk at a critical time. So the double tree would swing wildly toward Tony and then toward Prince. Not what you want when trying to position a section of flooring (12x18ft) onto a new foundation.

Dad used a stick to jab Prince in the butt to get him to match Tony for the pull, but that only made things worse. Finally Dad lost his temper and grabbed a piece of 2x4 and beat Prince about the head and neck. It was difficult to watch Prince being punished and to see my Dad become so angry; I left and did not see how the floor section was finally put in place. Perhaps Dad levered it into place using lumber as a pry bar.

Charlie Magini, Gene's older brother, had worked as a carpenter on several neighbor houses. Dad hired Charlie to help build the new addition - a living room, a bedroom with closet and a bedroom in the attic. To accommodate all of this a number of other changes were required, described next referencing drawing 4-04.

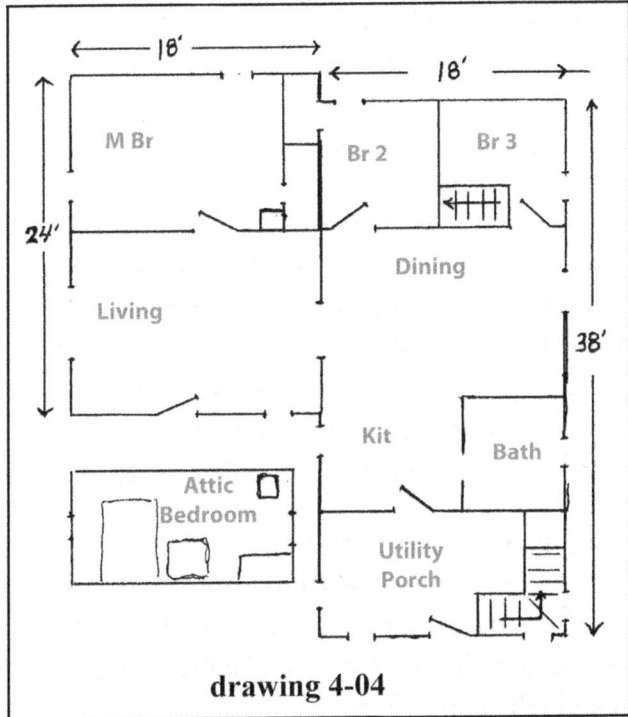

drawing 4-04

The window on the west side of the living room was taken out to make a double door width opening into the new living room. The doors to the bedrooms on the north end of the house were moved to the outside walls. This opened up the center of the old living room to make a more comfortable dining room, and to accommodate entry to the stairs inside bedroom three. The window in bedroom three was moved from the north wall to the east wall; the window in bedroom two was moved to the west side of the room and a door opening was added to enter a closet inside the new addition. Stairs were added to the bedroom side of the dining room wall beginning inside the bedroom three door and continuing to attic floor inside the new addition, which took up part of the floor space in the bedroom three and intruded in the wall and ceiling space of bedroom two.

The attic bedroom was about 9x16ft, a big room. But the ceiling was low, from stub walls about three feet high on the outside to six feet in the middle. There was a flush mounted ceiling light with switch beside it and a small window on the west wall. At the top of the stairs was a space to hang some clothes to the left and to the right was a clay pipe and brick chimney from the new living room below. A pull-string light was in the center at the top of the stairs.

This pull-string light also had a switch at the bottom of the stairs, not a two-way switch arrangement. The routine was to turn the light on at the bottom and turn it off at the top going up, and the reverse going down. If you broke the routine you had to walk the stairs in the dark.

There was room for a bed and an old parlor table along the south wall between the chimney and the window. My brother and I slept here until we left home, he on the chimney side and I on the window side. I built a small shelf and added some coat hooks to the right of the window where I emptied my pockets and hung my clothes at night. Norman had the old parlor table and a small chair for his things. It was a very cozy bedroom for us except on hot summer days. I remember lying uncovered until after midnight before it was cool enough to sleep comfortably on hot summer nights.

Mom and Dad now slept in the new-addition bedroom, Patsy and Lavon slept in bedroom two and Gordon slept in bedroom three.

The original part of the house was not insulated; the new addition did have minimum wall and ceiling insulation. So the new living room, bedroom and attic room were the warmest parts of the house in winter. Gordon's room was the coldest. All of the windows were single pane glass in wood frames and during the winter months collected a good bit of frost. The window in Gordon's room built up frost to a quarter inch or more on cold days then melted dripping water onto the sill and floor.

Concrete steps were poured off the porch with walkway to the edge of the driveway and steps were also poured off the new living room door. I don't recall that we ever used the living room door; we continued to enter/exit via the kitchen and porch. And I don't think that either of the doors was ever locked, or that we even had a key. The entire outside of the house was covered with new and popular white asbestos cement shakes. A green asphalt shingle roof completed this addition. It all looked very nice.

It was a comfortable house and on par with the majority of our neighbors. The one thing that was forever disagreeable was the placement of the bathroom. It was behind the kitchen, and could not have been further from all the bedrooms. You had to walk through the whole house and past everyone present to get to the bathroom.

Once when I was in high school I came home from a night of beer drinking with my friends, and after getting into bed I became sick and needed to throw up. I knew I couldn't get down stairs and outside soon enough, so I opened the window on my side of the bed, stuck my head out and threw up. The next morning Dad asked how I felt, then said I had to wash the side of the house. After the side of the house was cleaned I did feel better. Can you believe that I drove home from Stevensville that night without incident?

photo 4-07

Photo 4-07 is how our house looked after this last addition in 1952. Notice the small window to the attic bedroom at the peak of the roof, my bedroom window.

More changes were made after Mom and Dad sold their farm on contract in 1979. Some electric baseboard heaters were added, a cement block chimney was built outside the east dining room wall and a rock surround was built in the corner of the dining and bathroom walls to accommodate a wood heater. A sliding glass door replaced the east window in the dining room, a concrete patio was poured outside and an island was built to the left side of the cook stove.

Four or five years later the new owners defaulted on the contract and my parents took their farm back. They moved back into their house and lived there until they died.

Document 4-01 is a copy of the contract my mother, Helen M. Wax, signed to buy lot 22 with the apple house. Note the $63.00 down payment and $50.40 plus interest at four percent for each of the next five years. "The Land" has more information about these contracts.

Mom and Dad had a sizeable investment in their small farm and house by the end of 1941 and were determined to keep it, where others before had failed. They added and improved for nearly 40 years to build a comfortable life for all of us, and later provide for their retirement.

In 2010 lot 22, with all the Wax farm buildings, was sold for a little less than $200,000. After more than seventy years, the Bill and Helen Wax farmstead belonged to someone else.

The 10 acre lots that my parents bought for as little as $45 today sell for $80,000 (and more). These lots are being developed by retirees who want privacy, and by younger families who want to keep horses and other farm animals. Some of these new houses are very nice with excellent views of the valley and mountains.

The initial owners dreamed of irrigating dry land, and then investors dreamed of apple orchards; economic problems caused the orchards to be converted to farms and ranches, and today new owners dream of pets and privacy. The land changes to accommodate the dreams of each generation.

CONTRACT OF SALE

This agreement, made and entered into this ___2nd___ day of ___October___, 19__39__, between the County of Ravalli, of the State of Montana, hereinafter called the Vendor, and ___Helen M. Wax of___ ___Stevensville___ of hereinafter called the Purchaser, witnesseth.

That whereas, the Board of County Commissioners of Ravalli county, Montana, by an order entered upon the minutes of its proceedings on the ___3rd___ day of ___May___, 19__39__ ordered sold at public auction at the front door of the court house the property hereinafter described; and,

Whereas, 20 days' notice of sale was given by the Board of County Commissioners as required by law by publication thereof in a newspaper printed in the county and by posting copies of such notices in at least five public places in the county, and which notice among other things stated the fair market value of said property to be $ ___350.00___ as determined and fixed by the Board of County Commissioners at the time of making said order for sale; and,

Whereas, __there were no bidder for said property on date of sale and now comes__ ~~madkx the highest bidder for said property and did the best hereinafter set out~~ __Helen M. Wax and offers to purchase said property for 90% of the appraised value;__

Now, therefore, it is hereby mutually agreed that the Vendor, in consideration of the payment, covenants and agreements on the part of the purchaser, hereinafter contained, agrees to sell and convey unto the Purchaser (and the Purchaser agrees to buy), all of that certain lot and parcel of land situated in the City of _____, County of Ravalli, and State of Montana bounded and described as follows, to-wit:

___Lot Twenty two (22) Block Two (2) Sunset Orchards, according to the official___ ___plat of the survey thereof on file and of record in the office of the County Clerk___ ___and Recorder of Ravalli County, Montana.___

For the sum of __Three hundred fifteen and No/100 - - - - - - - - - - - - -__ Dollars, ($ __315.00__) in lawful money of the United States of America; and the said Purchaser, in consideration of the premises, agrees to pay to said Vendor the sum of __Three hundred fifteen and No/100 - - - - - -__ Dollars ($ __315.00__) in such lawful money, as follows, to-wit:

__Sixty three and No/100 - - - - - - - -__ Dollars ($ __63.00__) on the execution of this contract;
__Fifty and 40/100__ Dollars ($ __50.40__) on the __2nd__ day of __October__ 19__40__
__Fifty and 40/100__ Dollars ($ __50.40__) on the __2nd__ day of __October__ 12__41__
__Fifty and 40/100__ Dollars ($ __50.40__) on the __2nd__ day of __October__ 19__42__
__Fifty and 40/100__ Dollars ($ __50.40__) on the __2nd__ day of __October__ 19__43__
__Fifty and 40/100__ Dollars ($ __50.40__) on the __2nd__ day of __October__ 19__44__

and the balance, _____ Dollars ($ _____), on the _____ day of _____ 19_____; together with interest at the rate of __Four__ per cent (__4__ %) per annum from this date on all deferred payments, which interest shall be due and paid annually thereon on the __2nd__ day of __October__

document 4-01

The Well

A major project, down and down again

I was not old enough to remember the history of the well from personal experience, but I do remember the stories that were told over and over again. Grandpa Wax and a neighbor both witched for the well. This is sometimes called witching for water, or more recently called dowsing for water. They both ended up in the same location. It was on a line from the house to the apple house, about two thirds of the way to the apple house. So, in October of 1940 Dad began digging the well.

Photo 5-01 is from late summer of 1940. That is me wearing Dad's hat; what a big boy. There are several things to note in this photo: no evidence of a well, the 1934 Chevrolet car hooked to the

photo 5-01

wagon, the apple house without windows and the ventilation stacks on the roof that vented the apple house basement. Dad used this wagon and a team of horses to haul gravel during the 1940s.

The apple house had a basement and an elevator platform that could move apples from the receiving floor to the basement for storage. It was powered by a wooden windlass with rope, pulley and hand crank. Dad secured the elevator platform to the wooden receiving floor and moved the windlass to the well site, about 30 feet west of the apple house. He cut the top off of a 10 gallon milk can just above the connecting ring that fastened the neck and mouth to the body of the can. This ring provided strong connection points for an iron rod bail to lift the can. I remember seeing this can and the wooden windlass when I was about five years old.

An interesting side note about the iron rod that was used for the bail; this rod material came from the wooden siphon that carried the Big Ditch water across Willoughby Creek. The wooden siphon was replaced with a steel siphon sometime before Dad began digging the well. I remember seeing many pieces of this rod material, and the connecting brackets, around the farm yard. I also used some of this rod material on one of my shop projects in high school.

A side note about the Big Ditch; the official name was the Bitter Root Irrigation District canal, or BRID canal. The maps in the Appendix use this designation. We always called it the Big Ditch, and so will I here.

Dad began digging a four plus foot diameter well with pick, shovel and crow bar. When the well was deeper than Dad could throw the dirt with his shovel he used the windlass with rope attached to the modified milk can to lift the dirt to the surface. Dad dug the first 60 feet of the well entirely by himself. He lowered the can to the bottom; blocked the windlass handle with peg and strap, then slid down the rope. He filled the can with fresh diggings, then climbed back up the rope hand over hand to the windlass and cranked the can to the top. Then he emptied it into a wheel barrow which was dumped away from the well site. This was repeated time and time again until he had completed the first 60 feet of the well.

Let us assume that the well excavation was four foot eight inches in diameter (the cement casing is four foot in diameter) and 60' deep. The math: 2.33x2.33x60ft x 3.14 (pie) = 1022 cubic feet of dirt Dad excavated by himself. That is almost 38 cubic yards at 2300 lbs per cu yd = 43.7 tons carried to the surface.

How many cans full (10 gal) did it take, how many trips up/down the rope? Each foot of excavation equals 17 cubic feet (cu ft) of dirt. The can held between 1.1 and 1.33 cu ft per trip depending on how loose the dirt was packed in the can. Let's take 1.25 cu ft as an average, or more than 13 trips up/down the rope per each foot of excavation, when Dad began using the rope and can method, let's say at the 10 foot level.

It took 650 trips up/down the rope to dig that first 60 feet.

It makes you think of the line "you load 16 tons and what do you get?" from the Tennessee Ernie Ford song "16 Tons", and wonder just how hard that was compared to digging this well. I ask you to compare that to the tough men of today! And Dad was 5' 8" and weighed about 145 lbs. You shouldn't think that was all he did during the days digging the well. He also milked the cows by hand, separated the cream, and fed the cows and pigs before he began digging for the day.

I don't know how long Dad took to dig that first 60 feet, but if I know my Dad he averaged two feet per day. So he probably spent 30 days digging before quitting to cut fire wood for the winter.

During the fall of 1941 Dad hired two young neighbor men to help him continue digging the well. Don Chapman and Orvalle Rasmussen were recent high school graduates with no work experience off the farm. Dad had worked for a year in the tunneling operations that were required to build the Fort Peck Dam in eastern Montana on the Missouri River in the 1930s. He understood a little about earth formations, tunneling and the dangers involved. So Dad continued to do the digging and gave the windlass operations to Don and Orvalle.

The windlass crank handle was long enough for two sets of hands; one cranking forward and the other backward (if they faced each other). It was necessary to always have a set of hands on the crank handle because this homemade windlass did not have a ratchet mechanism to prevent it from running backwards when under load. If they lost control of the windlass the can full of dirt would drop to the bottom. Not good! The three of them continued digging for the next 60 feet, to the 120 foot level - another 42 tons of dirt.

One evening Don and Orvalle emptied several wheel barrows full of snow down the well hole after Dad went to the house. They wanted to play a practical joke on Dad. They reasoned that the snow would melt during the night leaving a small pool of water. Dad would find the water the next morning and think he had hit water.

The next morning (Dec. 21, 1941) Don and Orvalle were acting rather silly, but were serious when lowering Dad into the well. Dad yelled back up, "we have water"! "Yah, yah, we know" they yelled back laughing. Dad was puzzled by their response. He tried to dig, but the water came in faster and faster. Finally he asked to be hauled up. They had to confess when Dad got to the top. But Dad explained that there was much more water than a few wheel barrows full of snow. They all finally agreed that they had indeed hit water. The next morning the water was 10 feet deep; the digging was a success.

Dad next built forms to begin pouring concrete around the inside of the well. With the help of Don and Orvalle they began at the 60 foot level and poured in three foot increments every few days working upwards. Dad again worked in the well with Don and Orvalle working on the surface mixing the concrete. I may not remember correctly the depth of the concrete casing; it may have been cased to around 110 feet. I do remember that the last few feet of the well were treated differently.

If I did the math correctly that was 1.4 cu yd of concrete per each three foot set, or 28 cubic yards of concrete for the first 60 feet of casing, or another 33 tons of material muscled into the well. You will need to multiply times 1.83 if the well was cased to the 110 foot level. Think about it for a minute; 60 tons of concrete poured into the casing of this well all by muscle power. Nothing like that would ever happen today.

A galvanized iron pipe was lowered into the well and attached to wall supports embedded in the concrete casing. A hand pump was mounted on the top of the pipe, and now water was available 70 feet from the house. Prior to getting water from our well, a pair of water cans (10 gallon milk cans) were filled at the Webster well about 450 feet to the south and carried in a wheel barrow special built to carry two cans. These cans were still used to get the water to the front porch from our new well, now only about 70 feet away (see Our House).

A wooden trough fed water from the pump to a stock water tank for the animals. Later, an electric motor driven pump jack was attached to the hand pump so getting water was as easy as throwing a switch. This was used until the house was plumbed for water.

After thinking about this a little more, I may have the digging and casing reversed. It would make more sense to install the concrete casing on the first 60 feet before continuing the digging. It would be much safer to secure the dirt wall with concrete and then continue the digging down to the 120 foot level.

Dad knew the dangers involved. Dig the first 60 feet and case it, then dig the remainder and case the last 60 feet. I am sure that was the sequence.

photo 5-02

Photo 5-02 is probably from the winter of 1945. You can see Grandpa Zimmerman's car to the left of the house and our 1934 Chevrolet to the right. Note the clothes line and outhouse to the right of the house. If you look carefully there is a cow drinking water at the bottom right of the pump house. The stock water tank was located just outside the pump house wall on the south side. There is no evidence of windows for the apple house basement and you can see the apple trees in the background on the back half of lot 23.

This well faithfully supplied all of our water needs for the rest of my parents' lives. The state began measuring the water level in the 1950s and has continued to this day; so they have more than six decades of water table history from this well alone. I have seen a copy of those records which indicate the water depth in the well measured between 12 and 36 feet. The water has been tested a number of times over the years and always tested pure.

Dad later poured a concrete foundation and built a permanent pump house. He also poured a concrete floor in the pump house and a concrete cover for the well hole. A new Jacuzzi (brand) pump was positioned in a covered pump basement beside the well when our house was plumbed for water and the stock water tank was moved further south near the corrals. All of this was done by hand before hydraulic machinery was available to help. It is the story of "moving a mountain".

The well provided a sense of accomplishment, especially for Dad, but also for the rest of us who felt that we must accomplish something someday. It was the one thing of all the things that were built on the Wax farm that gave the most pride, not only for the well itself, but also for the water that came from the well. I remember neighbors, even strangers, would stop at our house and ask if they could fill up from our well. It was the drink offered most often to any visitors, hot black coffee was the next.

Some years later when a salesman (Culligan) sold Mom and Dad a water softener system, Dad insisted that one faucet in the house continue to have untreated water. We always drank from the untreated faucet, or from an outside faucet.

Many farmers and ranchers used tightly woven canvas water bags when working in the field. The evaporation of moisture on the outside of the canvas kept the water cool. Dad would not use these bags because they left a slight taste of canvas on the tongue after drinking; he wrapped glass gallon jugs in several layers of burlap and stitched it all together. After filling the jug with water the burlap was thoroughly soaked (evaporation for cooling) and we drank pure, good tasting water in the field.

I once drank one of those gallon jugs of water by myself one afternoon while stacking bales in the hay field. It was one of those hot, dry and dusty days in the full sun of mid July that is seared into your memory, and being able to sit a few minutes in the shade and drink cool good tasting water was a real pleasure.

Experience is the knowledge gained from the lessons of living. Some lessons come with a cost and some are free. And I did not realize that I had learned anything until I began writing this account. What did I learn?

I learned that every job or project will forever remain too big if you do not start. I learned that what seems like the impossible will always remain impossible if you make excuses for not starting. I learned that once started, the end of the job or project will provide the motivation to finish. A big project well done will be appreciated by everyone, but perhaps the most by strangers.

I received these lessons free, the only cost was being the son of my father. I was too close to Dad's accomplishments; I saw things day by day and little by little. Even though I sometimes helped him I didn't see the plan or project through his eyes.

He was always making life better for his family. From the distance of my seventy-five years I can better appreciate everything he did. Some years later in my career at GE (during the leadership of the legendary Jack Welch) I attended a class on Continuous Improvement, which is making things better over time. After finishing the class I understood that I had learned this concept many years before from Dad.

Document 5-01 is a copy of the form for registering the well with the state. My Dad wrote this himself in December 31, 1963. He describes the type of dirt at various levels and says that the concrete casing extended to the 110 foot level.

I am not aware of any other hand-dug well this deep on the Sunset Bench. It would be interesting to know if Montana has registered any other well like this one. Most hand-dug wells were in the 20 to 50 foot range. Drilled wells are typically 100 to 500 feet.

County..................

STATE OF MONTANA
ADMINISTRATOR OF GROUNDWATER CODE
OFFICE OF STATE ENGINEER

Declaration of Vested Groundwater Rights
(Under Chapter 237, Montana Session Laws, 1961)

1. .....*Montana Wm. Hof*........., of ....*Stevensville*.........
   (Name of Appropriator)   (Address)   (Town)

County of ...*Ravalli*.................State of ...*Montana*......
have appropriated groundwater according to the Montana laws in effect prior to January 1, 1962, as
follows:

1/4. Sec. *7*. T. *F*. R. *9*.
Indicate point of appropriation
and place of use, if possible. Each
small square represents 10 acres.

*Lot 22 Blk 2
Sunset Orchards*

2. The beneficial use on which the claim is based. *limited irrigation
   stock water, and home use.*

3. Date or approximate date of earliest beneficial use; and how
   continuous the use has been....*Sept. 1, 1941*.....
   Used every day since appropriated.

4. The amount of groundwater claimed (in miner's inches or gallons
   per minute)........*50 miners inches*........

5. If used for irrigation, give the acreage and description of the lands
   to which water has been applied and name of the owner thereof
   *1 acre on Lot 22 Block 2
   Sunset Orchards*

6. The means of withdrawing such water from the ground and the location of each well or other means of withdrawal. *1 Jacuzzi
   jet pump and 1 lift pump with
   relief.*

7. The date of commencement and completion of the construction of the well, wells, or other works for
   withdrawal of groundwater...*Sept. 1920 and was completed Dec. 21,
   1941.*

8. The depth of water table....*Approx. 35 ft.*

9. So far as it may be available, the type, size and depth of each well or the general specifications of
   any other works for the withdrawal of groundwater...*Hand dug 4 feet in
   diameter, 120 ft. deep.*

10. The estimated amount of groundwater withdrawn each year....*50 acre feet*

11. The log of formations encountered in the drilling of each well if available. *80 ft. hard pan
    and gravel, 2 ft. clay, 25 ft. hard pan and rock,
    2 ft. of clay, then 8 ft. of sand and gravel.*

12. Such other information of a similar nature as may be useful in carrying out the policy of this act,
    including reference to book and page of any county record...*this well is
    cemented from top to with in 8 ft. of the bottom.*

Signature of Owner *Montana Wm Hof*
Date...*Dec. 21, 1962.*

Three copies to be filed by the owner with the County Clerk and Recorder of the county in which the well
is located.
Please answer all questions. If not applicable, so state, otherwise the form will be returned.
Original to the County Clerk and Recorder; Duplicate to the State Engineer; Triplicate to the Montana
Bureau of Mines and Geology, and Quadruplicate for the Appropriator.

document 5-01

Food & Fuel

Teamwork providing the necessities

All of our food came from the farm in the 1940s and most of it in the 1950s. During the 1960s and later the farm became less and less important as a primary source of food.

Many of my first memories are from the garden. As I remember it now, it seems that Norman and I were in the garden pulling weeds soon after we began to walk. That is probably a bit of an exaggeration, but we did pull weeds from a very young age. We didn't like to pull weeds very much, so Mom and Dad had to ask, demand and scold to get the weeds pulled. When we were older we could use a hoe and chop the weeds, still not much fun.

The growing season was too short to grow good big corn every year, but we always had peas, string beans and potatoes. We also had lettuce, carrots, beets and radishes, and sometimes onions, squash and cucumbers. I remember the plants sometimes were frost damaged, and had to start growing again from the ground up.

Dad applied manure and plowed the garden with horses; he prepared the ground for planting. We all helped with the planting. Mom cut the potato eyes from last year's crop stored in the basement and Dad opened a furrow for us to drop the potato pieces into. Then he covered the furrow. We usually had six rows each of corn and potatoes, three rows each of peas and beans and six rows with a combination of other vegetables.

photo 6-01

Photo 6-01 is from the fall of 1945 of me, my sister Patsy and my brother Norman plus the dogs. Notice the young silver leaf maple tree to the right and the remains of the garden to the upper left. The trees in the background are in the coulee that began just to the left of our garden. This coulee was a favorite place to play.

Like all productive land on the Sunset Bench our garden needed to be irrigated. Dad made a small ditch around the north side of the house and down the west side of the yard then under the driveway to the garden. This fed the water to a ditch along the north side of the garden. The rows were always running north-south to allow the irrigation water to run down the rows. Norman and I would help with the irrigation too. We made a small channel between the rows using a hoe as a plow. We pretended to be farmers and turn a small stream of water into three rows at a time. We would move the water to the next set of rows irrigating the garden. Dirt, mud and water! It was a lot more fun than pulling weeds.

It was a really big treat to eat the first fresh vegetables from the garden each summer. I can remember it now - new little potatoes and peas cooked with fresh cream and seasoned with salt and pepper. Very tasty! Last year's potatoes stored in the basement had all sprouted and were pretty mushy. Not much taste.

Mom began canning the peas and beans soon after the first harvest was eaten. She also canned beets and corn when we had them, and sometimes carrots. The potatoes and raw carrots were stored in the basement each fall. It was our starch and vegetables for the coming season. I don't ever recall growing any fruit in the garden.

photo 6-02

Photo 6-02 is the remains of the garden in the fall of 1945. Note the bare feet on two of us three. Would you trust your vegetable supply for the coming year to these two weed pullers?

Mom did can fruit that we bought by the box from the store or from Gene Magini. Gene had 1½ ton Ford truck (a 1946 model) that he drove to southwestern Idaho each fall and brought back boxes of peaches and pears. He took orders from neighbors on the Sunset Bench and some people in Stevensville. Mom would store the fruit until deliciously ripe, then prepare and can it. She also made jam and jelly.

Mom had a large pressure cooker for canning. It had a gauge and a pressure relief valve on top. She prepared the jars, filled them with fruit or vegetable and put the jars in the pressure cooker, then placed the cooker on the wood stove. A fire of apple wood would soon have the pressure cooker up to the correct pressure and then its position on the stove was adjusted to maintain the pressure for the correct time. The cooker was then placed into a sink of water to cool and when the pressure had reduced to zero it was opened and the jars set aside ready for storing in the basement. It was a long and tiring process on a hot August afternoon.

A community cannery once existed in the southeast corner of Baldwin and Middle Burnt Fork roads. It was a small wooden building painted white; an old steam tractor was parked near the east side with a steam pipe running inside from the boiler. A group from Stevensville started it up in the fall and people came to do their canning. I was never inside the building to see any of the canning, but I do remember seeing some of the unlabeled tin cans that were produced there.

A pie cherry orchard owned by a man named Bass (historic name in Stevensville) was located on the south side of Pine Hollow Road where it joined the Eastside Highway. We picked cherries at the Bass orchard and Mom canned these too. (Dad refers to this orchard in one of his letters. We paid!) And we had many remaining apple trees that sometimes gave us a good crop of McIntosh apples for juicy pies and cider. The apples would last in the basement until about Christmas time.

One year we had an extra good crop of apples, so Norman and I gathered up several burlap bags of apples and loaded the bags into my first car, a 1935 Ford. We were 12 and 13 at the time. We drove down to the cider press which was owned by a man named Munger. It was in the corner of his pasture near the corner of Pine Hollow and Logan roads. We made gallons of cider filling a 5 gallon milk can. Then we gathered up the pulp to take to the pigs and washed the press with water from the irrigation ditch. We thanked Mr. Munger and drove home. The can was stored in the basement and we had fresh cider for a couple weeks.

Our milk, cream and butter came from the milk cows (see Outbuildings). We churned our own butter. Mom did the churning in what I guess was a six quart square sided glass jug with a crank and gear mechanism on top. Turning the crank caused a steel rod which descended into the jar to turn, and attached to the rod were four paddles. She made it look easy, so I wanted to churn butter. I turned the crank for 10 minutes and grew tired. It would take Mom another 20 minutes to finish the job. She poured out the butter milk and scooped out the butter, then added a little salt and we had fresh butter.

We delivered the cream to a small creamery in town. We could trade the cream for ice cream and cheese. Our food sources are beginning to fill out nicely; we just need some meat, eggs and bread.

Mom and Dad usually bought hundred pound sacks of flour and sugar in the fall. It was expected that these would last until the next fall. The sugar was for canning and the table. Mom baked all our bread, always white. She sometimes baked cinnamon rolls and cookies and when we had fruit she baked pies.

The eggs came from our chickens. Some people today don't know that chickens don't lay eggs all the time. We usually bought baby chicks in the spring. They arrived in a flat cardboard box delivered by the mailman or picked up in town. Most of the roosters would become fryers and the hens would supply our eggs. This process would usually provide a continuous supply of eggs, but sometimes we traded or bought eggs or went without (more about the fryers later).

While I'm thinking about it, some people today don't know that cows don't give milk all the time either. One year, probably in the fall of 1949, Dad was late in getting a new bull and all of our cows went dry. For three months that fall we did not have fresh milk. Dad bought cases of condensed milk and we drank reconstituted milk instead. It took several cases to get through that dry spell. Not bad for Norman and me, since we didn't have to help milk the cows.

What's left? Oh, yes the meat. Dad always butchered a pig for our pork. Once we had a pig butchering party; it was soon after the war before controls on meat were lifted. We weren't affected by the controls, but those who lived in town were: Grandpa and Grandma Wax, Aunt Doris and her man and Mr. and Mrs. Walz. The Walz family lived next to Grandpa Wax; Mr. Walz worked for the railroad and played the fiddle. They all came one day in the fall to butcher pigs.

Dad set a barrel on some rocks, filled it with water and built a fire under it. The hay stacker was moved from the feed lot and placed next to the barrel. The water was soon steaming hot and everybody had arrived. The pigs were selected and brought from the pig lot north of the house. Dad used the 22 rifle to shoot each pig between the eyes and then puncture its throat to cut the jugular vein. He cut slots in their heels to hook both feet onto a single tree. The single tree was then attached to the stacker and the pig hauled up so it could bleed out. This one was laid aside and the next pig was treated the same. The pig carcasses were dipped into the boiling water and laid on a wagon where we took turns with scrappers removing all the hair. It took a number of such dips in the water and turns scrapping to finish the job. Each pig was then gutted and the carcasses were covered with a sheet and hung up for the night.

Sleeping at our house that night was cramped: Grandpa and Grandma slept in Mom and Dad's bed, the Walz's slept in Patsy's room, Aunt Doris and her man in the basement, Mom, Dad and Patsy slept on the kitchen floor and Norman and I in our usual bed on the porch. Next morning after breakfast the carcasses were split into halves, each of the visitors got a half and we kept 3 halves. The halves were wrapped in a sheet and laid onto the back seats for the drive back to Missoula.

Dad cured the hams and bacon with salt, pepper and brown sugar, and smoked them with apple wood. They were then wrapped in clothe flour sacks and buried in the center of one of the grain bins. This was a good environment for storing cured pork; rather dry, cool to cold with moderate swings in temperature and away from vermin and insects. Chops were cut and sausage ground and wrapped in paper to be frozen in the refrigerator. We had our pork for the year.

Where did the refrigerator come from? The REA (Rural Electrification Administration) brought electric power to the Sunset Bench sometime before the war. The house we lived in (see Our House) always had electricity. I am going to guess that the new electric washing machine and refrigerator were bought about the same time.

I do recall that we had an old chest-type ice box, maybe 24x30x30 inches which must have served for food storage before the refrigerator. I remember that it was later used in the basement to store carrots. We put a layer of sand, a layer of carrots, a layer of sand, and so on. The sand prevented the carrots from drying out and they remained fairly crunchy until spring. This ice chest would end its useful life in the apple house milk barn as a grain storage bin.

In the later 1940s Dad rented space in a cold storage room in town for storing meat. The freshly prepared meat was transferred to town for long-term storage. The room was not big, maybe 12x18 feet, and divided into three foot cubes. These cubes (lockers) were made of wire hung on wooden frames with a door and hasp for a padlock. Each renter supplied their own padlock. The outside door to the room was not locked. There were cubes three levels high and six columns deep and three rows wide. We had a locker there until mid-1950s for storing meat.

Beef and game were more varied. Dad did butcher a beef now and then, but he also liked to hunt deer and elk. Some years he was very successful hunting, so we ate only game and on those years when he was not successful he butchered a beef. He chose the biggest and best from the herd to butcher. It was choice hamburger and steaks.

photo 6-03

Photo 6-03 is of Dad with his big bull elk, in the fall of 1955, hanging on the head pole of the gate between house and farm yard. Notice the three young cows playing behind Dad. There were also times when the kill was hung up in the dark and covered during the day and was not talked about.

Deer and elk meat can be tough, dry and smelly depending on the animal's condition. Much of the meat was ground and mixed 50-50 with pork and seasoned. We called it deer sausage or deer burger which was pretty good eating. We also had deer and elk steaks. One year Dad killed his limit of elk, but they were all in poor condition. I remember he had two elk carcasses at one time hanging on the pole over the gate between the house and barn. The steaks were tough, dry and smelly. Toward the end of winter Mom had had enough, and told Dad that if he wanted another elk steak he would have to cook it himself. I must admit that I was tired of elk meat too.

Photo 6-04 is Norman, in 1955, with his big buck deer. Notice behind them to the right is my car undergoing an engine replacement. Norman was more interested in guns and hunting. I never did kill any game animals.

Norman and I usually each had a baby calf as our own. It was to teach us how to be responsible and take care of an animal. If we bought the calf we could sell it in the fall and keep the profit. If it was one of Dad's, it just remained in the herd when sold. One year during branding my calf was roped and thrown. It hit the ground hard and soon began to show signs of dying, so Dad slit its throat and we butchered it. During the butchering we discovered that it had a ruptured lung. That was the only time we ate veal.

photo 6-04

So, now you know the sources of most all our food. Now, let's talk about the fuel.

In the early 1940s the fire wood for heater and stove came from the remaining apple trees that occupied the back half of lots 21 and 23. Each winter Dad cut the trees down with a double bitted ax and cut the trees into fire wood with a buck (hand) saw.

He put the ax head into the stock water tank at night so its temperature was above freezing and to maintain good moisture in the handle to prevent the head from coming loose. After the cows were milked and cows and pigs fed, he and the ax would be off the orchard. Sometimes Norman and I went with him to help gather the small limbs. We usually didn't last very long on cold winter days. Soon Dad was working in his bare hands and shirt sleeves; powerful and accurate strokes of the ax would have a tree down in a matter of minutes, and the limbs trimmed a few minutes after that. It always amazed me how much my Dad could do with simple hand tools.

By the fall of 1945 we had our first tractor, and a buzz saw which Dad used to cut the tree limbs into fire wood. I was recruited to catch the cut pieces from the saw and throw them into a pile. Our buzz saw was a stand-alone type that Dad staked to the ground and connected with a belt to the tractor pulley. It had a hinged table on one side that allowed moving the limbs into the saw blade which was about 30" in diameter (newer blades were larger). The saw blade was not covered and totally unprotected. It could be a very dangerous cutting machine; Dad carefully instructed me how to stand and to catch the cut pieces from the saw. I caught and tossed many pieces of firewood from that saw over the years without incident.

The crooked apple tree limbs required turning to find the safest way to make the cut with the buzz saw. Patience and care were required.

I don't know how the first stumps were pulled from the ground, but they were cleaned of dirt and cut for fire wood too. If the saw hit a rock Dad had to sharpen the teeth with a file which allowed me a short break. Dad split the pieces if they were too big for the stove. Norman and I carried the wood to the house every day after school.

A side note about apple wood and Grandma Wax. Whenever she visited she would go the orchard where the pigs were kept (back of lot 21) at the time and gather bundles and bundles of twigs for the stove. These twigs were good for starting a fire, but didn't last long enough to provide much heat. Mom and Dad didn't know what to do with so many twigs. Grandma Wax spent many years in eastern Montana gathering such twigs and cow chips for her stove, so to Grandma it was very important and she was helping us with one of the chores.

Son Of Montana

The last of the apple trees were cut in the early 1950s. I remember pulling the last of the stumps on the back half of lot 23 using the 1948 Case tractor. Dad took the cable and pulleys from the old hay stacker (we had a new hydraulic stacker now) and rigged a block and tackle system to amplify the power of the tractor. Dad would chain/unchain and organize the cable and I drove the tractor. Sometimes the tractor was just a little light in the oomph to pull a big stump, so Dad used a shovel to open several feet of the roots on the backside of the stump. That'll do it!

Together we could go down a row of tree stumps in rather sort order. I remember this well because it was during this time that Dad had a fight with Mom and left for several days. He stayed in Missoula with his sister and parents. While he was gone I pulled some of those stumps by myself. Mom finally convinced me that I should leave the rest until Dad returned.

After the apple trees were all gone we began to harvest lodge pole pine from the mountains for fire wood. Dad cut a new longer pole for the spine that held the front and back of our wagon together. He removed the hay rack, installed the much longer spine and we had a wagon twice as long as before. Some longer bolster stakes were added and we were ready to go logging.

Our 1948 Case tractor would go about 10 mph in fourth gear full throttle. The trip to the mountains took one and a half hours on dirt roads, about 12 miles. We began selecting lodge pole pine for our needs: fire wood, fence posts or building material. Dad took the cable and pulleys from the old hay stacker and with the pulley fastened on the opposite side of the road from our harvest area we could pull the trees up onto the road with the tractor.

We selected downed or dead trees for fire wood, larger live trees for posts and smaller live trees for building material (corral poles, studs, etc.). Dad used the double bitted ax and buck saw. He also had a two-man cross cut saw and I was the second man when harvesting the larger poles. The full length poles were carefully stacked and balanced on the wagon. The butt end of the pole hung out over the wagon tongue close to the tractor seat and the longest poles would drag their tops on the ground on our way home. It must have been a sight to see us coming down the road; Dad driving the tractor with two boys riding on top of a wagon full of lodge pole pine.

How did Dad know where to go? The Forest Service was actively trying to spot forest fires and in the mid-1940s one of their men saw that we had a very good view of the valley and mountains from our house. So they asked if we would help and we said yes. They planted a post in our front yard and mounted a flat board with map on top. The map covered the Sapphire Range to the east and the Bitterroot Range to the west. This map also included a sighting iron and pivot point. The map had all the Forest Service detail needed to find their way in the mountains. They asked us to report any fires and lightning strikes we saw and provide location details from the map. Can you guess how this map was most often used? Yes! Dad used it to plan trips for hunting and harvesting lodge pole pine on Forest Service land.

When Norman and I went with Dad we sat on the back bolster of the wagon as there was not enough room for two to stand behind the tractor seat. Dad thought that if we should fall off the back bolster we wouldn't get hurt very bad; no more wheels to run over us. We never did fall off, but it was rough on our rumps. We were both very happy to arrive at the harvest area.

I remember one time Dad and I went without Norman, Dad in the tractor seat and I standing on the drawbar holding on to the seat. I soon discovered the disadvantage of standing on the drawbar with no opportunity to move around or wiggle your feet.

Son Of Montana

This work was usually done in the late fall and there would often be snow in the mountains. It was cold and my feet were soon very cold. I later learned that my toes were frost bit; they itch and tingle when healing after being frost bit. We did see several deer and a mountain lion that morning. Anyway, we soon began our work harvesting lodge pole pine, ate our lunch, loaded the wagon and were on our way home. I rode home sitting on the load.

I will interrupt here to tell you a personal story. I was born with a deformed little toe on my left foot. It grew from the top of my foot and lay across the other toes at their base joints. This toe was always an irritation, in the way and overly sensitive to cold because it pressed against the top of my shoe.

During the Christmas vacation from school of 1951 I went to the hospital in Hamilton and the doctor removed the toe. He numbed up the base of the toe real good and then carved around the toe down to the base joint, then he took a pair of side cutters and crunch. I watched the whole thing. It was gone. He stitched up the wound. I was pretty sore for the first few days (no Vicadin), but I went back to school in January in new condition. A number of times since I wished that the doctor had trimmed my right foot to match the left. I have a size eight left foot and a size nine right foot.

The lodge pole pine was cut up with the buzz saw, the same as with the apple tree limbs. Most of the fire wood was large enough to require splitting. By the time I was 14, I was doing most of the wood splitting. Lodge pole pine is easy to split. I was getting pretty good at it and became a little over confident; I could handle the double bitted ax with my right hand and the wood with my left splitting piece after piece from a large block.

One afternoon I was busy splitting at the wood pile and caught the end of the ax handle on the block of wood which threw my aim off. I tried to correct without stopping the swing. But on the way down I saw that I could not correct enough and began to pull up. Just not in time! The corner of the ax blade cut through the index finger of my glove and I felt a sting.

"Oh shit, I cut my finger," I yelled! I heard a scream from the yard. I didn't know anybody was around! Mom was hanging clothes on the line. She came over right away and we pulled the glove off. The finger was still on my hand but I had a long cut (from knuckle to 2nd joint) in the flesh on the side of my index finger.

We wrapped it in a clean hanky, jumped into the car and headed to town. On the way down Pine Hollow we met Fred Longpre on the road and he flagged us down. We exchanged greetings and he noticed that I had a problem; he asked and we explained. Then he told me it better not be serious because he wanted me to help with the haying again (see Earning Money) and sent us on our way.

The doctor pulled the cut open and found it was full of sawdust and wood chips from inside my glove. He had to wash and clean until it was all gone. He put 10 stitches along the top and 1 stitch on the bottom of my finger. No wood splitting for a while and then with more care after my finger healed.

Lodge pole pine and other species of wood from the mountains would continue to be fuel for the heater for the rest of my parents' lives. The kitchen stove was replaced with an electric stove during the 1960s.

The post material was peeled with a draw knife and stacked to dry. A point was cut with the buzz saw on posts to be driven with the post maul. They were then set into a barrel filled with a mixture of fuel oil and wood preservative. After a few days of soaking in the preservative they were taken out and a new batch placed in the barrel. Many of the posts treated in this manner lasted for the next

30-40 years.

Dad built several corrals over the years with treated posts and lodge pole rails. Some are still standing today. He also built the pole barn that replaced the straw barn and a large machine shop building using the lodge pole pine material after I left home.

A side story when Dad was in his 80s. He and a neighbor loved to go to the mountains to harvest fire wood. One August when I was home on vacation we decided to split wood using Dad's hydraulic splitter. I muscled the blocks into position and Dad operated the splitter. Things were going along just fine until some black clouds came roaring in from the northwest; a cold wind and spitting snow drove us inside for the rest of the day. The wood heater sure felt good on that August afternoon. Ah yes, that's life in western Montana!

In photo 6-05 I am next to the heater in 1995. My sister Lavon still has the splitter.

photo 6-05

photo 6-06

Photo 6-06 is of Dad and neighbors, Keith Liss in white shirt and Whiskey Dave (I don't know his real name), with a load of those big blocks.

I almost forgot to comment about the young chickens that became fryers. By the time I was doing most of the wood splitting Dad was trying to unload any work related to the chickens. There was a time before the chicken house was built that the chickens were kept in the south side of the apple house. He probably developed a certain hatred of the chickens because they sometimes got into the grain bins. They were not fenced and always around the apple house where they left droppings in the places that were unfortunate for Dad. Anyway I was recruited to kill the fryers.

Mom and I would select two or three for butchering and I cut their heads off. Mom didn't like the head cutting off either and because I could handle the ax with one hand and the chicken in the other I got to do the job. The part I didn't like was catching the headless chicken; it would run, jump and splatter blood all over. After catching the chicken I tied its legs together and hung it on the fence to bleed out.

Mom had a large pot of boiling water on the stove where she dipped each chicken for a few minutes before taking it outside to pluck the feathers. After the feathers were gone she made torch from rolled up paper and burned off the fuzz. The bare chicken was then gutted. She cut each into pieces and wrapped the pieces tightly in freezer paper. On the next trip to town the wrapped chicken pieces were transferred to the cold storage locker. We ate fried chicken that night for supper; Dad liked fried chicken.

During my first vacation at home after joining the Army Dad was cursing the chickens. They were still not fenced, so I said that I would build a fence. I selected several posts from the post pile and set the posts for an enclosure next to the chicken house. I added some lodge pole rails, bought a roll of chicken wire and stapled the wire up for a six foot fence. The chickens were finally fenced, and they stayed fenced until Mom no longer had chickens. Then this chicken yard became Mom's strawberry patch where she grew some nice berries.

Fish? It was not common in western Montana, but there were times when we had fish. Once in the early 1950s Dad bought a case of frozen fish from a supplier in Duluth, Minnesota. These were Great Lakes species and not familiar to our taste, so that was the end of that experiment.

Dad learned about the supplier from a neighbor named Joseph Stang that we cooperated with during threshing. The Stangs were Catholic and Dad probably ate fish at their house on a Friday (more about threshing in The Harvests). Descendants of Joseph Stang own and operate a grocery store in St Regis, Montana.

In the late 1950s Dad spent some time in the winter fishing for white fish in the Bitterroot River which he processed and smoked. A nice treat when we tired of meat. And of course the occasional fishing trip to Burnt Fork Creek in the summer gave us a meal of brook trout.

Mom and Dad learned from their parents how to grow, kill, and process their food supplies, and how to provide an energy source for heating and cooking. We were there to listen, learn and help. It was a family effort.

Today, we pick our food from a vast array packaged in plastic or metal. We can eat fresh picked strawberries in January with a glass of Chardonnay from California paired with a blue cheese from France and English crackers. Fresh and packaged foods are available from literally around the world. Life is very, very good.

Our Neighbors

On adjacent property or close relationships

My intention here is to introduce you to a few of our neighbors. These are the ones that we had the most contact with, and about whom I can recall interesting stories.

The Chapman's lived directly east of us, on the east side of what became Chapman Lane. Their farmstead was next to the middle supply ditch (Baker ditch) for the Sunset Irrigation District. They lived there all the time I was living at home.

You remember Don Chapman was the young man who helped Dad dig our well. Don was the only child of Mr. (Frank) and Mrs. Chapman; I don't remember her given name. They were both quite old when Don was born and now were very old. I don't know when Don's parents no longer lived on their farm or when they died; Don continued to live there until he died in a logging accident (age 50 plus) and his widow lived there for some years after that.

Don was like an older brother (15yrs) to Norman and me. We were all over him every time he came to our house, and begging him to play with us. Don visited often, sometimes to work, or just to talk with Mom and Dad and play with Norman and me. Dad was interested in Don's courting life, and teased him a lot.

Norman and I often visited the Chapman house. Mr. and Mrs. Chapman were kind, and Mr. Chapman would tell us stories. It was my impression that Mr. Chapman was born in Montana and that his father told him stories about life in frontier Montana. One story that I remember was about a murder, a shooting related to gambling in Virginia City. The shooter ran on horseback. The sheriff formed a posse and gave chase. The posse chased the shooter for several days, finally catching him in the Bitterroot Valley where they hung him.

The reason I remember this story is that the tree where he was hanged was along the Eastside Highway (according to Mr. Chapman). The bus passed by this tree on the way to school. The tree and road had a curious relationship. The road approached the tree from the north and south in such a way that the tree was visible in front of you. The road made a slight curve just before the tree. Mr. Chapman said that the tree was left standing to remind citizens of frontier justice. It was a big old tree, and the only large pine tree in this area of the river bottom land located a little north of Bell Crossing. That's the story as I remember it.

Recalling this story got me interested in doing some research to see if there was any truth to this tale. I looked on a Google map and believe that the tree was located a little bit south of present day Higgins Lane and the Eastside Highway, which is about three miles from Stevensville. There is a division between the fields at a slight curve in the highway and a tree might have occupied this corner beside the highway. It is where I remember the tree was located.

In Frederick Allen's book A Decent Orderly Lynching (see the Appendix, Additional Reading), he describes the vigilantes of Virginia City capturing a Bill Graves near Fort Owen. When preparing to hang him the vigilantes were asked to move the execution out of sight of the encampment so as not to offend anyone's sensitivities, especially the resident Indians. So the vigilantes proceeded out of town and completed their mission a short distance away and out of sight of the encampment at Fort Owen and Saint Mary's mission.

Fort Owen and Saint Mary's Mission were the settlement areas that later became Stevensville. So it seems that Mr. Chapman's story might indeed have some truth to it.

The Chapman house was a curious mix of stone and wood. The main part of the house was made of stone masonry with solid walls that contained the sitting room and a bedroom. The kitchen/dining area was made of wood. There was a cook stove in the kitchen and a heater in the sitting room. The cook stove had a hot water manifold to heat water in a large wood barrel behind the stove with an open top. The barrel was filled by bucket from a hand pump that sat on the counter next to the kitchen sink and hot water was dipped from the open top. Their kitchen was always very warm and humid because of the steam from the open barrel.

Don bought a new Dodge pickup sometime after WWII. It had the old style flat head six cylinder engine with running boards that continued inside the doors. If you looked down you could see a portion of the running board below the door.

Don was chewing tobacco by the early 1950s and found it inconvenient to carry a spit can or to roll down the window to spit. So he spit toward the inside portion of the running board, frequently hitting the inside of the door. The inside of the driver's door was covered with tobacco juice the last time I rode in his pickup. Not a very pleasant sight.

The last time I remember visiting the Chapmans was when Don broke his hip. In mid-1950s Don was farming some dry land in the foothills up east of our place. He bought a new John Deere model

A tractor a couple years before and was share cropping where he could. He had taken to drinking - some said up to a fifth a day. His tractor was one of the tricycle types and not very stable in the steep fields. One day he tipped his tractor over and it rolled on top of him the seat pinning him at the hip. A neighbor saw what happened and came to his rescue. Don was confined to his bed in the ante room between the stone living room and wooden kitchen parts of the house, in a cast that extended from his chest down to his knees. A sad and uncomfortable visit.

Today their house, outbuildings and corrals have all been cleared away and the land restored to pasture. It is amazing how man can make such changes and how restorative nature can be.

Photo 7-01 is of Grandpa Wax, Norman and me about 1951. I was 12 and Norman 11. Grandpa Wax recently retired from the railroad, and would have been 70 years old. He frequently visited us when he was free, ready to help with any farm activities even for the neighbors. We are at the Rasmussen farm; Carl's machine shed is in the background.

photo 7-01

Son Of Montana

Mamie (Mary J) and Carl (O) Rasmussen lived a mile northeast of us on what is now known as Miller Hill Road. Mamie was a former school teacher and Carl a farmer from north central Montana. They were in their forties when they married and did not have any children. Carl's nephew Orvalle Rasmussen helped Dad dig our well. Orvalle's parents farmed somewhere in remote north central Montana near Havre, so Orvalle came to live with his uncle to attend high school.

Mamie and Carl milked cows; they had a small dairy of 20 to 30 cows (big for us). Mamie most often did the milking. It was a sight to see! Mamie dressed in bib overalls and rubber boots moving the cows in and out, washing teats and attaching the milking machine. Just like a pro. Sometimes we would help. Then Mamie was off to the house to wash up and change clothes, and offer Norman and me a piece of pie or a cookie. Carl did the feeding, corral cleaning and all the field work with his hired man. They were like our favorite grandparents, kind and friendly. We were lucky boys, three sets of grandparents!

I remember eating our treat with Mamie. We pulled the chairs from the table up next to the propane wall heater in the dining room. A cozy warm heater and a tasty piece of pie or a cookie. On a cold day, it would make anyone happy.

Mamie was the more serious one; she scolded us when we misbehaved or showed us how to do things correctly (always the teacher). Carl on the other hand was always laughing and joking with us. Sometimes he got scolded too. Stop it! Sit down! Finish your plate!

Mamie and Carl had one thing in common - they liked to play cards. As soon as there was any free time, the table was cleared and out came the card decks. Mom and Dad liked to play cards too. So a visit from/to the Rasmussen's often ended with a card game, either cribbage or pinochle.

Dad used to tell a story of Carl and his hired man. Carl bought a new tractor after WWII, a yellow Minneapolis Moline with new implements: mower, rake and stacker. Carl was already in his fifties and had worked only with horses. So, it was the hired man that operated all the new machinery. Dad said that Carl would tell the hired man, "You operate it until I learn how". That always generated a laugh. Carl did eventually learn to use his new machinery.

photo 7-02

Photo 7-02 is of Mamie and Carl, about 1960. It appears they are at an anniversary or retirement party. This is just as I remember them, Mamie the serious one with a small forced smile and Carl with an easy smile and a hint of fun in his eyes. Seeing Carl today makes me think of Cantinflas (Mexican comedic actor). Not because they are similar in appearance, but because seeing him makes me think pleasant thoughts.

The Brush family (Carl's hired man) moved to Oregon and Carl got a new hired man. Carl and Mamie would later retire, sell their dairy farm to the new hired man (Wetherall?) and move to Yuma, Arizona. They lived there for many years playing cards and entertaining children. They both died about the same time, Carl a little over 90 and Mamie a little under 90. Some years later Mrs.

Son Of Montana

Brush (Ilene?) would make a patch work quilt for my parent's anniversary (don't remember which one). My sister Pat still has that quilt.

The Kester family moved onto the Webster property south of our house in the 1940s. The Waxes lived on this property from 1936 until 1940, with Grandpa and Grandma Wax living in the main house and Mom and Dad in the hired help house. The main house burned down sometime before the Kester's came to live in the hired help house. As I remember, this little house had a kitchen, a sitting room and a bedroom. The Kesters were a few years younger than my parents and had a daughter (Mary Mae) my age and a son (Duffy, a couple years younger). Mr. Kester (Rupert, always called Scoop) and Mrs. Kester (Doris) became close friends with Mom and Dad. Doris was famous for her baking powder biscuits, fresh baked biscuits with butter and some jam. Hhhmmmm good!

Mary Mae, Norman, Duffy and I played together a lot. We were always exploring the buildings and fields. One summer there was a rumor that a mountain lion was seen in the coulee to the west of our house; we understood lions can sound just like a human screaming. The coulee was deep with lots of pine and cottonwood trees. The Big Ditch crossed the coulee about a quarter mile west of our house and it got deeper and wilder as it continued on west after the Big Ditch.

We four decided to find that lion. We carefully crossed the Big Ditch and cautiously crept along the edge of the coulee searching in the pine trees for a mountain lion. We were about to give up and go home when we heard the loudest scream you can imagine. We four scattered like frightened rabbits, each on his/her own and running like the wind. We flew over, or through, the Big Ditch and went immediately to our house looking for Dad. He was not in the house, so we breathlessly told Mom what we heard. We heard the lion in the coulee! We need Dad to go investigate! Soon Dad arrived and asked us what happened? Why some of us were wet, where had we been?

We told him where we were looking for the lion, and had heard it scream. He scolded us for being so far from the house and said we would get spanked if we went there again. We kind of withdrew and quietly began to listen to Mom and Dad. It soon became clear that it was Dad who screamed in the coulee. He had a good laugh at our expense; he watched us scramble across the Big Ditch and run to the house. I don't ever recall going into that coulee again.

Photo 7-03 is of the Kester family about the year Mary Mae and I graduated from high school (1957). Jim and Jack (twins) are on either side of Duffy (I can't tell which is which); Doris and Scoop on Mary's left.

photo 7-03

The Kester's had relatives that lived to the northwest of us. Myrtle Pope Potter was an old lady and Mavis Potter (sister-in-law), a younger woman. As I recall they owned 90 acres around their house and the 30 acres that Gordon later bought. Dad later owned half of the 90 and me the other half. Dad would own half of the 30 acres of the Webster place, the half without the buildings.

Son Of Montana

We were invited to a meal (7-04) at the Kester home with, left to right: Mavis, Mom, Scoop, Duffy, Gordon, Mae (Scoop's's mother), Myrtle, two unknowns, a twin (Jack/Jim) Mary Mae and Doris with Lavon at front center in 1956.

photo 7-04

Scoop and Mavis did the haying for Myrtle Potter, first with horses, bull rake and overshot stacker and later with tractor and baler. Once when helping Scoop stack bales we were resting in the shade of the stack for a few minutes and Scoop asked what grade I was in. After I answered he told me I should stay in school as long as possible because it was a lot easier than stacking hay. He was right of course. The attitude of many working men of the Great Depression era was you should begin working as soon as possible and your education was something that you got while you worked.

Doris Kester became pregnant with twins boys in the early 1950s. She grew very large. I was amazed at the size of her belly because she was a small woman. When Jim and Jack were three and four they were all over me when I was at their house like Norman and I were all over Don Chapman when we were little boys. Jim and Jack were a handful.

They moved to a much bigger house (after the twins were born) about a mile to the southwest of us on a hill that later became known as the Kester Hill. Later Doris moved to Stevensville and lived there with Jim (never married) until she died in 2013.

We all went to school riding the school bus with the driver, Howard Longbottom, who lived in town. He owned and operated a small lumber planer when not driving the school bus. His wife Ruby was the secretary to our school principal, Mr. Tamplin. Howard's brother, Reuben Longbottom, rented the Cook ranch two miles southeast of our house in the deep coulee off the McFadgen hill. A family from north central Montana bought this ranch in the early1950s. Their name was Solomon - Mr. Solomon (Ted) and Mrs. (Rose) and four daughters.

Mary was the oldest, then Barbara, next Martha and last was Jeannie (Roberta Jean). Mary was 4 years older than me and Barbara was 2 years older. Mary was in my class and had her driver's license; she sometimes drove all of us kids to school in her dad's 1950 Ford sedan. She graduated eighth grade and married after the first year of high school, and I lost track of her. I later learned that she died of a brain tumor in her sixties.

Barbara helped her dad in the field, while Mary helped her mother. Their ranch had both irrigated and dry land. Thirty acres of the irrigated land was next to our 50 acre hay and grain fields. I remember Barbara raking hay on the 30 acres with her dad's model H Farmall tractor. Martha's age was between Patsy and Gordon, and Jeannie was about Gordon's age. Jeannie became very close friends with my sister Lavon. They both loved to ride horses and were together for days at a time riding, washing, brushing and feeding their horses. Jeannie would later marry Norman, and become my sister-in-law. They are together still and live in California.

Photo 7-05 is
of Norman
and wife
Jeannie at the
Solomon
ranch in the
1960s. This
was originally
the Ben (Nell)
Cook ranch.

photo 7-05

Mr. Solomon
(Ted) told me a story once about living in northern Montana. He
said their ranch was rather remote and it was sometimes difficult
for his girls to go to school. One winter, just prior to their moving
to western Montana, was extremely cold with a lot of snow and
wind. The roads drifted shut and he could not get the girls to
school for three long months.

Ted tried. He had a new Chevrolet pickup with chains and he tried
to push through the drifts. The engine began making loud knocking
sounds before he was through the first drift; he left the pickup and
walked back to the house. There was some oil on the porch of the
same type as was in the pickup crankcase and it had turned to jelly
like Vaseline. It was so cold that the oil would not flow and burned
out the rod bearings. It was the reason why Mary and Barbara were
so far behind the rest of us in school.

Photo 7-06 is of the Solomon family in the late 1950s: Jeannie,
Ted, Barbara and Mrs. Solomon (Rose). Barbara married a
neighbor by the name of Tom Redjou who had a dairy with his
father John. She now lives in Idaho. Martha married and lives in
central Montana. Jeannie has many interesting stories to tell about
the Solomon family.

Donald R Wax

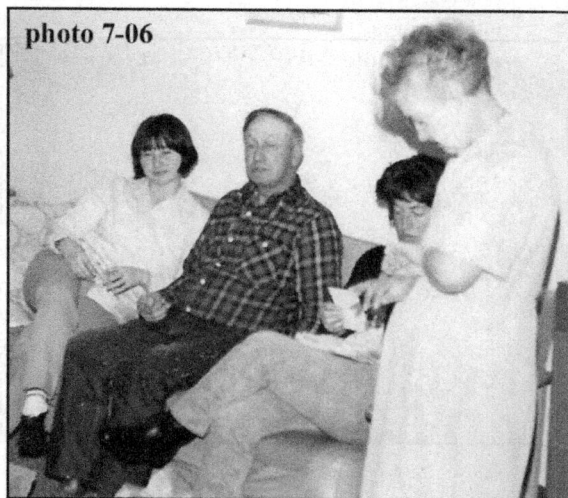

photo 7-06

It was well known that the Solomons were Jews. One day in the field, while we were taking a break, Ted told me he didn't understand why he had to work so hard. He said everybody knows that Jews don't work very hard. I didn't understand until I was older that there are very few Jewish farmers and that Ted wondered why he was not a jeweler or banker.

Ted did work hard and expanded their ranch with more irrigated hay land before he retired. A short time after selling the ranch he died of heart failure in June, 1973. Mrs. Solomon died in 2011 at age 95.

The land west of our house was owned by the Dayton family: Carl Dayton, Mrs. Dayton, and sons Neil, Morris, Wayne. I don't remember their ages but Wayne was about 12 years my senior. I remember riding the school bus with Morris and Wayne, probably during my first year of school. Howard Longbottom, the bus driver, once had a strong disagreement with Wayne and told him he could not ride the bus. The next morning Wayne tried to get on the bus and Mr. Longbottom pushed him down the steps and out the door. Wayne didn't ride the bus that day!

The Dayton's had a dairy at Bell Crossing Road and the Eastside Highway, and used the Sunset Bench land for hay and pasture. There were 90 acres of hay and 70 of pasture. They would bring a number of Holstein heifers and steers up to pasture in the spring and take them back in the fall. The haying began in mid-July and continued to mid-August.

Their house was about four miles to the southwest of us so we did not have a social relationship. But we did have a working relationship. We called them if any of their animals needed attention. I did help with the haying several times (see Earning Money) and the Dayton boys did help with the threshing. I remember shoveling grain into the apple house with Neil Dayton when I was 13. The reason I remember is that Neil had recently returned from the Korean War and was telling stories about his time in the Army. Sometime after that Carl killed himself with a shotgun. Later Dad and Wayne bought 90 acres of land (divided 50-50), and later I bought 40 of Wayne's 45 acres.

The McIntyre family lived about five miles southeast of our house: Ross and Jean, daughter Jeanette and son Rodney. Jeanette was about my age and Rodney was a couple of years younger. The McIntyres had a large dry land farm in the foothills and were somewhat better off than we were. We understood that Ross inherited his ranch from his father (Roscoe) who came from the eastern US (New York) during the investment rush of the early 1900s. Because of the distance we did not have much contact during the 1940s.

I remember visiting the McIntyre home and roaming around the hills with Rodney during the 1950s. Once we three (Norman, Rodney, I) were exploring near the tree line at the top of the foothills on a hot, dry and dusty July day and we came to a small pond. We decided to go swimming and stripped to our underwear before wading in. The water was so cold (snow melt) that our legs began to feel numb before we were waist deep. That was enough swimming for now, out we came. It was probably a good thing too; I know today that extreme temperature changes can be dangerous.

About three miles of road to the McIntyre house was unimproved. Those last miles could be a real bear during the winter time. It was a single lane of dirt along the canyon hillside, up and down and around corners. Rain, mud and snow made it a real challenge. Ross spent a lot of time helping with the transportation for his family (Jean, Jeanette and Rodney). Their car often passed our house covered top to bottom in mud. I remember driving this road in the summer time, it demanded your full attention.

I visited the McIntyre place on occasion during the summer to get fresh drinking water when working in the dry land fields. They had a spring below their house that gave especially cold water. There was a food storage box that the water ran through where they kept milk and cream. I always waved to Ross or Jean if I saw them, but I never felt that I needed to ask permission to fill up.

It became known that Dad and Ross had the same birthday, though Ross was nine years older. Dad and Ross would often have their birthday celebrations together and as they grew older they became good friends.

Photo 7-07 is of Jean and Ross McIntyre perhaps taken during one of the shared birthday parties.

photo 7-07

Jean was real outgoing and very social, but Ross was rather reserved and private. Around our house there was a response to a question that was considered too probing, "not too many" or "not too much". This response was attributed to Ross. How many calves did you have this spring? Not too many. How much did you get for your wheat? Not too much. The question was answered and the conversation continued, but you didn't learn anything. I later used this response in my work as a technician for General Electric. How long until it is fixed? Not too long was my answer.

Photo 7-08 is Dad's 80th and Ross's 89th birthday party at our house.

I visited Ross one summer day in the mid-1970s wearing a pair of shorts. We didn't visit very long, it was Ross's lunch time. All the time he kept looking at my legs and short pants. I guessed that he had never seen a man wear shorts.

Nov 19, 1993. Bill Wax (80) & Ross McIntyre (89) birthdays

A PENNY FOR YOUR THOUGHTS

HOW DID I END UP HERE?

photo 7-08

Many years later (1990s) when Ross was having some health problems I visited the McIntyre farm for the last time. He had had an operation to replace a knee joint and it became infected. The doctors couldn't cure the infection so they removed the implant, cleaned and closed the wound. He had no knee joint! There was just skin holding his leg together. It was sad to see him this way, a man so active all his life now crawling around on crutches.

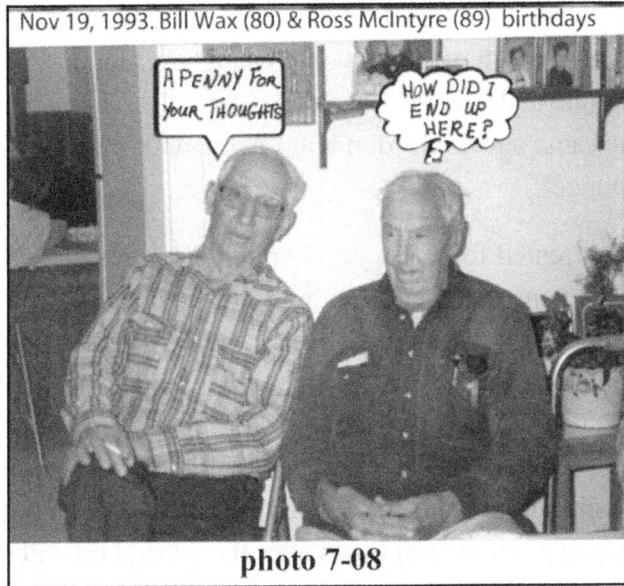

Rodney inherited the place from his parents and has continued to farm there until recently. He never married and has no children. I have on occasion met him in town over the years. Jeanette married and had several children, but I never met any of her children. I always wondered what would happen to the McIntyre farm after Rodney and Jeanette pass on.

The Bugli family came to the Sunset Bench in the late 1940s. They first rented the Myrtle Potter place northwest of us. Zack and Shirley Bugli would have two daughters and a son, Lynette, Vonnie and Jay, if I remember correctly. The two girls were about the same age as Gordon and Lavon, and Jay was 13-14 years younger.

Zack rented for a few years and then bought some land east of the Chapman's on what became Bugli Lane. He built a house and they lived there all the time I lived at home. I remember visiting Zack one day when he was haying on the rented Myrtle Potter land. His tractor was broken (no money for repairs) and he was raking hay with a jeep. Zack was always taking on projects with the bare minimum of what was needed, but somehow he got things done. I helped Zack several times over the years, and will cover those experiences in another chapter (Earning Money).

Zack did some rodeoing as a teenager and young man. He was a small slight built man and suffered some injuries; he had to give up the rodeo. Shirley and the girls were always involved with horses and horse related activities. I guess you could say Shirley was an over achiever. She was always on the go. Once she made Zack some shirts. She laid out several layers of cloth and cut it to one pattern; she sewed them together like an assembly line. Zack had half a dozen new western shirts, each very attractive.

In the 1960s I visited the Bugli's while on vacation and remember seeing Jay when he was about three years old. He had on a big cowboy hat and was telling me how he was going to drive the combine. Zack was servicing the combine that day. Today Jay Bugli owns a helicopter repair business located in the coulee off the McFadgen hill. Jay did indeed drive the combine and much more.

Helicopters are seen and heard flying around the Sunset Bench being tested, and going to/from Jay's shop. Gordon and I visited Jay one day a few years ago (2000s) and Jay was rebuilding an old helicopter (Vietnam era Huey) from Australia. It had been converted to agricultural use.

Gordon and I stopped to visit with Zack too. Shirley had died some years before and Zack was living alone near Jay. He told us a story about his big John Deere tractor and red Ford pickup. He drove over to the tractor one cold fall morning, parked and started the tractor so it could warm up. He forgot to lock the brakes; the tractor began to roll backwards hitting the side of the pickup and leaving a deep scratch the full length of the pickup. He had insurance on the pickup and reported the accident to the insurance company.

The back and forth with the insurance agent went something like this. *Who was driving the pickup?* No one, it was parked. *Who was driving the tractor?* No one, it was parked. *Was the pickup engine running?* Yes. *But no one was driving the pickup?* That's right. *Was the tractor engine running?* Yes. *But no one was driving the tractor?* That's right. *Did anyone see the accident?* No, not right away. *Where were you?* I was relieving myself on the opposite side of the pickup. *When did you first discover the accident?* When I heard the tractor hit the pickup. *So the tractor moved and hit the pickup?* Yes. *Didn't you see the tractor move?* No, I was watching something else. *Who was driving the tractor?* No one. After satisfying this insurance agent, more people from the insurance company called, and Zack had to explain the same thing two more times. I looked over at the pickup and it was all new again, so the insurance agents must have received satisfactory answers to all their questions.

The Bugli girls married local boys and live on the Sunset Bench.

There are of course a number of other neighbors that I did not mention here. Some of them will get mentioned in other chapters. I don't want to slight anyone, but this is my story and I'm choosing to end this section.

The Outbuildings

Temporary to permanent, few to many

A term we hear today is "strawman" which is not really about straw or man, and of course the Three Little Pigs once built a straw house. We had a straw barn. It was a warm and functional barn that served for almost 20 years. It probably was built in the fall of 1939 or 1940. I really do not know, but after describing how it was made we can draw some conclusions.

Large posts were set in the ground to define the four corners with a door opening facing south. A frame of lodge pole pine was then attached to form the walls with a window opening to the east and a flat roof. Over this frame was attached woven wire as would normally be used for sheep or pig fencing. Every fall the threshing machine was parked to the west of this pole and wire frame, and the straw was blown into a large pile over the frame. The excess straw was cleared away from the door and window openings, and you have the straw barn. This straw barn was there from my earliest memories. I know that Dad and Grandpa Wax had grain crops in 1939 and 1940, and Dad had a contract on lot 21 in the summer of 1939.

Dad added stanchions for six cows. He milked cows by hand in this barn until 1948 when the apple house was converted into a milking barn. He milked three or four cows in the early 1940s and by the end of the 1940s he was milking eight to nine cows by hand.

The milk was carried in a wheel barrow to the apple house basement where the electric separator separated cream from milk. The cream and whole milk we used at home; the excess cream was sold to a small creamery in Stevensville and the skimmed milk was fed to the pigs.

The straw barn was a warm, inexpensive and functional milking barn. Fresh straw was spread on the ground inside for the cows and when soiled it was pitched out through the window. Fresh straw was taken inside from the pile outside to replace the soiled straw. The cows could also bed down around the periphery of the pile outside. After each threshing season the barn had a new exterior and a fresh supply of bedding for the animals. The soiled straw and manure was then spread each spring to fertilize the fields. I guess Dad was an organic farmer! He later built a feed lot east of the straw barn, so the cows were always close at hand.

The straw barn was used for birthing in cold weather after the cow milking was moved to the apple house basement. We once had a sow in the straw barn with a new litter. I carried a five gallon bucket of skimmed milk and grain over to feed her, and while emptying the bucket into her trough she took a swipe at me. Her mouth covered my right hand which was on the bucket handle. I pulled away as quick as possible missing most of her bite, but it did leave heavy scratches across the top and down the side of my hand. I was about 13 at the time and was ever after careful around new mothers.

It was also a cool place for the cows to get out of the hot summer sun. That's enough about the straw barn, more about threshing in The Harvests.

I am reminded of a story about this same sow and Lavon when she was about 2 years old. The sow somehow got free and was roaming the farmyard with her litter. Lavon wandered beyond the yard fence into the farmyard; she saw the piglets and approached them. When the sow noticed Lavon, she charged and knocked Lavon down. Patsy saw the charge. She yelled and ran to help Lavon. Mom and I heard Patsy yell. Patsy got to Lavon and quickly assured us that Lavon was OK. We separated Lavon from the sow and her piglets.

The apple house is next and a short history of how it came to be called the apple house.

Beginning in 1910 the bench land was divided into 10 acre plots; planted with apple trees and sold to investors in Minneapolis. The Sunset Bench had hundreds of acres of apple trees by the 1920s. It was sort of an "apple boom" for investors until the crash of 1929.

Roads, fences and irrigation systems were built. Some investors came to live here and built very nice homes, but most invested without ever seeing what they bought. After a few years the investors were expecting to receive a return on their investment and apple crops did on occasion provide a nice return. It was during one of those good years that the apple house was built in the 1920s.

One of our neighbors, Paul McFadgen, helped build it when he was a teenager. It was built by an investor to sort and store apples, hence the name apple house. It had a basement for frost free storage with a double set of doors opening to the south and a larger ground level with elevator platform for moving apples to the basement. It was made of rough cut number two fir boards, double layered on the floor and walls. It had a steep pitched cedar shingled roof and was not painted.

During the depression years of the 1930s the apple crops were mostly failures due the short growing season. Many owners lost their investments due to unpaid taxes. Mom and Dad bought their lots for back taxes, one 10 acre lot for only $45.

An old timer (Ed Sims, the ditch rider) told me that he helped clear acres of apple trees in the 1930s. He described how they pushed the cut trees off the south side of the bench and burned them (Sims once owned lot 17 which extends over the south edge of the bench). They built a heavy duty buck rake which was powered by four horses (a team on each side). It was probably a beefed-up buck rake normally used to harvest hay. Can you imagine seeing this buck rake pushing apple trees and tree parts across the Sunset Bench to the bluff overlooking Willoughby Creek and setting it on fire?

The first changes to the apple house (after we moved from the Webster place in late 1940) were made when Dad removed the elevator windlass (see The Well). Then Dad built a work bench along the west side of the center section where he sharpened tools and sickle bars for the mower. To the east and west of the center he built grain storage bins. Dad bought number two fir flooring (tongue & groove) to cover the bare studs on the outside walls for two sides of the grain bin. Wall studs and fir flooring were added to complete the other two walls. He strung several strands of wire and turn-buckle tighteners north-south and east-west to strengthen the walls.

The wire was surplus from the phone line that was installed by the farmers and ranchers before the war. Dad mentions harvesting the poles in one of his letters to Mom in 1938. They had formed a co-op and the line was connected through the telephone exchange in Stevensville. In the 1960s the Bell Telephone Company absorbed this co-op and the farmers took down the poles and wire. Dad used this wire for electric fencing for many years.

Bette Magini (in my class) worked at this phone exchange after graduating from high school in 1957.

By 1945-46 these bins were being filled with oats and barley. That is when Dad bought a grain grinder (hammer mill) and placed it directly over the old elevator platform in line with the door. The new tractor was lined up outside the door with a belt to power the hammer mill. He could now grind grain for the cows, horses and pigs. Ground grain is like course flour which is more completely digested by the animals.

In 1948 Dad converted the apple house basement into our milking barn. The basement did not have any windows, so Dad cut three small rectangles at the ground floor level into the west wall and cut open the floor between the joists to allow light to penetrate into the basement area. These openings were enclosed and windows installed. I don't recall any widows on the east side though there may have been.

He then poured a concrete floor with troughs to drain the liquids and installed drain pipe out to the coulee to the south. He installed stanchions for 10 cows and feed troughs so the cows could have some grain during milking. A Surge (brand name) milking machine system was installed and the double set of basement doors were cut in half. These half doors allowed us to open only a quarter of the door way to get the cows in and out, thereby conserving the warmth during cold weather. There was room for storage in the southeast corner, and the cream separator and vacuum pump occupied the southwest corner. We had two electric lights, one in the southwest corner and one in the middle.

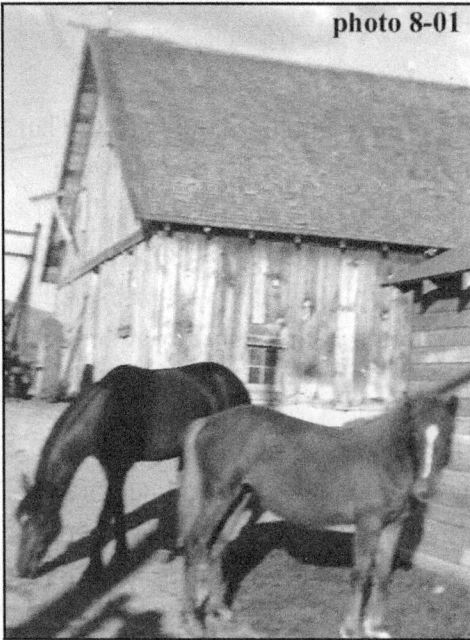

photo 8-01

Photo 8-01 is from about 1956. Notice the window low on the west wall and the brackets; one on the north wall (above tractor) and one on the peak of the roof. The one on the north wall was to hold the dust collector for the hammer mill and later to hold a carcass when butchering. The one on the roof was to hold the radio antenna. To the right on the roof you can see one of the lightning rods. The horses are my sister Lavon's pets, Bunny and Trinket. The shadows indicate that it was late evening in early summer

After Dad began milking cows in the apple house basement (1948) the dust collector was moved back inside and he built a small bin in the northeast corner of the east grain bin. A small chute was attached to the bottom of this bin that allowed the ground grain to drain into a small box in the basement so we could conveniently feed grain to the cows during milking. The dust collector spout was turned to exit a window for filling a large tank parked outside. The tank (mounted on skids) was then moved to the pig lot for feeding the pigs. Norman and I were doing most of the grain grinding by the mid-1950s.

By 1949 Norman and I were old enough now to help Dad with many of the chores. We gathered the cows from the feed lot across the field to the south beside the straw barn. We also helped during milking by giving the cows grain and guiding them in and out, and locking/unlocking the stanchions. Cleaning the barn was a chore we didn't like. The fresh manure was scooped out of the troughs after each milking and about once a week we connected a hose to the faucet at the stock water tank and washed the floor. The cold, ice and snow during winter made this job more difficult.

There was a single light mounted high up on the apple house south wall for the dark winter nights that provided enough light at the entrance, but it was only a guide when coming from the feed lot across the field.

I remember once gathering the cows from the feed lot on such a night. As I was walking toward the apple house light I heard heavy footsteps approaching fast from behind. The cows were all in front of me, so who/what could it be? I turned around to confront our Holstein bull face to face. He was large, young and frisky, so Dad had put a ring in his nose with 4 feet of chain to slow him down. If he walked with his head down in the normal confrontation position he could easily step on the end of the chain and jerk the ring in his nose. Ouch! So he was forced to walk with his head held high enough to prevent the chain from dragging on the ground. When I turned he lowered his head, remembered the chain and stopped dead in his tracks. He did surprise me, but I was not frightened because I had seen him do this many times before.

On another night in August gathering the cows, just as it was getting dark, I saw a lightning strike behind our house. A large fire ball appeared just as the strike faded and continued for several minutes. WOW! What was that? It was not our house, but was close. The next day when driving past the Gene Magini house I saw the result of the strike. The lightning struck a large pine tree opposite their house burning off all the needles and upper branches. It also blew off a quarter round section of the tree down to the root. The stomp is still standing left of the cattle guard opposite the house at 619 Pine Hollow Road on Google maps street scene.

By the time Norman and I were 13 and 14 years old we were doing much of the milking at night; Dad milked in the morning. We three did not have a schedule system, but was sort of catch as catch can. Whoever was home and free would milk the cows. Norman and I were not free in the mornings because we had to get ready for school, but were free in the evenings most of the time. There were a few occasions when we missed a milking, and there were a few times when Norman and I did the milking morning and night.

One of those times was when Dad decided to work in a mine in the mountains south of Darby in the fall. He had to leave home about 5:00am driving our first pickup, a 1946 red International (½ ton) two plus hours to get to the mine. He operated a jack hammer for eight hours getting home late, tired and hungry. It was tough on all of us because Norman and I had to milk mornings and evenings, so Dad quit after a week. Another time Mom and Dad had a big fight and Dad went to Missoula to stay with his sister (Aunt Doris) for four days. As I recall this happened during the summer so Norman and I had more time to do the milking.

One evening Norman and I were milking the cows when little sister Lavon wandered into the barn. We didn't pay much attention as she was always outside even though she was only about 2 years old. Norman and I continued with our work not thinking much about Lavon being in the barn.

The vacuum pump and motor were mounted on a plank that sat on the floor and did not have a cover over the belt and pulley. She heard the noise, saw the motion of the belt and walked directly to it reaching out to touch it with her right hand. The pump pulley caught her right thumb and cut it off at the base joint. I saw it happen, grabbed her and rushed out the door toward the house. As it happened, Mom and Dad had just now returned from town so they drove straight to the hospital in Hamilton. Lavon lost her thumb.

I always felt bad about that accident because I could have prevented it if I had taken Lavon out of the barn. Dad raised the vacuum pump and motor to head height and installed a cover over the belt and pulley.

Photo 8-02 is from about 1956. Notice Dad standing in one of the open door panels, there was another set of doors about 4 feet back from these doors.

Someone is carrying a sack of potatoes.

During this time we were buying cull potatoes from (James) Duard

photo 8-02

Higgins and storing them in the southeast corner of the apple house basement. Every few days Dad filled a barrel setting on some rocks with potatoes and water; build a fire under it and boiled potatoes for the pigs. The smell was rich, the potatoes hot and the pigs loved them on cold days. Notice a barrel and can on the stoneboat. A can of skimmed milk, fresh boiled potatoes and some ground barley and oats; those pigs ate very well.

A stoneboat is a crude sled, just 2 runners usually of lodge pole pine with a platform built on top. A stoneboat is used to carry things a short distance, especially things that are difficult to load and unload. They were commonly used during the 1940s and 50s.

Sometime after Dad bought the new 1948 Chevrolet car he built a garage and wood shed. As with all the buildings before, he dug and poured a concrete foundation by hand. He filled the foundation interior with dirt and gravel, and poured a concrete floor. He bought number two rough cut pine boards from a small sawmill near Woodside north of Hamilton. The wall studs and roof beams were made of lodge pole pine.

Dad made a jig for the buzz saw which he used to cut a slice from the lodge poles creating a flat surface on which to nail the pine boards. The top and bottom plates and window and door frames were made of rough cut 2x4s. Using the pole studs and beams meant that each piece was custom fit to make a square and even structure.

photo 8-03

Photo 8-03 is of Patsy (six) and Norman (nine) during the summer of 1949 standing on the sidewalk leading to the porch. That is Uncle Jack's (Aunt Doris' husband) Studebaker pickup behind them. He bought it just after the war ended without a metal box so he built the wooden box.

Notice the garage/wood shed in the background. We see the north side in this photo, the side facing the house. The garage also had a window on the east wall. Behind the pickup east of the garage was the wood pile.

One incident that I remember very well about the garage happened in the summer of 1950. We moved our bed from the west side of the porch to just inside the door in the northeast corner of the garage. The firewood was still stored in the southeast corner during the summer months. Norman and I slept there during that summer. If we lay on our stomachs we could look out through the large spaces between the boards. The spaces were created when the green pine boards dried. One evening there came a thunderstorm rolling across the Sunset Bench with lightning, wind and rain, maybe even some small hail. We were uncomfortable and afraid, so we watched out through a crack at all the activity. KERR BOOOMM! Blinding light and sound all in the same instant. Holy smokes, that was close! But the storm didn't give much more after that and we soon fell asleep.

Next morning we dressed and went to the house for breakfast. We asked Mom and Dad if they heard the lightning as we had not spoken last night during the storm. Yes they heard, and explained that it had entered the house and burned out the radio. Norman and I began to investigate; we moved the radio away from the wall and found a large black spot around where the antenna wire entered the house. We ran outside to look for the antenna wire. It was completely gone, every last inch of it from the house to the apple house. Vaporized, gone!

No more radio. No more news or entertainment from the outside world. I remember that we listened to the news and market reports during our midday meals from the local station in Missoula. We received a good signal from Missoula during the day but power was reduced at night, and the Missoula station was no better than signals from places like Los Angeles, Salt Lake, even New Orleans and Del Rio, Texas

In the evening we scanned the dial looking for a good signal to listen to shows such as the Grand Ole Opera, Amos n Andy, George Burns & Gracie Allen, and my favorite show Jack Benny. Weather was a big factor in determining which station we could get and which show we listened to. We sat near the radio, quietly and intently listening to a show until the fading signal gave us only noise and static. If the signal didn't fade and we listened too long, Dad would give us a stern warning. It's time to milk!

photo 8-04

The radio (photo 8-04) was one of those popular pre-war floor models. It had a nice cabinet of two-tone wood, a large lighted dial on the top and a large grill with speaker on the bottom. I don't know how we happened to have such a nice radio or the brand name or what happened to it after the lightning strike, but it was missed.

An interesting follow up to this story is that a traveling salesman came to our house a month or so later. He was selling lightning rods! Can you believe the timing? Just after a strike had smoked our radio! It was the easiest and quickest sale he ever made. In a week or so the workmen came to install the lightning rod system on our barn and house. Safe at last! As far as I know lightning never did strike those rods.

In 1951 after the addition to our house was complete; Dad built a shop and garage using the kitchen section of the old farm house that I mention in Our House. Dad built a foundation and concrete floor in the same manner and method as the garage, and moved this old building onto the foundation. Garage style doors were built and hung on the open east end. Dad added a workbench along the south wall and built a forge in the west end. All shop activities were moved from the apple house to this new shop. The center area was available to park the model SC Case tractor. This is where Norman and I worked on our bikes and cars.

Dad used the forge to work old automobile leaf springs into new teeth for a John Deere cultivator that we called a quack machine. He built a hot metal shear from two old plow shares and a long cultivator lever. He would heat the spring material in the forge until white hot, cut a 12-14 inch section, reheat and cut two corners to form a point on each end. The center was then reheated to white and two holes were punched. Some final heating, hammering on the anvil, drilling on the drill press, tempering in water and the point was ready for use. Dad made several sets of these points which we wore down to half their size on the quack machine preparing the fields for planting.

In this shop building I made a tire bead breaker and attached it to the north wall. This was before tubeless tires and we were often patching the tubes because of age and the many hazards on the farm and dirt roads. None of us was heavy enough to break the tire bead from the rim to extract the tube by standing or jumping on the tire. It was always a struggle. I made an angle iron frame attached to a long cultivator lever attached to a bracket mounted on the wall. I could now lay the tire on the floor, place the frame end (8" wide) on the tire next to the rim and squeeze down on the lever and break the bead with ease.

I make a tool during my career with GE and was told that I was wasting my time. It was a software tool to test the functions of a control program. It was not an accepted practice at the time, but in the end it served me well.

Sometime after the last addition to the house, the outhouse was moved to the southeast corner of the garage. We had inside plumbing since 1946 and Mom didn't like that the outhouse was visible from the house and yard. It was now only visible when approaching the farm from the south. As mentioned before, we men continued to use the outhouse often (our second toilet). It is still there today.

I don't ever recall having toilet tissue in the outhouse, only the catalogs. The Sears and Montgomery Ward catalogs were dispatched to the outhouse after the new ones arrived. Catalogs were an important part of our education; we learned about new machines and technology, female underwear, even new words from catalogs in both houses.

It soon became difficult to find our way in the catalogs because the index pages were the first to be used. Those pages were the lightest and softest in the catalog. The routine was to select a couple of the best pages from the catalog; tear them out and crumple them into a ball and unfold them. Then repeat several times to soften the paper, tear the page in half and proceed to cleanup. Job complete!

photo 8-05

Photo 8-05 is from 1966 and shows the main outbuildings of the 1950s. It is cut from a large photo of our farmstead taken by a studio that flew over farm properties and took photos (farmstead portraits) to sell.

Notice the outhouse at the bottom right corner of the garage, between the garage and the chicken house you can see the wood pile. At the upper right corner you can see the shop building, to its left is an old metal building used for oil/grease storage and a gasoline storage tank. In the center is the pump house and to its left is the basketball backboard. Notice the apple house basement doors are open for summer ventilation. The chicken house was not always where you see it in this photo, in the bottom right corner.

Norman and I built a basketball backboard; we dug post holes and set two poles to mount the backboard. We then bent some rod material to form a basket, drilled a pair of holes and mounted it to the backboard. We could now shoot baskets in the driveway in front of the garage.

About the same time as the shop was built the Sunset Irrigation District (SID) replaced the wooden flume with steel pipe. The wooden flume brought the water from Burnt Fork Creek up along the north side of the bench. I cannot describe the location exactly, but do remember visiting the old flume several times and even swimming in it once. The SID members were allowed to take as much of the old flume wood as they wanted. Dad, Norman and I spent several days hauling home wagon loads of planks.

The Abstract of Title papers indicate that the bonds were sold in the summer of 1948, so the flume wood was probably harvested soon after. These planks were redwood from California around 1900. I saw some of the original planks in Rollie Lewis's house in Corvallis many years later. They were very fine tongue and groove inch thick planks of redwood.

The redwood planks were used to build the water side of the flume. A second layer on the outside was of rough cut fir and cedar planks. The redwood planks were not very useable and for the most part became firewood.

We recovered many weathered, but useable, planks from the outside of the flume. They were used to build the chicken house. It was initially built on skids so it could be moved around the farm yard and pasture. Dad used the same jig with the buzz saw to cut lodge pole studs as was used building the garage, but this time he trimmed front and back so we could line the inside with planks. We poured saw dust into the wall cavities for insulation.

One day I was helping Dad fit the inside planks around a window opening. He was spending too much time (I thought) getting the plank to fit perfectly, and I said "Just nail it up, no one will ever know". He replied "I will know". He was right. If you don't take pride in your work how can you expect others to appreciate it.

One time when the chicken house was located east of the shop Norman and I were given the job of cleaning it. Dad removed a window, parked the manure spreader outside and gave us each a fork. An hour later Dad came back to see how things were going. Norman and I had been arguing and fighting the whole time, nothing was done. Dad was tired of our fighting, so off came his belt and we got a whipping. Shortly after that the manure spreader was full and the chicken house was clean and ready for fresh straw.

Later the chicken house was moved to the spot seen in the photo and mounted a foundation with concrete floor. A large machine shed/shop was built east of the apple house by 1966 and later a second garage for was built west of the garage/wood shed. Most of the outbuildings were covered in painted or galvanized metal sometime after the second garage was built.

There were other sheds built on skids for the pigs and cows. Most of these sheds were temporary in nature and most did not last long, or serve a need beyond their initial purpose. A permanent pole barn was built in place of the straw barn.

Photo 8-07 is from 1966 and shows the main farmstead. The pole

photo 8-07

barn is located out of view to the right. In the upper right corner are the hay feeders for winter feeding and to the upper left side you see sheds for the pigs and calves. To the right of the apple house you see the large shop/machine shed and to its lower right corner you see a shed with corral for the young calves. To the upper right side you can see the corrals for working the cattle. The stock water tank is to the right of the chicken house.

photo 8-06

Photo 8-06 is of the farmstead in the 2000s, about 40 years after photo 8-07.

The Harvests

How we made our money

The Wax farm produced a variety of crops during the 1940s and 1950s, some were consumed and others sold. I will describe the crops, as best I remember, except the garden which is described in "Food & Fuel".

Dad began milking cows when the straw barn was built. This was discussed in The Outbuildings. The most we ever milked was probably 14 or 15 cows in the mid-1950s.

Dad preferred the Shorthorn breed at first because they were a good combination of milk and beef cow. Later he bred our Shorthorn cows with a Holstein bull (The Outbuildings); the resulting mixed breed cows gave more milk and good meat. By the 1960s he was into Hereford cows for beef. Dad wanted to cut down on the milking after Norman and I left home, and soon had only beef cows. During the 1970s he was selling 90 Hereford calves each fall.

For a cow to produce milk year after year she must have a calf. A cow can produce a good flow of milk for about eight months, after that the flow drops off until she stops producing. So, the cows were bred on a 12 month cycle and the cycles were staggered to provide a continuous flow of milk. In the early 1950s we had 10-16 new baby calves from our cows; we also bought additional baby calves for a total of around 20 each year.

photo 9-01

In photo 9-01 we see Dad's Hereford cattle plus the cow shed that replaced the straw barn, and to its left is the feed lot in 1970.

The new calf was left with its mother for the first three days to get a good start with mother's milk. Then they were separated; the cow was added to the milking herd and the calf went to the calf corral. The new calf was fed by hand for another week to ten days with whole milk. Feeding baby calves is a messy chore; they can only suck until taught to drink.

Norman and I taught the calves to drink. Fill a two gallon bucket half full of milk, and standing at the head of the calf, place your two middle fingers in its mouth and it will begin to suck. Then lift the bucket to the calf so that its mouth is in the milk. Some milk will enter the calf's mouth and it will begin to suck faster. The calf will also buck its head upward as would be natural when nursing its mother. Do you get the picture? There is milk and calf slobber splashing all over.

We switched the calf to skim milk at two weeks, it could now drink from the bucket without help. We set out three or four buckets at once, and then made sure each calf would drink only his milk. We had to prevent the bigger calves from stealing milk from the smaller calves. At three months or so the calves were weaned off milk, and ate hay and/or grass supplemented with a little ground grain. A little after that and it was time to make some decisions about each new calf: bull, cow or beef.

Photo 9-02 is from 1949 'working' the calves. I am sure about only two people; Norman is on the ground facing the

photo 9-02

camera and I am behind him. I think Dad is on Norman's left and Duffy Kester to Norman's right in the dark hat. I think Scoop Kester is on horseback. Scoop has a rope around the calf's rear legs and Dad is holding down its head. It might be Patsy in the scarf. I don't know who was holding the branding iron (spread leg stance to my right).

In the background you can see some apple trees, a couple of pig sheds and perhaps some pigs. We were not sit-on-the-fence observers, but in the mix helping even if it was not always necessary. Notice the dog in the right corner waiting for his little round piece of meat. The dog ate the testicles with great anticipation and delight.

In the beef producing regions of Montana many small towns have a Rocky Mountain Oyster Festival each year during roundup. The calf testicles are gathered, prepared, breaded and skillet fried. They are served with hot sauce and cold beer (the best I know); I've never eaten them myself. They are called oysters because after the sheathing membrane is removed they are split open and after frying have the appearance of fried oysters. There is another reason that I will not describe that has to do with how oysters are eaten.

Dad selected two or three of the heifers to become replacements for the milk cows. A bull might also be identified for later service, not on our farm, but traded with a neighbor for a bull of equal value. All were treated the same as to branding and dehorning. The bull calves not selected for breeding were castrated and they became beef. It took a full morning to corral and process the new crop of calves one time per year.

Those selected for special purposes were watched during the rest of the year, and if they did not meet expectations they lost their special status. Dad knew his animals well, so that didn't happen often.

Each fall we would have 16-20 calves to sell (most were Dad's), but sometimes Norman and I had one or two of our own to sell. If we had our own calf, market day was looked forward to all summer long. Counting our chickens before they hatched!

This was the time of year that the new catalogs were in the house and studied carefully for what we wanted to buy. It was when all our new school clothes were bought: a pair of pants, a shirt, some socks or underwear, perhaps a new coat or shoes and overshoes. Depending on the need and the price of calves we might also get a new cap and mittens or gloves.

The pigs were a crop we sold twice each year. In the 1950s we had three or four sows and we could typically get 30 to 40 piglets to market age in the fall and spring. Each sow can have up to 16 babies, normally we had 8 to 14 with an average of 10 surviving to market age.

Little pigs grow fast and at about eight weeks it is time to 'work' the pigs. All the piglets get rings in their noses to prevent them from rooting and males get castrated. Three rings were normally used, one in the middle and one on each side. Sometimes they would root anyway or lose a ring and we had to add a couple more rings.

Dad had a favorite pocket knife on which he honed one blade to razor sharp. It was the castration blade. He also had a nail keg (12-13 inches in diameter by 22 high) that was just the right size to stuff a piglet into. We separated the piglets from the older pigs, caught the males by their hind legs and stuffed them head first into the nail keg. A piglet was long enough that its butt and hind legs were outside the keg. Dad held the keg between his legs facing the piglet's belly and I held the hind legs pulling them up toward its back. This would tip the buttocks and testicles toward Dad. With three swift and sure strokes of the knife the testicle was out; one last stroke to cut the cord and it was gone. It was all done before the piglet had time to squeal; putting rings in its nose caused more squealing.

Ring pliers have cupped ends on its jaws to hold the ring. The ring is trapezoid shaped with one shallow corner open and the ends sheared at a diagonal to make a sharp point. Dad held the piglet between his knees, sat on its back and lifted its head with one hand. I placed a ring into the opened ring pliers in his other hand, then pliers to nose squeezing the ring closed. I reloaded the pliers twice more and the job was done.

Processing of each piglet didn't take much time, but catching those little buggers could sometimes be fun, but other times frustrating. In either case, it was what took the most time.

In the 1950s Dad had a ¾ ton Ford pickup with a stock rack in which he could haul 16-18 pigs to market. Before then, Gene Magini or Scoop Kester hauled our pigs to market. Dad selected the most even bunch at just the right market weight and off to sell the load. Because of this selection process Dad often got top price for his pigs. A week or two later a second batch was carried to market when each was at just the right weight.

We sold the pigs at auction in Hamilton or Missoula, or to the Daly slaughter house in Missoula. We stopped butchering in the 1950s, it was messy and too much work. Daly's did custom butchering and curing, so Dad would select one or two pigs for them to process for us. Our pigs made some fine bacon and ham cured to Dad's specifications.

I have a short side story to tell. It was maybe winter 1944 and one of the sows had her babies at night. It was bitter cold that night and Dad had gone out several times to check on them, but by morning he found some of those little guys were freezing. He picked the baby pigs up by their tails, so as not to alarm their mother (they don't squeal when picked by their tails), and loaded them into a burlap bag. He brought them into the house and rubbed them warm, then put them back into the sack and the sack was placed behind the kitchen stove. By mid morning that sack was moving in every direction and it was time to take them back to their mother.

Harvesting the grain and seed crops was the exciting time for me. Big machinery was involved and I could watch, and as I grew older I helped. The threshing was always done by Harley (L) Williamson. He was a small man (like Dad), very likeable and attentive. Harley was someone I liked; I marveled at his caring for those big machines. Harley had a small farm near Victor, but much of his cash income was from custom threshing.

Photo 9-03 is the way I remember Harley Williamson's 15/30 tractor with rubber tires on the back and steel wheels on the front. Note the exhaust exit at the top of the frame above and behind the front wheel.

photo 9-03

Harley was related to the Williamson families living around Stevensville. I went to school with two Williamson boys.

Harley's machines were old and each winter he spent time servicing and repairing them. I don't ever remember any major failures during the threshing season on the Sunset Bench. If something did happen Harley knew his machines inside out and would soon have it back working again. Both thresher and 15/30 tractor were pre-1930s McCormack Deering, and a Chevrolet grain truck of the similar vintage.

Harley came up on the Sunset Bench from Bell Crossing along the South Sunset Bench Road. We could see him when he crossed over the Big Ditch. He was strung out like a train. The 15/30 was pulling the thresher and the old Chevy truck was attached to rear of the thresher. The 15/30 could go about four mph, so it would take Harley an hour more to get his thresher into place and be ready to start after we spotted him. Threshing was a busy day; we saw Harley coming and picked up the pace.

Mom had to cook and feed seven (or more) men besides tending to a baby brother or baby sister, so Patsy stayed home to help. Norman and I helped with the wagons, tools and water. As we got older we were on the working end of the forks or shovels. And all of our normal chores had to be completed: milking cows, feeding pigs and cows.

Harley had been on the road since 6:00 am and was in no mood to wait for anyone not prepared to thresh. We were ready. By 9:30 in the morning under a low fall sun we threw the first bundles into the thresher.

Our grain had a lot of straw and the men sometimes overloaded the bundle conveyor on the thresher. The governor would open the throttle on that 15/30 and the thresher would groan and shake; the flow from the straw spout would look like a big snake wiggling out to the straw pile.

photo 9-04

Photo 9-04 is a McCormick Deering thresher similar to Harley's. Search YouTube.com for threshing or binding grain to see examples of such work.

The 15/30 did NOT have a muffler; the exhaust manifold ended pointing down at the side of the frame. It was a 4 cylinder and ran at about 1000 rpm. All of that sound and activity, and the low grumble and growl from that tractor would raise goose bumps on my arms. It was a sight to see and feel.

Son Of Montana

When the threshing started Harley was all over his thresher adjusting air flow, speeds and sieves, and checking the straw flow; he was on top, the sides, in the back, up front, checking the belts and all the adjustments. If something got stuck in the thresher Harley stopped the 15/30 and crawled inside to correct the problem. It was like that thresher swallowed Harley. What if Harley didn't get out?

That reminds me of a story. Once when I was five years old Dad and I were returning from town when we saw Lou Miller with his crawler tractor across from Charley Magini's house, so we stopped. As we walked up to Charley and Lou we had to pass in front of the crawler tractor when Dad told me to be very careful because those tracks could squash me like a bug. Lou and Charley told me the same; I believed it and I was frightened. It was the one time I was truly afraid of a machine.

Harley went from farm to farm up the Sunset Bench usually ending up at Shorty (August) Baumgartner's place on the Burnt Fork. There are a few places that I remember, one was the Zimmerman (Maurice?) place. It was different. Mrs. Zimmerman didn't cook a meal for us at noon. Mr. Zimmerman asked us to bring our own lunches or go home to eat. I think one time he even went to town and brought back burgers and such when everyone complained. We were always shorthanded, never enough wagons or men which meant that everyone had to work harder and faster. No Breaks! Nobody liked to thresh at the Zimmerman place.

Next was the (Joseph) Stang farm, nothing usual except one time we threshed field peas. Norman, Francis and I drove Ford tractors with buck rake heads. We pushed pea vines to the thresher like crazy. Each of us trying to get our load back to the thresher first, boys racing. We were 11 and 12 years old, and it was fun.

Then it was on to Shorty Baumgartner's place where there were more men than wagons. The wagons had to get in line to off-load at the thresher. Elsie brought out pie and coffee at mid-morning. There was a full meal at lunch time. The men ate, talked, drank, smoked, loaded some bundles and then repeated the process. So Zimmerman asked "Shorty, how come you have so many men and I never have enough?" Shorty (born in Austria) laughed and said "Dats easy cahz everbody like ole Shorty". And it was true; everybody did like Shorty and Elsie.

That reminds me of a story. One time when we were 10 and 11, Norman and I rode our bikes up to visit Francis Stang. We found Francis and discussed what to do next, finally deciding that we should visit Shorty and Elsie Baumgartner because we might get a sweet. It was a hot summer day and we were hoping for ice cream. So away we went.

No one answered the door at Shorty's house; they must be in the barn. No one was in the barn, but we did look at all Shorty's pinup girls lifting the cloth patch that Elsie pinned over them so we could see everything. Doors open, pickup and tractor in the yard, but we couldn't find Elsie or Shorty.

Finally we noticed Elsie's hat on the ground out in the pasture, Oh my God! They were both very old. What could have happened? We ran toward the hat, it moved! We ran faster. The hat moved again. Suddenly we saw Elsie hidden behind a ditch bank. She was setting on the ground with her legs spread wide and a young ewe between them. Elsie's sleeves were rolled up past her elbows and she had one hand into the birth canal of the ewe.

Her greeting was short and to the point. Be quiet boys! Stay put till I finish pulling this lamb! We did and she did. Soon the young lamb was dried off and nursing and we were headed back to the house. Just as we arrived at the house Shorty appeared in his boots from the other direction carrying a shovel (irrigating). Shorty waved and yelled, "Elsie, da boys n me want pie". Elsie washed up and we ate pie with ice cream. It was worth the trip; we went back home riding down South Burnt Fork Road like the wind.

The first time I remember threshing was in 1944. Norman and I climbed into Harley's truck were we found a box of matches in the glove box and began to strike the matches. Harley saw us, told Dad and that was the end of that. We could stay, but we had to stay where they could see us and not get into any more trouble. Mom didn't want us in the house, so the choice was stay put and behave.

The last time I remember threshing was on December 1, 1954. We were threshing clover seed in the west half of the 50 acres. Since it was so late in the fall we were starting rather late in the morning, after 10:00. We had to wait for the sun to burn off the dew. Just as we were about to start Patsy came from the house running straight to Dad; Mom was going to have a baby and it was time to go to the hospital. Dad went to the house and took Mom to the hospital.

It was a real crisis! Mom had called Shirley Bugli and asked her to finish the meal preparations. Finally the crisis was under control and we decided to continue threshing. Back to work about 11:00. Just after the midday meal Dad returned to the threshing. Later that evening we learned Mom had given birth to a baby boy, still born.

I remember loading clover onto the wagons all day in my bare hands, with a jacket at first, then in shirt sleeves. The thresher was parked in the field; I didn't like off-loading the wagon into the thresher. Mature clover has fuzz on the stems causing a cloud of fine fuzz around the thresher.

One of the crew was a young fellow that came from a farm down by the river, (James) Jim Winters. He had been in school at the university and soon after we had eaten our midday meal he was complaining of blisters on his hands and asking for gloves. I thought what a pansy we have here. I looked at my hands in the places where he had blisters and I saw only calluses. No blisters for me.

Another member of the threshing crew was a deaf and dumb man who lived with his parents near the junction of the Eastside Highway and Pine Hollow Road. Dad went to fetch him in the morning, and told me he was to work with me in the field (not anywhere near the threshing machinery). I don't remember his name. He was pleasant, attentive and eager to work.

I haven't described how we prepared a crop for the thresher. Let me start with the grain. Dad cut the grain with the McCormick Deering binder using horses until 1945 when he bought the first tractor. It is a one man job with horses; the reins in one hand and the other to adjust the levers and right foot on the pedal to dump the bundle basket. If you are using the tractor you need someone to ride the binder to adjust the cutter head height, reel height and trip the bundle basket.

Photo 9-05 is from fall 1945 of Dad on the tractor and Grandpa Wax on the binder. A few years later Norman and I were the ones riding that binder.

photo 9-05

Photo (9-06) is in the fall of 1947 of Patsy, Norman, Dolores and I on a stack of straw bales. Stripes were in fashion!

photo 9-06

There was so much straw left in the field that Dad cut, raked and baled the excess. I believe that Howard Van Vliet was hired to do the custom baling. See Earning Money.

The bundles were then set into a shock of ten bundles with stem down and head up. A shock of grain is like a small teepee, the bundles set in a circle leaning toward the middle. This would allow the grain to dry. Dry grain is easier and more efficient to thresh, and can be stored without overheating or developing mold.

The binder sometimes didn't tie a good knot closing the twine around a bundle and the grain would fall loose on the ground. While I was helping shock the first grain crop on the Prather land (lot 17) Grandpa Wax taught me how to retie a bundle without using twine: gather the loose grain together, take a few strands of grain, divide in half and twist the heads together, wrap the strands (now double length) around the bundle, pull tight, twist the stems together and tuck the ends into the bundle. There you have it! It's a new bundle ready for the shock.

The clover seed harvest was about the same amount of work. The first crop of hay was cut early (in late June) and the second cutting was allowed to grow to maturity. In early September we would begin cutting with the mowing machine. Dad had a special windrowing attachment for the sickle bar. It had flat strips of metal every few inches that curved up at the ends. The shortest strip began near the end of the sickle bar and the longest ones were near the tractor. This attachment would cause the cut clover stems to roll up very gently into a windrow so as to not shake any of the seed from the dry blossom. The trouble was that often the stems would lodge in these strips. So I was recruited to walk behind the mower with a fork and help the clover maintain a nice continuous roll.

This crop had been growing undisturbed during July and August, and the field mice had large families. They were plentiful, big and fat, and not afraid. Some would stand up and get cut in half by the sickle bar, others ran and the sickle bar trimmed the skin off their backs and a few hunkered down and escaped the sickle bar. I would stab the ones that escaped with the fork tines, and empty my fork at the end of the row. The tines were sometimes full of dead mice. Yuk!

Why were we threshing in December? Well normally we would be threshing the clover seed a couple weeks after cutting, just enough time to let it dry completely. But in 1954 there came an early snow just before we were ready to thresh. I think the thresher and tractor were already in the field when it snowed, and remained in the field until we did thresh. It was an anxious 8 weeks waiting for good weather. Dad had to turn those windrows by hand to get them to dry out. That was the last year we harvested clover seed.

The threshed clover stems were fed to the dry cows, wintering calves and horses.

Clover seed is about the size of a grain of sand, fine sand. It feels like silk in your hands when reaching into a bag of seed. A whole field (25 acres) of clover would yield 500-600 pounds of seed. The thresher emptied the seed into 100lb cloth sacks setting on the ground and attached to the seed spout. They were the most precious sacks, maybe $100 per sack when delivered to the mills in Stevensville or Missoula.

While I'm thinking about it I'll tell about the grain we used for seed. In the 1940s Dad shoveled seed grain from the bins while I held the burlap bags. He then sewed the bag shut with bag needle and thread. A bag corner was rolled into an ear and the thread wrapped around the ear several times, then the top edges were tucked under and the opening sewn shut to the other corner which was again rolled into an ear and the thread wrapped around several times to close the sack. Before we had a pickup truck the bags were loaded into the back of the car and taken to town. The local grain mill did custom cleaning and treating of the grain for seed. They would call us when ready and back to town in the car to bring the seed home.

After the mid-1950s Dad began hiring a combine to harvest the grain crops. It was faster and required less labor.

Photo 9-07 is of stacking hay in 1937. I can't tell where, or who was doing the work. But I have seen these tools being used in the mid-1940s. I remember seeing the hay hook (holds load of hay) in our farm yard. I remember Scoop Kester using a horse powered buck rake like this with an overshot stacker on the Myrtle

photo 9-07

Potter place. We used a stacker like this one until after 1948 when Dad bought the hydraulic stacker for the Case SC tractor.

Dad did the haying with horses until 1946, when his new Case tractor and mower were used, see photo 9-08. That's me on the wagon, Norman on the tractor fender and Patsy on the tractor hood.

photo 9-08

I don't know when Dad got the hay loader, he may have used it with the horses. Again, with horses it was a one man operation but with the tractor it took two to work efficiently. Dad hooked and unhooked the loader in the field and the wagon at the stack. Dad drove to/from the field; Norman or I drove the tractor down the hay rows during loading.

This is the same wagon chassis you saw before with the large diameter wheels. I believe it was from an early 1920s vintage Jewet car with steel disc wheels, 32 inch diameter if I remember correctly. I think this car came from eastern Montana in 1936.

With the tractor and wagon straddling the windrow the loader picked up the hay and emptied it onto the wagon. Dad had four hay nets for each wagon load. These nets were like large hammocks made of rope with small wooden cross beams and hardware at each end to connect one to the other (used in pairs) and for connecting to the stacker. Each pair of nets would hold half a wagon load. One pair was laid on the floor of the wagon for the first half and the second at the level of hay in this photo. The ends of each pair were hooked to the front and back of the wagon rack. When we got to the stacker the two ends were pulled together and hooked to the stacker pulley. I drove the tractor raising this round bundle of hay; Dad swung it into place over the stack and tripped open the nets. The trip mechanism is what held the two nets together in the middle.

Dad had to be careful not to overload the nets. If overloaded, it was very difficult to pull the two ends together to connect to the stacker pulley. Also with an extra heavy load the stacker boom would creak and bend, and the stacker base would begin to rise off the ground against the stakes holding it in place.

This was a labor intensive way to stack hay, but it did have some advantages. The hay stack was in the feed lot so feeding was easy in the winter. The other was that the hay arrived on the stack with most of the stems parallel which formed a uniform and weather tight stack. I remember looking at the stacks from our house, they looked like giant loaves of bread. Being weather tight meant that the stack had very little spoilage on the top and bottom. Dad had a hay knife that he used to cut the stack in half when feeding in the winter. It was beautiful hay, fresh and clean.

Beginning in 1949 we were using the Case with hydraulic stacker to stack in the field. The Case didn't have power steering so the heavy loads made it hard to steer. And it didn't have live power-take-off (pto) which meant that you had to shift to neutral to raise the stacker when adjusting the ground speed. In 1954 Dad bought a new John Deer model 50 tractor which had power steering and live pto. It was a welcome improvement.

Dad built a buck rake head for the Case tractor. Dad was on the stack, Norman on the Case and I on the John Deere with stacker. We could put a 25 acre field into the stack in one day. This method of haying was very efficient, but it did have some disadvantages. The stack was in the field so we had to haul the hay to the feed lot in winter. The buck rake pushed the hay along the ground so the hay was dusty and was pushed into a ball in the buck rake head. The stems were not parallel with some areas packed tight and others loose which meant that even the best built stacks had more spoilage on the top and bottom.

Photo 9-09 is from 1954 of Dad with his new John Deere 50 tractor. Notice the V shape on the back side of the stacker head. These were like elbows on folded arms, two pipes paralleling the main lift arms at the top of the stacker were activated by a hydraulic cylinder just behind Dad's head that caused those arms to push the hay off the head teeth. It was easy to position the load anywhere on the stack. Notice how lumpy the stack looks.

photo 9-09

In the early 1960s Dad bought a second-hand baler and this stacker was used to pick up the bales in the field and lift them up onto the stack. My brother Gordon was now commissioned to stack the bales. He learned from Dad to build straight and strong stacks. We three boys were good baled hay stackers.

Over the years Dad developed a reputation as a wizard at fixing the twine tying mechanism on balers. Neighbors came to Dad from all over the Sunset Bench to ask Dad, "Can you fix my baler?" He was more than generous at giving neighbors his time, but didn't like to lend machinery. He did do a little custom haying, but Dad really didn't like taking his machinery into a strange field.

Photo 9-10 is of Gordon in 1959 with the SC Case tractor and buck rake head pushing hay to the stack. We three worked in the fields during harvests from this age and younger. Dad trusted us as long as he saw that we followed his instructions and didn't play around.

photo 9-10

This is Dad (photo 9-11) raking hay in late summer 1959.

photo 9-11

photo 9-12

A Wax family gathering in 1959 at our house (photo 9-12), from the left: Uncle Jack, Lavon, Nancy Bluhm, Herb Bluhm (my cousin, Aunt Marie's son), Gordon, Roxy Bluhm, Gary Bluhm, Aunt Doris, Grandpa Wax, Dad, Mom and Patsy. Notice the wood heater to the right

Our Health

The usual stuff, then a family crisis

I am not aware that my parents had any health problems before I
began to remember events from my own experience. They simply
did not talk about those kinds of things. I did learn from reading
Mom's diary notes that she suffered colds. So this discussion will
be limited to the health issues that I remember or that happened to
me personally.

I had the normal childhood diseases of the 1940s: measles, mumps,
earaches, colds and flu. I remember that measles were very itchy
and uncomfortable, and that Mom used a lotion to quiet the itching
and soothing words to provide some comfort. In a week the
measles had passed and were forgotten, all better. The mumps
caused a swelling in the throat and neck with a rather severe ache
and difficulty swallowing. Some aspirin and liquid foods with
plenty of rest were prescribed, and again after a week all was better
and forgotten.

Colds seemed to affect everyone almost every year. Sometimes
they were mild with sneezing and drippy nose (actually this might
have been an allergy). The colds that caused a cough and settled in
the chest were uncomfortable and difficult to get rid of.

Earaches occurred several times until I was about 9 years old. The
earaches were especially painful; I didn't like getting an earache.
The prescription this time was aspirin and hot compresses on the

infected ear to increase the blood circulation.

Later in life (1995) I did suffer an earache during a trip to China and it caused my right eardrum to burst. It was the most painful night of my life. When the drum broke and drained there was much less pain. It took several weeks of antibiotics to get well again.

I never suffered any broken bones. I did visit the hospital to have my tonsils removed when I was about 10 years old. And to have the little toe on my left foot removed when I was 13. There were also a couple of cuts that needed stitching. Once when I was in the first grade to patch a cut over my right eye, and then when I was 14 to sew up a cut to my left index finger. I did have to visit the dentist to have the two upper wisdom teeth pulled, a shot of Novocain and then his strong hands with pliers did the job. Otherwise I was healthy in my later teen years.

A family health issue that occurred in 1944 was probably an infestation of bed bugs. We had to leave our house and spend the night at a neighbor's house. We packed up and went outside, then Dad activated a grenade type device that sent a cloud of smoke throughout the house. It was suppose to kill all insects. We returned the next day, aired out the house and washed all the bedding. Dad said the bugs came from some old clothing or bedding that Grandma Wax brought from Missoula.

Dad did have a ringworm infection about this same time. It was treated with a sticky tar-like lotion that was applied morning and evening and required a covering. It left a round red rash on the back of his head and neck. There was no hair on the area (maybe the hair was removed?). It took about two weeks for this treatment to cure the problem. His hair soon grew back.

Mom was pregnant with Patsy and Dolores during those middle 1940s and visited the doctor for checkups. I don't remember any particular problems except she did occasionally have rashes and allergies. After the birth of a stillborn boy in 1954 she began to have problems with anemia, and later would have a hysterectomy.

It may have been on a trip to visit the doctor in Hamilton that I remember first eating in a restaurant. Mom and Dad discussed at some length the cost, finally deciding to eat at the lunch counter in a drug store. We ate a hamburger and drank a coke. It was a most delicious meal.

Photo 10-01 is of Patsy and Dolores in the spring of 1948 riding the original Daisy horse. We rode at a very early age.

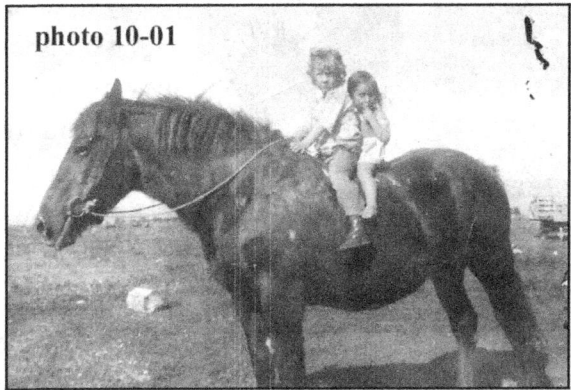

photo 10-01

Gordon was about the size of Dolores in this photo when he fell from a second Daisy horse and broke his collar bone. He also lost the first joint of his middle finger in a wagon and tractor accident. Lavon lost her right thumb in an accident in the milking barn when she was not yet two years old. The biggest family health issue occurred during the second half of 1949 and involved my sister Dolores.

Dolores was diagnosed with nephrotic syndrome, a kidney disease. She suffered considerable swelling in her face, legs, arms and stomach. Treatments for this disease were being developed and dialysis was still experimental. The main treatment was hospitalization with some drugs and blood transfusions. Over a period of a week or so she recovered, but a month or so later she would suffer a relapse. Then it was back in the hospital for another round of treatment.

photo 10-02

Photo 10-02 is of us four children probably in the fall of 1948. I was 9, Norman 8, Patsy 5 and Dolores 2+. This would have been after our summer trip to eastern Montana.

I remember visiting the hospital many times during Dolores's illness. I became friends with a boy my age that had polio. We talked and sometimes played board games. He was usually in bed or in a wheelchair, but on a couple of occasions he was in an iron lung. I remember the iron lung with its rhythmic puffing that aided his breathing. He had to lay in this large stainless steel and glass tube on his back with a gasket fastened around his neck. I stood by his side and didn't know what to do or say. It was a rather uncomfortable visit.

photo 10-03

Photo 10-03 is of Dolores during a short visit home from the hospital. She is sitting on the steps of the building where Aunt Doris was living in an upstairs apartment. You can see her puffy face. Mom and Dolores often stayed with Aunt Doris in Missoula near the hospital for several days at a time during her illness. It was a difficult time for the family.

One day in the fall of 1949 Mom and Dad

sent us three to school telling us they may not be back before we returned home. They gave particular instructions and asked me to look after my brother and sister. The bus dropped us off after school and we started walking home (half mile). Soon Norman and I were in a very heated argument. Remembering what Mom told me in the morning I told Norman that he must do what I said; he replied that he didn't have to do anything I said.

Photo 10-04 is of Mom and Dad and we five children. Grandpa Wax is holding Gordon, and Dad is holding Dolores in the fall of 1949.

When we arrived in the house there was some pushing and shoving, maybe even a few punches. Norman told me he was

photo 10-04

going to settle this once and for all. We were in the kitchen when he turned away and walked out to the porch. I returned to my after school snack. The next thing I heard was Norman saying that he was going to shoot me. I turned around and he had the 22 rifle pointed at my stomach just a few inches away. I stepped out from in front of the barrel and quickly moved toward him grabbing the stock and trigger guard.

I told him he didn't mean it and that I didn't believe that the gun was even loaded. He said it was. I said "Ok, let's see". I reached inside the trigger guard and pulled the trigger. Bang! The bullet entered a piece of the cupboard frame between a drawer and a door making a small hole. That really sobered us up; we quickly decided to cooperate and not tell Mom or Dad. We put the gun back in its place and were on very good behavior waiting for Mom and Dad. They never said anything to us, but later I learned they did know about the incident. Maybe Patsy told them.

The rifle was a single shot bolt action which Dad thought would be safe enough for boys to shoot. He showed us the safe way to handle a gun. The guns were hung above the clothes hooks on the wall of the porch next to the kitchen door.

He taught us how to load, aim and hit a target or small animal (rabbit, squirrel, bird). We did shoot several times at targets. I remember shooting magpies at age 10, and earning a bounty of 25 cents for a pair of legs. It was thought that these birds were undesirable and this was an attempt to reduce their numbers.

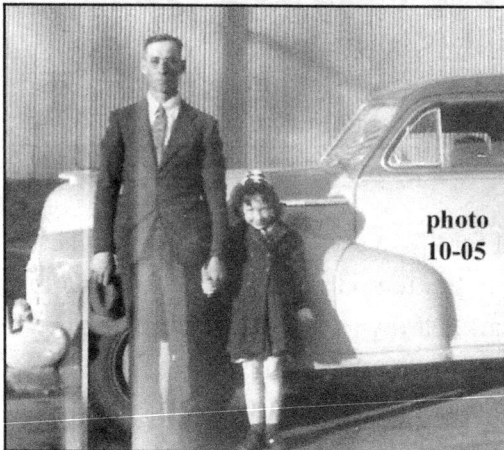

photo 10-05

Photo 10-05 is of Dad and Dolores in the fall of 1949. Dolores was probably on her way home after a stay in the hospital. Notice the expression on Dad's face, very sober, even sad. That is our 1948 Chevrolet car in the background.

The strain of Dolores being sick was getting to all of us. The hospital bills were often discussed around the dining table. There was a lot of anger and tears. It was a very difficult time. The neighbors were there to help when they could with haying and cooking meals. Dad and the rest of us managed for days at a time alone. The grain harvest that fall was largely done by the neighbors. We didn't know what would happen one day to the next. It seemed that it just could not continue.

Finally Dolores died at age 3 years 9 months in Mom's arms at the hospital in Missoula on December 14, 1949. She is buried at the Riverside Cemetery in Stevensville. Dolores's suffering ended; Mom and Dad could begin to mourn. Mom cried a lot. The sadness on Dad's face was very evident. It was not a normal year for us.

It was a very sad and quiet Christmas that year. Mom and Dad told us many times there would be no Christmas, period. Dad did get us a Christmas tree a few days before Christmas which he set up in the corner of the dining room. There was nothing under the tree.

On the day before Christmas Eve the mailman bought a brown paper package addressed to the Wacks Family without a return address. We untied the string, opened the paper and found inside a pair of knitted mittens for each of us three. It was obvious that the mittens were homemade by someone that heard our story and wanted to help. But we didn't know who to thank.

It did bring some joy into our lives that Christmas. I will never forget it. We knew that someone out there, someone outside of this family felt our pain. We could now begin the healing process.

Looking back on these events from my vantage point of today I see that the pain of this loss did continue to affect Mom and Dad for many years. They probably could have benefited from some grief counseling during 1950 and 1951. I see now that the family dynamics changed as Mom and Dad worked to overcome their grief.

photo 10-06

Photo 10-06 is of Patsy and Dolores in the fall of 1948. The photo was enlarged to 10 x 12 and colored. It was framed and hung in Mom and Dad's bedroom for the rest of their lives.

Dad began to self-medicate with alcohol and toward the end of the 1950s his drinking caused him to be more distant from Norman and me. Fights with Mom were more frequent and disturbing. I now understand the pain they were suffering. I just wished it could have been handled differently at the time.

There may have been other health issues that I was not aware of.

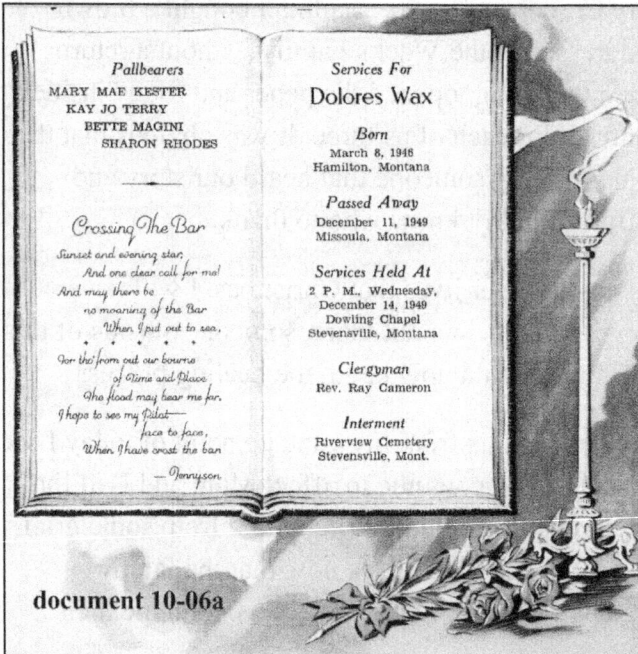

Pallbearers
MARY MAE KESTER
KAY JO TERRY
BETTE MAGINI
SHARON RHODES

Crossing The Bar

Sunset and evening star,
And one clear call for me!
And may there be
no moaning of the Bar
When I put out to sea,

For tho' from out our bourne
of Time and Place
The flood may bear me far,
I hope to see my Pilot—
face to face,
When I have crost the bar

— Tennyson

Services For
Dolores Wax

Born
March 8, 1948
Hamilton, Montana

Passed Away
December 11, 1949
Missoula, Montana

Services Held At
2 P. M., Wednesday,
December 14, 1949
Dowling Chapel
Stevensville, Montana

Clergyman
Rev. Ray Cameron

Interment
Riverview Cemetery
Stevensville, Mont.

document 10-06a

144

Son Of Montana

I don't want you to leave this chapter with sad thoughts, so I'll include something a little more cheerful.

On many other years Mom and Dad bought a large bag of unshelled nuts during the Christmas season. The Christmas tree was up and decorated, and each of us had a package under the tree. After supper the table was cleared. Norman and I sat on the floor and cracked open nuts with a hammer.

There were pecans, walnuts, almonds, Brazil nuts (we called them nigger toes) and hazel nuts. Each time we cracked a nut the shell pieces would fly in every direction and soon the floor was covered in nut shells. The heater was burning nice and warm, the nut meats tasted good and it was fun for boys.

Dad sat in his chair at the table cracking his share of nuts too. We didn't have a nut cracker. He didn't need a hammer. He placed two nuts in the palm of his hand and squeezed the two nuts against each other and one would break open. He could break every type of nut, even the hardest Brazil nuts in this manner. Dad used his pocket knife to extract the last pieces of nut meat.

Soon we had eaten our fill and it was time for bed. Norman and I made a few guesses about what might be in the package we would open on Christmas Eve before falling asleep.

Mom swept the floor; ready for tomorrow.

photo 10-07

This photo is of the Wax farmstead in the late 1960s looking east from Pine Hollow Road.

Vehicles & Tractors

The parade of cars, trucks and tractors

Mom and Dad's first car is mentioned in Mom's note (see Mom & Dad) and is described as a grey Ford "Gideon". I never saw a photo of that car. I did see a photo of an old "run-about" car from eastern Montana. I don't think it belonged to my parents, but the photo does help explain Mom's term "Gideon". I think she was just writing what she heard, such as "git-ty-on". Just as one would say gitty-up to a horse; the passengers were told "gitty-on". Get on board, gitty-on, to my mother's ears was Gideon. It is my guess that this first car was a cut-down run-about kind of vehicle.

The next car my parents owned was a 1934 Chevrolet 4 door sedan (photo 11-01), brown in color. I recall it had a six cylinder valve in head engine, independent front suspension called "knee-action" and of course the standard 3 speed transmission with clutch and mechanical brakes.

photo 11-01

Photo 11-02 is of Mom and baby sister Patsy in the fall of 1943. The shadow on the car (not our car) is probably Grandma Wax snapping the photo. If you look carefully you can see two little boys, one kneeling on the front seat looking back and one standing

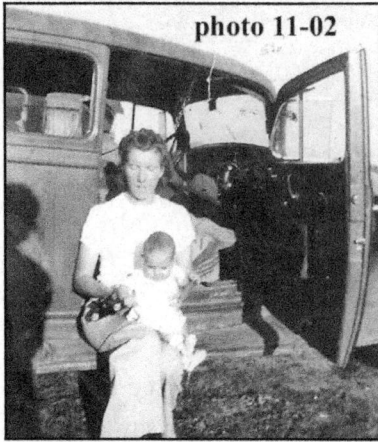

photo 11-02

in the back facing forward. Guess who those two monkeys are?

Once returning from town, Mom drove off Pine Hollow road with the 1934 Chevy while going up the Magini hill. I guess that was sometime in 1944. Mom and Patsy were in the front seat and Norman and I were in the back. Norman and I were wrestling, yelling and fighting, and causing Mom some grief. We were quiet for a few minutes after she told us to behave, but soon were back fighting. Finally, upset, she turned around and took a swing at us.

Bang, bump, zing, pop, bang! The car went off the north side of the hill above a steep bank, knocking down a fence post and breaking several strands of barbed wire. We finally stopped inches short of a large pine tree at the edge of the road. The incident got everybody into a sober mood. We slowly got out of the car, and after some yelling and a few tears, we surveyed the damage.

Gene Magini heard the noise and came to investigate. He helped Mom back the car onto the road and checked everything carefully. He said that no serious damage was done, just some dings and a number of scratches. Mom drove us home. The Wax boys sat motionless in the back seat, not a peep. Dad had to address the damaged fence. He set a couple of posts and patched the broken barbed wire. Our punishment was that we had to go with him to help with the patching. If you break it, you fix it. I'm not sure we were much help, but I do think we rode more quietly in the car after that, at least for awhile.

Photo 11-03 is of Patsy in 1944 about the time of this accident. This car had the suicide-style back doors. Notice that the door handle has been removed apparently to disable opening the doors. Need to keep those two boys safely locked inside the car.

In the summer of 1948 Dad bought a brand-new Chevrolet. It was a 2 door sedan, two-tone green, 6 cylinder overhead valve engine with shift at the steering wheel and hydraulic brakes. What a nice car - shiny chrome and paint, black tires and a new smell. My dad was eager to travel and show off his new car.

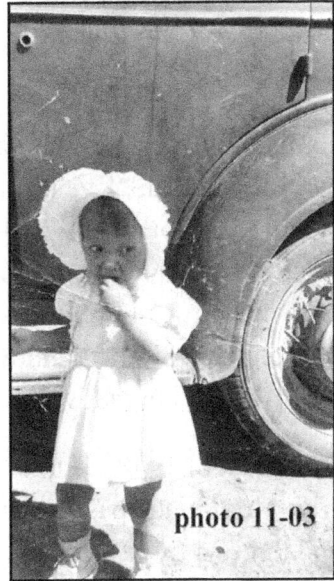

photo 11-03

Photo 11-04 is of Uncle Jack (Aunt Doris' husband), Patsy and Dad in winter of 1949. The nail keg next to the house was for working the pigs, outhouse to the right.

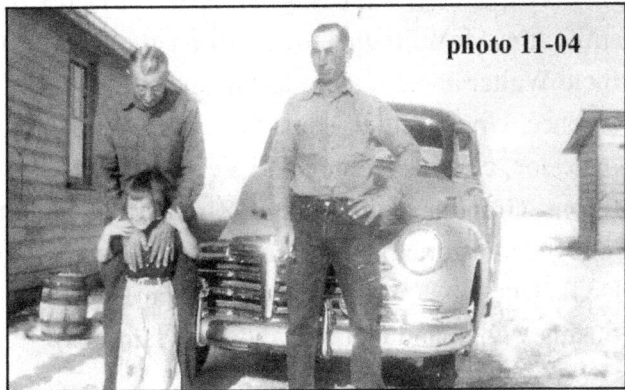

photo 11-04

This reminds me of something that happened during that summer. Dad was working in the farmyard east of the house. Norman and I were helping him, then we left and returned to the house. We were busy talking to Mom when the window you see to the left of Uncle Jack broke scattering glass all over the floor.

What was that? We looked out the broken window and saw Dad coming to the house with rather tight jaws. "Is everybody deaf here", he yelled. "I've been yelling for some help". We all looked at him dumbfounded. Finally he cooled down and explained that since we could not hear him he would get our attention by throwing a rock to hit the roof. The rock came up short by about four feet and hit the window. He did get our attention, but now he had to repair a window.

In August of 1948 we took a trip to eastern Montana. Dad drove with Mom in the passenger seat holding Dolores (born in 1946) and three of us in the back. Norman and I sat by the windows with Patsy in the middle. Being separated we were able to travel without fighting. It was a long day to get to Grandma and Grandpa Zimmerman's house east of Jordan.

On this trip we visited many of Mom and Dad's friends and family: the McWilliams, the Nelsons, the Bluhms (Aunt Marie, Uncle Walter and cousins Herbie and Willie), the Burchets (Aunt Florence, Uncle Lloyd, cousin Wayne), the Schmidts (Aunt Pearl, Uncle Joe, cousins Ronnie and Verna), Hirth Mahoney, the Hiltons, Grandpa and Grandma Zimmerman and others around Cohagen and Jordan. We then drove to Glendive to visit the Waxes (Dad's Uncle Al (William Allen), Aunt Josephine, and Dad's cousins Vivian and Octavia and their families).

One day we drove to the driveway gate of the vacant Grandpa Wax homestead and saw the remains of the old sod house. The windows and doors were gone and part of the clay roof had caved in. It was not tiny as homestead houses often were, but rather a nice-sized rectangular house. We didn't go any closer. It was behind a hill and would have been somewhat protected from the wind.

Son Of Montana

While visiting the McWilliams's, Ralph McWilliams told a story about his brother (Elton, Doris' ex-husband) buying an airplane. He said Elton thought that he could save time conducting business in different locations if he had an airplane. And often he did save time, but not on a trip to Minneapolis. He was following the highway (so as not to get lost) and flying into a 40-45 mph head wind. The cars on the highway were going faster than he was. No time saved on that trip.

I have driven in the North Dakota 'breezes' a few times. They are real and not a joke. Driving into the wind and maintaining your cruise speed will net about a 20% reduction in miles per gallon. If driving with the wind it is real easy to go over the speed limit, and you can get a 20% boost in mileage. Once I caught a strong wind in Nebraska and at a gas station I told the attendant that it sure was windy. He replied that they didn't have any wind in Nebraska. What? He said it was a Kansas wind in a hurry to get to South Dakota. I guess he was right, that wind was in a hurry.

The 1948 Chevrolet was wrecked in December 1951, something I learned when I read Mom's note (see Mom and Dad). The accident was not discussed at home as I recall. The replacement was a used dark Blue 1950 Chevrolet 4 door sedan. I wrecked this car.

I had an appointment to visit the chiropractor in Victor, probably after school in the winter 1956. I had my driver license by this time and my own car, but for some reason took the family car. I started out the door about 4:30 pm and, with Patsy riding along, drove to Victor.

After my treatment we started home. The main street of Victor forms a "T" junction with the west side highway. I stopped and looking right saw some headlights a long way off. Looking left I saw nothing, so I quickly pulled out onto the highway. Just as I was straight in my lane I heard tires screeching. BANG! We bolted forward.

Patsy and I weren't hurt and quickly got out. The car that hit us emptied as well revealing four young people with several beer cans (empty and full) that they threw away. The driver started cursing me, but I said nothing. The Highway Patrol took all our names, accident photos and measurements, and wrote up the reports. The officer told me that the other driver reported going 50 mph, but the officer said they were doing 70 in this 35 mph zone. I had judged that they were far enough away that I could enter the highway safely assuming they were traveling the speed limit. I didn't figure on them going 70 mph.

We looked the car over carefully, there was no damage to the front end. The trunk however, was kind of tucked under the main part of the body. I got in and test drove it a short distance. All seemed ok, so we slowly drove home. The next morning we had a closer look and saw that the frame was bent, but the sheet metal was not damaged that much. Dad got an estimate for the repairs. We were told the repairs would be expensive, and the car might never drive properly again. It was not until summer that a final decision was made about this car. Dad would buy a new car.

photo 11-05

Photo 11-05 (probably 1955) is of the 1950 Chevrolet, Mom, Dad and the 1952 Ford pickup. I don't know where they were going all dressed up. Maybe Norman's eighth grade graduation?

In the summer 1956 they decided to buy a 1957 Chevrolet 2 door sedan with a small V8 engine and three speed transmission. The 1957 Chevy was a light aqua green color and without any accessories. I did not drive this car very often, and was very careful when I did. Norman had a wreck with this car a few years later when he was home on leave from the Marine Corp.

In the 1960s they bought a Ford car, and owned several Fords until they could no longer drive.

Dad bought his first pickup in 1951, a red 1946 International ½ ton with 6 cylinder flat head engine and three speed transmission. It had a wood and iron slat floor in the box. I replaced all the wood in the box floor during shop class the first year I was in high school. I unbolted the metal strips that fastened the board edges together and cut new boards from select fir, then bolted everything together again. It was a nice looking box floor.

We only had the International pickup for a couple of years; Dad traded it for a newer and bigger Ford ¾ ton. It was a 1952 model with four speed transmission, overload springs and flat head V8 engine. It also had a slide-in stock rack that was big enough to carry two cows, 4-5 calves or 15-16 pigs. Rollie Lewis and I hauled fence posts from the mountains with this pickup. We hauled many loads of cull potatoes from Duard Higgins cellar to feed our pigs. This was a useful pickup and Dad kept it for several years.

After I left home he bought an International one ton truck. It was a used Forest Service truck. His last pickups were ½ ton four wheel drive Fords.

Dad's first tractor was a 1945 Case VA tractor, a 4 cylinder engine with 4 speed transmission, foot clutch and gas pedal. It also had a hand throttle and came with a mower. This was the first tractor I learned to drive while helping Dad stack hay. If I placed my butt on the front edge of the seat I was able to reach the clutch and brake pedals. Later I could sit on the seat and drive.

Photo 11-06 is of Patsy and Grandpa Zimmerman in 1945 on the Case VA tractor.

photo 11-06

Dad farmed with this tractor until fall of 1948 when he bought the bigger Case SC with single front wheel. It had the "crow's perch" steering rod, 4 cylinder engine with 4 speed transmission and hand clutch. The crow's perch steering rod (rod on side of tractor in photo 9-11) connects the steering gear box arm to an arm that turns the front wheels. Search YouTube for a Case SC tractor to see an example of this steering configuration.

He used it with the single front wheel for a couple of seasons and then bought a two wheel wide front end. The single wheel was very maneuverable, but was rough riding. It also left a track down the middle of a hay swath which Dad didn't like. That old single wheel front end lay around the farm yard for several years.

photo 11-07

Photo 11-07 is of Jimmy Mike Burchett (cousin) in the wagon and Gordon (brother) on the tractor in 1961 with the Case SC and the rock wagon. In the background is the shop where Dad's forge was located.

This is the tractor and wagon tongue that cut off the tip of Gordon's middle finger 9 years earlier (see The Land). This wagon chassis with a longer spine was used to haul lodge pole pine from the mountains (see Food & Fuel)

Dad kept this tractor until he retired in 1980 and sold it to a neighbor. Many years later (1990s) he bought it from the neighbor. During a visit home while on vacation, he and I cleaned the carburetor, gas lines and filter, put fresh gas in and it started right up. I told Dad that he was the reason we were having a recession. The economy was in a slump and farmers were not buying new tractors. I said farmers like him caused the slowdown because they waited fifty years before buying a new tractor. He just looked at me with that "what stupid thing is he saying now?" look in his eyes.

Dad worked this tractor hard (we all did) winter and summer, and it never failed us. I remember driving it with the quack machine, grinding away in first gear at full throttle hour after hour. At full throttle the engine ran about 1800 rpm, a nice steady purr. But Dad still hungered for a John Deere tractor because of their legendary simplicity and power.

In the fall of 1954 Dad purchased the John Deere of his dreams, a model 50. It had the famous 2 cylinder engine, 6 speed transmission, power steering and roll-a-matic front end. But the love affair didn't last long. The transmission failed when doing heavy field work, and the popping sound of the 2 cylinder engine was harsh. The John Deere did have some advantages, but could not overcome the long relationship Dad had with those faithful Case tractors. A few years later Dad traded it for a little-used Case 530 diesel which soon became his favorite tractor. He purchased two additional Case tractors over the years, and when he retired owned three.

Photo 11-08 is of Dad on his Case 530 with Case-o-Matic transmission and hay rake in the mid-1960s. My brother Gordon still owns this tractor. I once mowed hay on Gordon's 30 acres with this tractor while on vacation. The automatic transmission was nice. It also had power steering.

photo 11-08

Profits from the farm were invested in newer and more efficient tractors, machinery and trucks. Dad took good care of his working equipment; he spent many hours during the winter months getting the equipment ready for the next season. He serviced the cars too, but they were second priority.

Bikes & Cars

Lessons learned and skills acquired

I was apparently born to explore the outdoors. Mom told me that she once lost me in the fall of 1940; unable to find me anywhere she called Dad and he went looking. She said that he found me in the stubble of the grain field just back of the house. The stubble was my height and my blonde hair blended with the grain stubble; I was not easy to see.

By ages five and six Norman and I were exploring the fields for up to a mile around our house. The walk to the school bus was to the ends of the mile long Webster Lane. We got on the bus at the back side (½ mile south) of the Sunset Bench loop and got off at the front side (½ mile north). We went across the Big Ditch to the west, south over the hill to the Big Ditch siphon across Willoughby Creek, northeast to the Rasmussen place on Miller Hill Road, north to the Magini farm on Pine Hollow Road. All on foot, and although we always had a horse, we seldom rode it.

One day when Norman and I were eight and nine years old we came home from school to an empty house. Shortly Mom came driving home in our 1948 Chevrolet car without Dad. Right away we asked, "Where's Daddy?" We didn't get a good answer; we asked again and again. She said, "He's coming." So we ate our usual after school snack (saltines or bread with butter and jam, and milk) and started to play outside. Soon we saw something moving on the road approaching from the direction of Stevensville. It was moving faster than a man walking - it was Dad riding a bicycle.

We knew right away it was a bicycle for us and ran out to meet him. It was shiny new, red with a white stripe, rather plain by today's standards. But we didn't know any different; it was the most beautiful bicycle we had ever seen. It was a Hawthorne, as best I remember. There was one really big problem. Both Norman and I were too short to sit on the seat and reach the pedals.

From ages about four and five we were always about the same size. People often asked if we were twins until we were 14 and 15. Mom often dressed us in the same clothes when we were young. Norman would eventually be three inches taller than me.

What to do? A brand new bike and unable to reach the pedals! Dad removed the seat, wrapped the top frame bar with a burlap bag and tied it together. We could now reach the pedals, but it was very uncomfortable. So, we learned to ride standing. It was how we rode the bike until our legs were longer, then the burlap came off and the seat was reattached. We were now more mobile and could extend our exploring range. But two boys on one bike didn't always work so well.

photo 12-01

That's me on the new bike (photo 12-01). It is already customized, notice the front fender has been removed. Also note the "bad biker" look on my face. I think that is Aunt Pearl and Cousin

Son Of Montana

Verna in the background, about 1949.

I once tried to build a spring action shock absorber for the front wheel, but it never quite worked. They now have exactly the kind I tried to build made of shiny chrome and steel. I was just years too early. Ah, the shade tree inventor!

By the time we were 10 and 11 we had a second bike, a used one. Well, actually both our bikes were used. That new bike from two year ago now had a lot of miles on it and the usual scratches and dings. We learned to repair it, flat tires were the most common problem. We adjusted the brakes, replaced spokes and added accessories like a clothes pin and playing card attached to the front fork so the tip of the card would strike the spokes. When the wheel turned the spokes hit the card and made a snapping sound. If we rode fast it sounded like a motorbike engine. We were the bike outlaws of the Sunset Bench and our range was now miles.

One time in the fall during the beginning days of the school year (1951) we hatched a plan to skip school. Francis Stang, Norman and I would ask for lunches from home and say that we were going to ride our bikes to school. Norman and I got ready that morning, made sure we had nice big lunches and started off on our bikes. We rode to the end of our lane, turned east onto North Sunset Bench Road and rode to Stang's on the South Burnt Fork Road. We joined Francis and continued east away from school.

We rode up past the old grist mill and onto the Burnt Fork Creek Road. We rode and rode watching the sun to gauge the time. We were getting hungry, real hungry, so we decided to eat our lunches. Should we turn back? The sun was still more or less in front of us. It seemed to be telling us that it was still about noon. Finally we decided to turn back, as we were getting tired.

We rode back down the creek past the grist mill and onto South

Burnt Fork again. Now in familiar territory we saw it was late, the sun was well off to the west. Mr. Stang was now ready to begin milking and he saw Francis approach from the east, not the west as if he were coming from school. Norman and I beat a hasty retreat home.

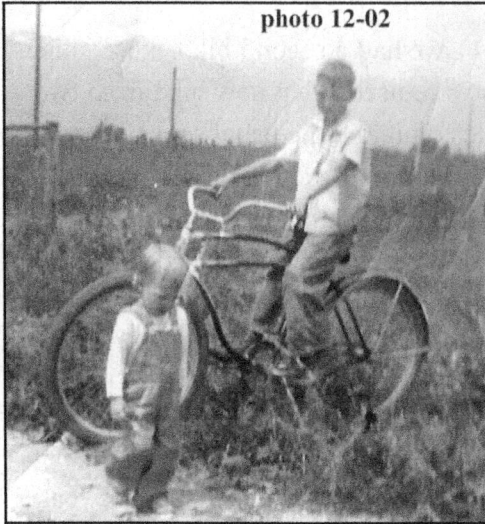

photo 12-02

Photo 12-02 is of Norman, also on the new bicycle, in fall 1949. That is our cousin Verna Schmidt. The Wax brothers will ride again!

The next day in school Francis said he had to lie to escape a whipping. He told his dad that we rode up the Middle Burnt Fork Road to the grist mill then back down to their house on our way home from school. It was the reason we were so late. Some quick thinking and skating over the truth is a good way to get past a lot of unpleasantness in life. He didn't get a whipping, and we had an answer if we were asked.

We probably rode 10 miles up and 10 miles back that day. We saw several deer including a well-antlered buck deer, and a porcupine. We had nine plus hours of physical exercise and plenty of fresh air. We saw the Burnt Fork Creek from bicycles, something I dare say few people have experienced. Were we bad? Yes, we skipped school and told a lie. But we were probably healthier and learned more than if we had spent the day in school.

I'll never forget it, and what it taught me about how things change when in a different environment. We didn't realize that Burnt Fork Road enters the mountains going east, but slowly circles around to the southwest. Gauging the time by the sun now has an additional factor (direction) in my calculations.

Norman and I probably rode hundreds of miles between the time we got that new bicycle and the time I bought my first car in the summer of 1952. It was a 1935 Ford V8 two door sedan. After my first summer of working for Fred Longpre at age 13 and getting paid $96 I was ready to spend the money and wanted a car. Dad agreed and one day in Hamilton we stopped at a used car lot and decided on this blue Ford. It cost $85 and I still had $11 left. Dad drove it home. I think it was a surprise for Mom and one that she did not particularly agree with. Anyway, the money was gone and the car was in our front yard.

This car (photo 12-03) had a small flat head V8 engine, clutch with 3 speed transmission and mechanical brakes. During the 1930s hydraulic brakes were becoming available on the more expensive cars, but not yet on this inexpensive Ford sedan. This car's mechanical brakes were a real

photo 12-03

weakness. The V8 engine gave it plenty of power and it would go, but stopping it could be a challenge.

I didn't get much time driving that first year because Dad wouldn't let me drive to school or on any of the main roads, only on the Sunset Bench and the Burnt Fork. Dad didn't always know where I drove. What!

The next summer (1953) I had a car to drive to/from Fred Longpre's for haying which allowed me to maintain a more precise schedule. Most of the year's haying money was used for gasoline and maintenance. My car needed a new battery, and repairs on radiator and tires. At age 14 I was still too young to get a driver's license, but I did drive to school on occasion. I didn't park in the school parking lot, but rather on a side street near school. Where were the police you ask?

Stevensville didn't have a resident policeman, only a night watchman on foot. He was out at night to make sure all the doors were locked and to keep order amongst the drunks in the bars on Main Street. We never saw him out by the school during the day, so I was safe. The only other law was the sheriff in Hamilton and the Highway Patrol out of Missoula. I didn't have any trouble with the law driving a car until after I was a senior in high school. I never had any accidents with my car or other difficulties other than having to walk home if I got stuck. Nobody at our house ever talked about car insurance; it was unknown to us.

During the winter I put chains on the car, first draining most of the air out of the rear tires and fastening on the chains straight and tight before pumping up the tires to normal pressure. I then had tires and chains as though they were married to each other. It allowed me to drive quiet and safe on all kinds of snow-packed roads at speeds up to 45 mph. I was very confident of my winter driving skills, even on unplowed roads with six inches of snow.

I don't remember why or where I was going; I crested over the edge of the Sunset Bench headed down Miller Hill. Six inches of fresh snow was on the unplowed road. I knew it wouldn't be easy, but the grade was rather steep and I thought plenty of speed (with my chains and driving skill) would get me to the bottom. I gave it the gas and hit second gear. Wrong!

There was a snow drift about 100 yards from the crest behind some sage brush and my speed carried me to the absolute crest of the drift where the car stopped and settled down into the snow. I was able to push the door open and step out sinking up to mid thigh into the snow. Oops! What was I thinking? I walked home, a little over a mile.

I came back with a shovel and moved snow until it was dark. I was now cold and tired, so back home again. Maybe I didn't need to go down Miller Hill after all. The next day after school was cold and windy, and I didn't feel like walking back to shovel more snow. I did worry some about the car because it didn't have a key like today's cars have, just a switch to start it. But I reasoned that if I couldn't drive it home nobody could steal it.

A Chinook wind began that night and soon the snow was melting big time. So I waited another day or two and then went back to my car. The Chinook wind had taken care of most of the snow so that only a little more shoveling was required; I could back up to the top of the hill, turn around and drive home. I was more careful after that when driving in snow.

Once I started my car with the crank (dead battery) and forgot to take the crank out and stow it away. I came from the house, jumped in and drove out to the road, turned right and shifted to second gear. About 50 yards down the road I heard something go Booi-ing, and I remembered the crank. I stopped, got out and looked for the crank. It was gone. It scratched the radiator on the way out and caused a small leak. It must have fallen out, the handle digging into the road, catching the bumper and was flung out like a stone from a slingshot. I never did find that crank; it maybe is still out there in Dayton's pasture.

The 1935 Ford was beginning to break more and more often and I had less and less money to fix it. The last thing that broke before I sold it was the clutch pedal. The mounting bracket that was the pivot point for the pedal broke and the pedal sank to the floor. I was not able to operate the clutch.

The transmission did have synchronizing gears and I had earlier tested my skill shifting without the clutch. I was now forced to shift without the clutch all the time. Starting could be a problem depending on where I was parked, and backing up was a real pain. I tried to find a downhill grade to park on because it was easier to start the car while in gear. And using compression could be a real challenge to slow the car. If I missed a down shift I only had those mechanical brakes to stop the car. The transmission suffered my abuse, but it stood by me to the end.

photo 12-03.5

My next car (12-03.5) was a 1936 Oldsmobile 4 door sedan, a light turquoise green. It had a big flat head 6 cylinder engine and the standard 3 speed transmission. It was rather nice with a well-built Fisher body, but it felt slow and heavy after my light and speedy Ford V8. It was quiet and sedate, and never gave me any trouble, but I longed for the power and speed of a Ford V8.

One time coming home from school (I had my license now) I could not make it over the little hill opposite Fred Longpre's barn and corrals. That little hill was later graded out when the road received an asphalt surface. The road was snow packed and it had sprinkled some rain that afternoon, so the road was iced over. I didn't have my chains and it was getting dark. I left the car on the side of the road and started walking. It was even difficult to stand on that ice.

The Longpre house was just three hundred feet up the road. I knocked and Fred answered the door. I told him my problem and he said he couldn't do anything because of the ice, but he did agree to go back to the car with me. I asked Fred to push, and he agreed. We made it over the hill. I dared not stop so I wasn't able to thank Fred for his help. I made it home, thanks to Fred.

Another time I was driving east on North Sunset Bench Road and a small squall was rolling across the bench from the southwest. I could see that the squall and I would intersect near the Mack Smith Lane junction. Soon I was in the middle of a little tornado, small hail and rain hitting the car from all sides. The dust, rain, and hail caused me to slow down and as I passed an old cottonwood tree at the side of the road a large branch dropped down just in front of me. Thump, thump as the front and rear wheels ran over a 2-3 inch limb. Wow! That was close. I didn't think much more about it until I reached my destination and saw leaves and twigs lodged on the bumper and in the radiator grill. Lady Luck was riding with me that day.

After my last season of haying for Fred I bought a 1948 Ford sedan. It was a nice looking car and an upgrade from my first Ford; it had hydraulic brakes and the shifter was by the steering wheel. The body and inside were still in good shape, but it soon became apparent why it was on the used car lot. It had bad engine.

What was the solution to this problem?

Photo 12-04 is a 1948 Ford sedan I took off the internet. It is the way my car looked when new and priced about $1250.

After some discussion and good advice I bought

photo 12-04

a rebuilt engine (short block) and began the work of putting it in my car. All the main parts of the engine, in a short block flat head V8, are new or rebuilt. I simply transferred the heads, carburetor, distributor, spark plugs and oil pan from the old engine to the new. Then I fastened it into the car connecting gas line, throttle rod and electrical connections. Ready for testing, it worked! A little more adjusting, pumping up the tires, and I was ready with a car I liked and one that should last. Later I put on new brake shoes; it served me well until I graduated from high school.

In high school several of the boys had cars and I learned some ways I could customize my Ford. I added a dual exhaust system and switched the shift lever around to the left side of the steering wheel. The shift pattern was now upside down, and if I didn't remember I could be in the wrong gear - going forward when I meant to back up. I soon became accustomed to the left handed shift.

It was said that you could drive with your right arm around your girl and change gears with your left hand without losing your girl or missing a shift. I didn't have a girl so didn't know if that was true.

photo 12-05

Photo 12-05 is of me and my 1948 Ford sedan. Notice the new jeans, western shirt and crew cut.

Once when working for the McPherson's in their dry land fields back of the Lewis (Rollie's parents) place I drove my car up to the field and on the way back I hit a rock in the road. There was a pothole to the right side of the road filled with water and I saw a little hump in the middle of the road next to the water. It all looked benign so I proceeded without slowing.

Bang! The right front wheel dropped into the pothole and the front cross member of the frame hit the sharp edge of a large rock buried in the road bed. I didn't think much about it until I heard a little bang bang sound from the front of the car a little further down the road. I stopped, got out and under the front end. The front cross member was bent enough to catch the edge of the front axle when the spring flexed more than one and a half inches. No problem on the highway, but on rough dirt roads I heard bang bang when the front wheels hit the bigger bumps. I was never able to straighten that cross member.

I once got stuck in the snow with this car. Rollie Lewis and I were in town one night during the winter and he didn't have a way home. There wasn't much snow in town but several inches up at the Lewis home. I drove Rollie home and then started driving back to our house.

It was not a problem driving on the upper road to Rollie's house, so I decided to drive back using the lower road and perhaps save some time and miles. I drove about a mile from the Lewis house and got stuck (think I slid into the ditch). My chains were in the trunk, but I decided not to put them on in the dark. Instead, I walked back to the Lewis house and spent the night there.

The Lewis house had an attic bedroom like our house (only bigger), with six cots. There were seven Lewis boys and a couple of the older ones were not sleeping at home that night, so there was a free cot. I just opened the back door, walked up the stairs, undressed and crawled into the empty cot.

The next morning when Rollie and I went down to breakfast Mrs.

Lewis said "So you're the one". She laid awake and counted the footsteps on the stairs that night. The boys she expected home were now in bed; she was dosing off when she heard one extra set of footsteps on the stairs. Mrs. Lewis said she couldn't sleep after that. Which boy was it? Why did he come home in the middle of the night?

I felt sorry for Mrs. Lewis. It never occurred to me that I might cause loss of sleep. It became a good story for Rollie and me to tell at high school reunions.

Another story about Rollie and me involved drag-racing down Main Street in Stevensville. We lined up at the feed mill and let her rip. On the way past the bank Rollie saw the night constable on the sidewalk. I didn't see him. We stopped our racing at the end of Main Street and Rollie continued out of town on his way home. I turned around and headed back into town going toward home.

The night constable stepped out into the street and stopped me. I was in trouble. He asked my name and I answered. He then asked if that other guy was one of the Lewis boys. I nodded. He told me not to do that again, and told me to tell that Lewis boy the same. I said ok. "Go home and drive carefully" were his final words.

You know, it was a good thing that 'zero tolerance' was not the policy of the day in Stevensville or many of us high school boys would be wearing stripes.

I once lent my car to some guys I didn't know very well to make a quick run to their home. It was late one night in town. They didn't return when they said and I waited. I needed to go home so I caught a ride with a friend. I called the next day and was told, "Oh yeh, we got back later, but left the car where we said we would."

I went to town, but the car was not there. After driving most streets I finally found my car by the train depot up on blocks and all the wheels were gone. Luckily I had spare wheels and tires enough to re-float my car and drive it home. I did not lend my car to anyone after that.

I was not the only one that worked and earned money, Norman did too. Sometimes he drove my car or I drove him, but we two managed our transportation needs with one car until Norman bought a motorcycle. He bought it from Rollie Lewis. Rollie bought it from the Sears catalog. It was made in Austria, imported and sold by Sears. Rollie had to assemble the main parts and used it for a year or so.

Photo 12-06 is of Norman on his motorcycle in 1954. Notice the lace-up boots. All of the boys in school had these lace-up logger boots at one time or another. I had a pair too in the seventh and eighth grades. He is in front of the garden gate.

photo 12-06

I once borrowed his motorcycle to ride down to the Solomon house and caught the front wheel in a rut and it bucked me off. I landed with my arms protecting my face and skinned my forearms. Think I'll stick to the car! I never rode a motorcycle again.

After I graduated from high school Norman and I decided to pool our resources and buy a car together. He sold his motorcycle and I sold my 1948 Ford sedan. We went shopping and found a nice Pontiac. It was a 1951 with a Hyda-matic transmission. It had the Berkshire green metallic paint and a large 6 cylinder flat head engine with that famous Body by Fisher. It did not have all the accessories, but it was the Chieftan model. It was a smooth and quiet ride. We were proud of our newer car.

That's me (photo 12-07) in my uniform and the Pontiac. I was in

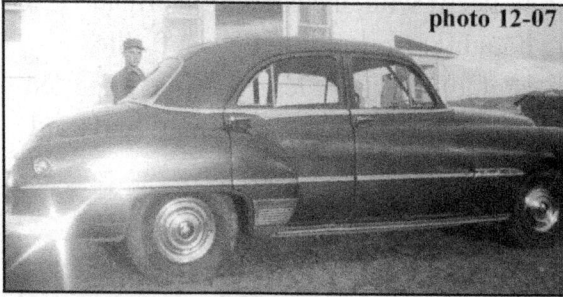

photo 12-07

the Montana National Guard during the first half of 1957 and was discharged after just 6 months service without explanation (maybe over subscription?).

I drove the Pontiac to work in the saw mill (see Leaving Home). It was soon my favorite - quiet, smooth, comfortable and easy to look at. I remember driving to the saw mill, about a 100 mile trip. From Stevensville to Drummond was oiled highway, but the last 40 miles were on gravel and dirt roads. I learned to drive 40-45 mph on these roads to quiet the rattling and shaking from the rough surface. If I drove over that speed I felt the car begin to lose control. Norman got the short end of this deal for the summer since I had the car with me most of the time.

I sold my share to Norman at the end of summer and headed to college. He sold it the next spring before he joined the Marine Corp. I wish I could buy another car like that one today.

Norman and I learned to repair our bikes and cars; the mechanical skills we gained would serve us well. Learning to ride bicycles and drive cars in a variety of conditions gave us self-confidence, something that helped us during our adult working years.

Earning Money

Seeking work, the jobs find me

Some may think what I tell here is an exaggeration, a stretching of the truth. There may of course be some, but it is what is in my head, my memory. I did do many different jobs from a rather young age, and if I didn't do them myself I was at an elbow watching and learning.

The first job was with the Dayton haying crew in 1947 across the road from our house on the south side of the Sunset Bench. Carl Dayton (Mr.) and his three sons would appear in mid July to begin haying on 90 acres of grass hay. The Dayton farm and dairy was about four miles south of Stevensville on the Eastside Highway at the junction of Bell Crossing Road, and about four miles southwest of our place. Normally we didn't see the Daytons much except at haying time.

The Dayton's had an old pre-war John Deere model D tractor that they used to cut the hay, then horses to rake and buck-rake. They had a standard over-shot stacker and a pre-war Chevrolet truck they used to pull the cable on the stacker.

Dad usually finished our haying (25-45 acres) before mid-July, so I was free. One day I was roaming the fields in search of interesting activities and I visited the Dayton haying operation. It was a flurry of activity with the four (Carl and three sons) at their jobs, one on the stack and another driving the truck with two others on buck rakes.

Carl was driving the truck and asked me if I wanted to ride along. Yes! I jumped in. He noticed that I was very attentive and soon asked if I wanted to drive the truck. Yes! So he took time to fit me behind the steering wheel and sat beside me to coach me on what to do. I had two seasons of haying with Dad and driving our little Case VA tractor under my belt: clutch, brake, gas pedal, steering wheel and gear shift. It was all familiar stuff.

The cable was tied to the front bumper and the truck driven in reverse to raise the stacker and dump the load of hay. In this way you could see the stacker and man on the stack, and know exactly when to stop the truck. There was no need to see what was behind you - just an empty hay field. After dumping the load I had to start the truck forward and let the stacker pull the truck back into its starting/stopping position. This was marked with a fence post laid on the ground for the front wheels to bump, like a curb.

Carl asked if I could do this job for them after several trips dumping the stacker load with Carl's coaching. Yes! I was eight years old and with my butt against the front edge of the seat I could reach all the pedals, and see out through the steering wheel to watch the stacker. There was no need to turn or steer the truck, just straight back and forward.

It would be my first paying job, but a salary was not discussed at the time. Back and forth I drove each day that they were stacking hay. Carl was now free to begin cutting the next field. It was a day or two of stacking, then a day or two off while the next field was raked and the stacker moved.

Photo 13-01 is an example of overshot stacker and a horse drawn buck rake. Actually those are mules, but the equipment was the same as what the Dayton's used. We can't see what is pulling the stacker cable, it is out of the photo to the right.

photo 13-01

When it was all finished Carl told me that I did a good job and gave me some money. It was a ten dollar bill and eight silver dollars. Surprise must have shown on my face as Carl took a minute to explain that it was worth two dollars a day to them and that I did a good job (again). Did I feel proud? Yes! Did I think I was a big boy now? Yes! So much money and it was mine. I had been given a quarter for my lunch at school and I had seen my parents with paper money, but this was all mine.

Montana used dollar coins until the early 1960s. It was difficult to find a paper dollar. Occasionally I got a dollar bill for Christmas and thought that it was special (real folding money). When I was older and had money to give as a gift I had to go to the bank and request paper dollar bills. Sometimes they had them, if not they ask me to come back after receiving the next order. Since paper dollar bills were not used in Montana they were usually fresh off the press and very crisp.

I remember going back to the Army in Alabama after vacations in Montana with silver dollars in my pocket. It always generated a lot of questions and often took some convincing before clerks in

Alabama would accept those silver dollars for a purchase.

Well, let's get back to the story. I had $18 dollars cash in my pocket and eight years old and no idea what to spend it on. Yes, it was burning a hole in my pocket. I wanted to buy something, but what? I ask Mom and Dad; their suggestion was to save it. That's not what I wanted to hear! But I did soon find something to buy. One day while Mom and Dad were in town shopping I was window shopping and saw what I wanted to buy. The Westfalls had a dealership for Farmall tractors and in the window of their store was a toy model H tractor with several toy implements. It was love at first sight.

I went in and asked the prices. I did the addition, and discovered I could buy the tractor and two implements for $15. So I was able to buy three pieces and still have a little money left. They wrapped it up for me and I returned to the car. Soon Mom and Dad returned and off we went for home. They now became very curious about my purchase, proudly I showed what I had bought and they were not happy. They suggested that I take it back, but I pleaded and finally won. They were concerned about how much these three toys cost - both said it was unreasonable. Anyway I was able to keep those toys and I played with them for hours a day pretending to be a farmer. A few years later I had outgrown the toys; they were well used by the time I found other interests.

This is not the end of the Dayton haying story. The next summer I was ready to drive the truck again, but the Dayton's had changed their haying equipment and were now using a baler. It made sense for them because it was easier hauling bales than loose hay down to their dairy. The John Deere model D was still used for mowing and a smaller model B was used for raking, and the model D again for baling. None of these jobs were simple or easy for a nine year old boy, so I was unemployed. But that didn't keep me away. I was there every day and ready to do anything I could.

Son Of Montana

The only time I was of any help was when they gathered the bales from the field. They had a wagon sized stoneboat (platform on lodge pole skids) and the model D pulled it through the field while the Dayton boys loaded the bales. Sometimes they let me steer the D, just keep it pointed straight down the row of bales and away we would go pop-popping along.

I was there in the morning when they started the D. They even let me try to start it and I did finally succeed a year or two later.

It was exciting to learn about such a big old tractor. I still remember the procedure: open the compression relief valves, open the gas valve, set the throttle and choke, rock the fly-wheel into the compression position, set your feet and give the fly-wheel a spin. Sometimes it would take a couple of spins on the fly-wheel, but it always began pop-pop popping away, spitting smoke out of the relief valves. Next adjust the choke, close the relief valves and adjust the throttle. We had a running tractor.

You can find examples of starting this tractor on YouTube; search for John Deere model D.

I rode in the fender wells out to the field at which time the tractor was warm enough to run on kerosene when I was allowed to shut off the gas and turn on the kerosene valve. If I was there at the end of the day I turned off the kerosene valve to stop the engine. It would shake, pop and sputter in its dying moments rattling the fenders.

I had fun with the Dayton boys, Neil, Morse and Wayne (if I remember correctly). I learned a lot, but it was several years until I got my next paying job. I had small chores here and there that paid small change or sometimes even a dollar or two, but nothing of consequence until the summer I was 13 when I worked for Fred Longpre.

Donald R Wax

The Longpre family lived two miles from us down in Pine Hollow. Their house was a small two story grey stucco right next to the road. It always amazed me how Mrs. Longpre (Ida) kept that house so clean because every car that passed on the gravel road would cause a cloud of dust to boil up beside their house. Fred always kept a nice green lawn around the house which probably helped some. Their daughter Ida May was Norman's age and rode the bus during all our school years. Mrs. Longpre lived to be quite old (100+), and her obituary was very interesting reading in the Missoula newspaper.

Fred must have called Mom and Dad to ask about me; the first thing I knew, Mom told me I had a job at the Longpre's and took me to work the next morning. I was introduced to Fred who told me if I did what he said he would pay me five dollars a day. I was ready and would do anything for that kind of money. I said ok! Fred and I went to the field in his old Ford model A coupe. I didn't know what to expect riding beside Fred. I did pay close attention when we arrived at the work location.

At the stacker I met the rest of the crew. There was an old man (retired miner from Butte) whose name I don't remember and Gertrude Compton. What a surprise! I knew Gertie. She worked in the drug store behind the soda counter. Gertie made milkshakes and served the ice cream cones. Well now, she was decked out in Levi's and long sleeved shirt with straw hat and gloves helping Fred hay. My job was to drive the tractor, a Farmall model A, probably a mid-1940s that would raise/lower the stacker which was a type of overshot stacker. I had learned this job before while working at the Dayton's.

A few words of explanation here about the Ford model A coupe. It was probably a 1927 model that Fred had modified for use on their ranch. The trunk door and rumble seat were removed and replaced with a wooden box such as you might find on a small pickup. It was sturdy enough that we could sit on the back edge and ride to the field. Fred could also carry gas cans, salt or grain sacks and canvas irrigation dams from the farmyard to the field. It had large diameter wire spoke wheels and rubber tires that Fred said allowed him to ride through all his pastures and grass hay fields to do his irrigating. I even got to drive it a few times to fetch water or salt. Fred drove it most of the time, everywhere on the ranch.

This (13-02) is Fred as I remember him, with cigarette in the corner of his mouth and handkerchief sticking out of the back pocket of his well-seasoned Levi's. Fred once told us that it was time to wash his

photo 13-02

Levi's when they could stand in the corner by themselves! Was he kidding?

The stacker was factory built, a combination overshot and a boom stacker painted green and red. It had a boom with a slight bend in the middle where it pivoted on top of an A frame structure. On one end of the boom was fastened the stacker head with a hinge and trip mechanism while the other end was attached to the pulleys and cables. In the center at the bottom of the A frame was a half-circle cast iron base about a foot in diameter with six holes, and a large round-headed pin. As the stacker raised the load it would swing the head clockwise toward the stack. The mechanism would trip the head, dumping the load at different points along the top of the stack according to which hole the pin was in.

Fred was always on the stack and I drove the tractor back and forth. The old miner's job was to throw a little mineralized salt on each load of hay positioned on the head and to set the large round-headed pin into the hole that Fred requested. The mineralized salt contains earth minerals that the cows need during the winter when the ground is frozen and they eat only hay, and it helps to cure the hay in the stack.

Gertie ran the buck rake, and did she run the buck rake! Fred had converted an old Buick car into a buck rake and the fields were smooth enough that Gertie could drive 20-25 mph fetching loads of hay. We could really stack hay, but I thought that such a large crew was overkill. I thought I could have done both my job and the old miner's job, but I never told Fred that.

Let me describe for you a little about the Buick buck rake. The Buick chassis was from the late 1920s. It was popular to fashion a buck rake from old cars or trucks in Montana during this time. The body was removed and the rear axle was turned upside down which caused the vehicle to travel backwards. The steering wheel was moved to a rear-facing position and the driver seat was mounted behind the engine facing to the rear. The clutch, brake and gas pedals were reversed and moved in front of the seat and the shift lever was extended so it could be maneuvered. A buck

photo 13-03

rake head was fastened to the rear frame instead of a bumper and it was ready to push hay. Fred changed out the original radiator for a big Caterpillar radiator (10-12 gal) for cooling.

Here (13-03) we have an example of old car chassis converted to a buck rake, similar to the one Gertie drove for Fred.

It was a sight to see Gertie perched on the seat (no seat belt) flying out to the hay and pushing a load back to the stacker. We were moving hay big time.

That old Buick engine (a 6 cylinder overhead valve) would run fine for most of the morning, but by middle of the afternoon it was boiling hot spouting steam and water from that big radiator. After a half hour or so of spewing out its contents Gertie would have to stop at an irrigation ditch and fill up the radiator again. It would take three to four trips to the ditch to refill the radiator with a small 2 gallon bucket she carried beside the seat. This was usually the time that she would disappear behind a tree or bush for a few minutes, and then back in her seat pushing hay. We soon became a close knit crew working our shift in the field.

I liked working for Fred for a number of reasons. The job was easy and the money was good, but also for some reasons not common on the farm. Fred always started work at eight o'clock in the morning and quit at five in the evening, and we always ate at 12 noon. I was not accustomed to such regular hours. Dad always let the job dictate the time to eat

photo 13-04

and quit for the day.

Photo 13-04 is the Longpre family in 1950, daughter Ida May, Fred and Ida.

About ten minutes before noon we stopped and headed to the house. The old miner and I were on the tail of the wood box in back, with Fred and Gertie in the cab of the model A Ford. We washed up and sat down at a square table with a place for each of us where a bowl of soup was waiting. When we finished Mrs. Longpre (Ida) cleared away the soup bowls and sat a plate of lunch for the day, just like in a restaurant. She then added a couple of bowls of the main dish items to center of the table. After the main dish, she cleared the plates and sat a small plate of dessert for each. Each day was a different soup, main dish and dessert, and always very tasty.

We did not talk as Fred always listened to the market reports on the radio and at 12:30 we were on our way out of the house. Fred stayed until 1:00 to listen to Nora Drake, a serial about a husband and wife pair of private detectives.

Fred and Ida Longpre were French Canadian and sometimes spoke a few words of French during lunch hour. I later learned that Ida (Mrs. Longpre) worked in a restaurant for some years before she married Fred; it was one reason that the meal was always so enjoyable. It was like a French restaurant, including the feeling that there should be some pleasure in dining (no wine). After lunch the old miner was by himself smoking; Gertie and I usually laid down in the shade beside the spring near the machine shed. Sometimes we talked or took a nap.

Gertie told me that she had worked many years for Fred. She also told me that I was not the first Wax to help Fred hay. She said that Grandpa Wax and my Dad both helped Fred at one time or another. My brother Norman also worked for Fred after I moved on to bigger things.

Fred worked in a saw mill for years saving his money to buy this ranch, according to Gertie. He worked at night and his skin was white. After he bought the ranch the sun burned his face so bad that the blood vessels became clearly visible on his nose and cheeks.

He also smoked Bull Durham and rolled his own cigarettes. It seemed there was always a cigarette in his mouth. He didn't smoke so many; they would go out and he would not light up again. He had a habit of moving the unlit cigarette back and forth on his lip with his tongue, first on the right then on the left. He was also on the hay stack with that unlit cigarette in his mouth, something that sent shivers through me.

Fred was not a chatty person with me. He was not unkind or mean, he just said what needed to be said and we went to work. It was difficult for me to adjust to the precision of Fred's schedule. During the first year Mom sometimes drove me down to Fred's, but more often I rode my bike. I was usually the last one there and frequently late. Fred never said anything, but once they left for the field without me. I had to walk up the hill to the field. Fred then told me that I needed to get there on time if I didn't want to walk. I was more prompt after that.

Once during that first year I decided to stand up in the back of the model A and ride leaning against the cab with the wind blowing in my face. You've seen the guy driving with his dog hanging out the window, well that was me standing up in the back. About half way up the hill my hat blew off, and I was so shy about talking to Fred that I didn't say anything. When we got to the stack Fred asked about my hat and I told him. I didn't ask to go back to get the hat, and he didn't offer.

I couldn't work in that hot sun without a hat so I made one out of the remains of a paper salt sack. It actually looked pretty good and did the job. We stacked hay like that until Fred came down off the stack for a drink and to relieve himself. After finishing he walked past me and said "let's go". We got into the model A and drove to retrieve my hat. I didn't stand up in the back again, and I always grabbed my hat if I felt the slightest breeze.

There is one more thing I remember working for Fred that is worth telling. Fred always wore long woolen underwear. I am not kidding. He would open the top couple of buttons on his shirt if he got warm. He would be up on the stack in the hot dry hay on a 100 degree day in long underwear. So, one day I was feeling confident and asked him, "Do you ever take off the long underwear?" He said yes he did. I asked, "When?" He said "On Creamery Picnic day". I smiled, but Fred was serious. Funny thing is I don't ever remember seeing Fred at the Creamery Picnic or in town for that matter. They were a rather private family.

When we finished that first summer we all gathered at the machine shed to be paid. Fred gave me a check. I knew what the amount should be, $80 for 16 days. I looked at the amount on the check, it was $96! So I told Fred there was a mistake. He said it was no mistake; the extra dollar per day was to make sure I would be back next year. I worked for Fred the next summer and also the summer I was 15 with the same equipment and same crew. It was now routine, almost like breathing. I did learn to get there before 8:00, and eventually to like Fred's schedule.

The summer I was 16 years old (1955) Dad had the new John Deere model 50 tractor and had mounted the hydraulic stacker on it to stack our hay. Fred was ready to try a different method of haying and wanted to try one year with Dad's new tractor and hydraulic stacker. He hired me again, but this time to drive Dad's new tractor which he rented from Dad. I got a check and Dad got a check. I drove the tractor back home when it wasn't being used at Fred's. I would remove the hay head and back home I went.

One time on the way back to Fred's place one of the stacker push-off arms bounced lose and jabbed into the road bending it into a 'U' shape. Dad and I went to Stevensville to have it fixed. Mr. Hardy (his son Dale was in my class), the blacksmith, cut the ends off the 'U' and welded a new piece in the middle. It was like new again, so back to work. That was the last year I worked for Fred. He bought a hay baler the next year. Gertie continued to work for Fred as far as I know.

Fred raised Hereford beef cows and had some of the best calves to sell in the fall. He was often in the Missoula newspaper as the rancher with the top dollar price and top weight for his calves.

Fred sold his ranch about 1960 and moved to the north side of the Pine Hollow Road where he built a one-story house well back off the road. He also bought a new Chevrolet pickup. He lived there until he died, December 1981.

After Fred passed that Chevrolet pickup was purchased by Bruce McFadgen, older brother of Mark McFadgen (I mentioned Mark McFadgen in The Land chapter). Bruce worked for the Chevrolet dealer in Missoula as a mechanic well into his 60s and was always very proud of Fred's almost new Chevy pickup. We talked about the pickup and Fred the last time I met Bruce at the Creamery Picnic. The McFadgen families (two) lived on the Sunset Bench and the children my age were grandchildren of the first McFadgen settler in our area.

photo 13-05

Photo 13-05 is of the Longpre hay crew in 1946. That is Ida May on the wagon and Gertie on the bale stack looking our way. The man bent over lifting a bale is either Fred or Grandpa Wax. Notice the steel wheels on the wagon and the model A Farmall tractor to the far left.

This may be a good place to tell you about a couple of smaller jobs I had at the age of 13 or 14. Let's start with Gene Magini. Gene was the younger brother of Charlie Magini and they lived near each other on the brow of the Sunset Bench where it dropped down into Pine Hollow. Gene and wife Mary had two daughters, Darlene and Karen, who were a few years younger than me. They rode the bus with the rest of us Sunset Bench kids. Gene was always friendly and seemed to enjoy the company of Norman and me, but Mary was very private and seldom visited outside their home.

Gene asked me to tend his place when they went on a trip. Not a whole lot to do: a bull in the corral to feed and water, a cow (maybe 2) to milk, a calf to feed and some eggs to gather. All small stuff I thought. The one thing I didn't have any real experience with was milking by hand. I knew all the mechanics, but no real practice. I got through all the chores easy enough the first day, but the second day was harder and the third was harder still. It was the milking by hand. The muscles in my hands, fingers and forearms were sore and getting weaker from squeezing those teats. I was able to finish the job and was very happy to see Gene and family return. That job gave me a new understanding and appreciation of what it means to "milk by hand".

We traded work with Gene especially during haying. I helped Gene stack bales a number of times on his land north of their house and on land he sometimes share-cropped. I remember eating lunch at their house a few times, not often.

The last time I saw Gene was at Creamery Picnic a few years ago (2004). We met in a bar (Plum Loco) and talked for several minutes. Finally he asked my name, explaining that he couldn't see anymore. I told him my name and he sighed, threw his arms around my neck and hugged me hard. A local artist painted his portrait which hangs in the local café. He died in 2007 at age 93, less than a year after Dad died at the same age.

photo 13-06

Photo 13-06 is from 1946 and is of Howard Van Vliet and his hay baler. Howard did custom baling. That is Howard on his John Deere model A tractor. This baler required two men to ride at the rear to insert and tie the wires that held the bales together. You see both men in this photo. Dad once hired Howard to bale some straw. I remember seeing this machine when I was about six or seven years old. Note the cigarette in Howard's mouth.

Howard Van Vliet and his wife lived in Pine Hallow just below the Gene Magini place. Mrs. Van Vliet worked at the creamery for many years and Howard farmed. They didn't have much land of their own (40-50 acres), but Howard did custom baling and share cropping. When I was 15 he was share cropping several large fields (80-90 acres) of dry land grain that belonged to the Solomons. Mr. Solomon (Ted) was too busy with all the other work, and didn't have a hired man.

In the late spring (mid-June) it was time to cultivate the dry land wheat fields that would be dormant for the season. We called this process "summer fallow". Howard had a new John Deere model A tractor and was suffering some health problems, so he hired me to do his summer fallow. I drove my car up to the field just below the McIntyre place with gas cans and a map to the correct field. There I found the tractor and cultivator, filled the tractor with gas and began working.

One day when I was dragging four sections of harrow hooked to the tractor with a log chain I caught the chain on a lug of the tractor tire during a turn and before I saw the chain it was up near the top of the wheel. Oh oh! I was in a difficult turn on a steep section of the field in very loose soil and had to get the chain off the right rear wheel. Go forward, turn, brake left then right, back up, turn and brake left then right, slide down the hill, over and over and inch by inch I finally got the chain off. Ever after that I kept an eye on the chain during my turns.

Once I saw two coyote mothers lope across the far end of the field with their pups. They were heading up toward the tree line, probably after a night of dining on some mice down in the meadows below. Another time there came up a snow squall in the middle of the afternoon. I thought I was dressed warm enough, but I was soon stamping my feet and slapping my hands to keep warm. The cold on that open tractor seat was getting the best of me, so finally I stopped and dismounted. I kicked the tires, stamped on the ground, walked around the tractor and hugged the exhaust pipe to warm up. Ok, mount up and finish the field. I was happy to go home at the end of that day.

A side story here about Howard and his next new John Deere, a model 70 tractor. His Model A that I used in the dry land had a sturdy and stable wide front end, but his new model 70 had the narrow front end (a tricycle type tractor). He was share cropping some hay on the fields that the Dayton family used to hay and got the front wheels caught in an irrigation ditch. This new model 70 was a big tractor and it had power steering. Somehow he managed to break those front wheels completely off the tractor. I walked down to see it. The wheels were lying in the ditch and the tractor front end was parked on the ditch bank. Poor Howard! I felt sorry for the tractor.

Photo 13-07 is of Mom raking hay in 1937 when she and her sister Pearl visited the Wax family on the Sunset Bench. Notice the cottonwood trees to the left of the rake wheel in the coulee west of our house. We are looking north-northwest.

photo 13-07

The only time I spent working with horses was when I raked hay on Howard's field above his house with a Gene Magini rake and team (like photo 13-07). I raked the entire 40 acres without complaint, so Gene and Dad teased me, calling me "iron butt". They both said they didn't like to ride that iron seat and couldn't understand how I managed it all day.

Howard drove us down to Smiley's restaurant in Stevensville and bought us the lunch special for each of the 2 days we needed to finish his haying. One day we had meat loaf with mashed potatoes, the next it was hamburger steak and baked potato both with green beans. We all kept looking at the dessert menu and Howard finally relented and added ice cream to finish the meal. We were smiling.

Another small job I had was during grain harvest. Mr. Zimmerman (no relation) lived about a mile east of our house. He hired me to ride his grain binder (see photo 9-05 in The Harvests). It was a job I did for Dad too, so it was not new or difficult. Mr. Zimmerman drove an Allis-Chalmers model WD-40 tractor and I rode the grain binder. He had 50-60 acres to cut and it took three days to finish the job.

Mr. Zimmerman told me that he would pay me $X (don't remember) per day, what he didn't tell me was how long those days would be. I was accustomed to a new schedule for farm work after working for Fred Longpre and when Mr. Zimmerman didn't stop at what I thought was quitting time, I complained. He said "What? There's still plenty of light". Do you know what time it gets dark in Montana? I wasn't happy with his answer, so every time we had to stop for anything I complained about it being too late. After three or four such complaints we finally did knock off for the day. I don't know if it was because of my complaints, or if he was ready to quit. I only worked for him that one year. He sold a year or two later and left the Sunset Bench. Ok by me!

A number of new kids joined our class from the Lone Rock School when I started high school (1953). Rollie Lewis was one, and we soon became good friends. We talked a lot about the jobs we could get for the summer, so after my last year working for Fred Longpre I was ready for something bigger. Rollie knew of a rancher (Arlo

Ellison) east of Florence that needed help for the summer, but wouldn't start until late June. So we made a plan to fill the beginning weeks of June. We would harvest lodge pole pine, cut and sell fence posts.

We scouted out a good place up in the mountains behind the Lewis farm, got a permit from the Forest Service and made our plans. Rollie would borrow their chain saw and a horse; I would supply a car and borrow Dad's pickup. Dad had his ¾ ton Ford pickup now, in the summer of 1956. We packed our food supplies, a bale of hay for the horse and a jug of fresh milk from the Lewis barn with our tools and bedding planning to stay a week. The first morning went real well. We cut trees and the horse pulled them down to the road where we cut them into fence post lengths. At lunch we got a surprise.

Our food went down real good but the milk tasted like soap. That was strange! Anyway back to work. We felt very good at the end of that first day and rolled out our bedding prepared to sleep a peaceful night on the ground. Next morning at daylight we were awake and sensing that something was around our camp. Sure enough! We caught a yearling black bear sniffing around. We were a little frightened, but crawled out and shooed him down the road. Ok, no more sleeping on the ground; we'll sleep in the car.

Today was another day of good production. The post pile was starting to look pretty good and we were counting our money. Time for lunch and the milk still tasted like soap. What the..? Now back to work and a night of trying to sleep in the car. The next day we were still making good progress, but we were looking for a home cooked meal. So back down the mountain and a meal at the Lewis place. We mentioned that the milk tasted like soap and Mrs. Lewis said that she didn't remember our milk request until she put the rinse water and soap into the separator, but thought that she had caught mostly good milk from the separator. No, not quite.

Problem solved. A little soap probably didn't hurt us.

I think we slept at the Lewis house that night. We also heard that Arlo Ellison wanted us to start on Monday, a week earlier than we had planned. The next morning we were back on the mountain and continued cutting for another day. The last day we only cut trees and dragged them down to the road; we would cut them into posts on another day. Then we took our camp and horse back to the Lewis place. I borrowed Dad's pickup the next day and we hauled out a load of posts that night. They were nice lodge pole pine posts. As I remember we sold several hundred to Mr. Woodberry for $1 each. His son, Leo Woodberry, was a year or two ahead of us in school. We had to leave the rest until fall because we needed to get ready for the Ellison job.

Arlo (C) Ellison was a Vo-Ag teacher and wrestling coach from some place east of the Bitterroot Valley, maybe from around Billings (don't remember). He was in his thirties, athletic, married and had 3 young children and a pregnant wife (Jean). He had rented the Antrim Ranch east of Florence, Montana. He had two Farmall tractors (models H and M), mower, hay rake and a big New Holland wire tie baler. He was also a cattle trader. He was a very busy guy and just getting started in the ranching business.

The Antrim ranch was big with irrigated hay fields and pastures, and dry land too. He and his family lived in the main house, and the ranch help stayed in an old house out by the hay fields. He hired Rollie and me for the summer season and an old chuck wagon cook to prepare meals for us. During peak haying Arlo also hired one of his ex-students who was a wrestler.

After the first payday the cook disappeared into town for the weekend and when we came to breakfast Monday morning there was a young Indian woman sitting at the table drinking coffee. What the . . . ! Where did she come from?

Son Of Montana

The cook explained that he got drunk Friday night and stayed drunk until late Sunday afternoon. When he sobered up he found a woman in his bed and his friends told him he was married. Don't think he even knew her name. So now we were three young men and an old cook married to an Indian woman living in the hired help house. He was a good cook and the food was tasty, but don't think this can last much longer. A week or so later she disappeared as mysteriously as she appeared. We just didn't know, and didn't care to ask.

Working for Arlo had its advantages and disadvantages. We got board and room and free gas. Free gas! Arlo let us fill up at his farm tank because he reasoned that we drove my car to/from the fields. We did of course, but we also drove all over the Bitterroot Valley between Missoula and Stevensville every weekend after work. It was a good thing my car had a rebuilt engine. The disadvantage was that we had to work long hours and there was no shower at the hired help house. We dipped water from a bucket and washed up out of a wash basin. So those long weekend nights cruising started with a stop at home for a shower and fresh clothes.

The days began for Rollie and me at 6:00am. We had sprinkler pipe to change for an hour in the morning, then back to do our daily toilet, wash up and eat breakfast. After a few minutes to let some digestion take place we headed for the field where we usually met Arlo. We three would plan the day's activity. Most days we baled and stacked hay, Arlo on the tractor pulling the baler and I on the wagon behind the baler stacking bales, his oldest boy shuffling the wagons to/from the stack yard, the ex-student wrestler on the stack and another helper unloading the wagons. Rollie spent the day on the mower or rake preparing the next field. Rollie would stop about 5:00pm and spend two hours changing the sprinklers by himself while we continued baling hay. We were at the supper table a little after 7:00pm and then off to bed. Other days Arlo was busy with the many other things he did - trading cattle, buying supplies, tending to his family.

Rollie and I finished the haying for Arlo on the Antrim ranch and then we split up. Arlo relocated me with the tractor and baler near Corvallis where he had contracted to do some custom baling. The next morning I drove up to Corvallis and started baling on my own, which lasted for a week or so. This was second cutting hay in late August; it was approaching the end of our working for Arlo.

The Farmall M tractor had a bad reputation for causing a steering wheel backlash. I had been warned to keep my thumbs away from the steering wheel spokes because the front wheels could cause a backlash. It happened! The front wheels caught the edge of a small ditch causing the steering wheel to spin rapidly against my left thumb laying it back on my wrist. It surprised me, and I quickly stopped the tractor. I took a deep breath and moved my thumb back to its normal position. Then I slowly resumed baling. Lesson learned!

After finishing up with Arlo, Rollie and I had time to return to our pile of lodge pole pine which we found exactly as we left it. We cut them to fence post length and hauled out a couple more loads for Mr. Woodberry. We earned $500-600 harvesting and selling fence posts, if I remember correctly.

Arlo Ellison would remain in the Florence and Stevensville areas and become a very successful rancher. He is well known in Stevensville because his ranch property is just outside of the city limits northeast of town. He developed part of his land creating a very attractive subdivision east of the schools and the railroad tracks. Arlo was a hard working no nonsense rancher and business man who was a good role model for two teenage boys.

Rollie Lewis would eventually own a large dairy north of

Corvallis. He began as a carpenter, bought a small acreage and milked a few cows before and after work. He built a milking barn, grew his herd of cows and finally quit carpentry to milk cows full time. The last time I talked to Rollie, he and his son were milking 250-300 cows three times per day. He added more and more acreage over the years and sold packaged fertilizer called MooPoo. He built and rents a number of storage units north of Corvallis. His brother Phillip also had a dairy for a time, then a trucking business.

During grain harvest that fall (1956) I worked for the McPherson family. Mr. and Mrs. McPherson and their son and his family had a dairy down by the river north of Stevensville. They also had several dry land grain fields up east of the Lewis farm. I stayed at their house working after school and on weekends. I also worked some for the Warburton's who had purchased the Combe dairy, south of the McPherson's. I also stayed there and worked after school and on weekends. These were both short jobs of a couple weeks each during spring planting and fall harvest.

I also worked at different times for a few days at a time for Zack Bugli. Usually it was to summer fallow on land he share-cropped, once down near Missoula and once in the dry land up east of Willoughby Creek. I need to tell about the time he asked me to help harvest grain. He was running the combine and I was to drive his old Ford truck to haul the grain to Hamilton. We had a truck load of grain after lunch and then he told me the truck didn't run very well, but he thought I could make it to Hamilton. He said I should stop at a particular garage to get a tune-up; the garage was expecting me.

It was a long slow trip to Hamilton (first and second gear only) to off-load and finally to the garage. An hour or so later I was on my way, and wow, what a difference. That flat head V8 was singing and we were rolling 50-55 mph on the highway and 30-35 on the dirt road back to the field. That truck had wings, but when Zack stopped to empty the combine we discovered that the slide-in gate at the end of the box was missing. It must have bounced out some place on the way back. Zack continued to combine and I drove up and down the road looking for that tail-gate panel. I could not find it. Zack didn't ask me back the next day.

It is difficult to find work during the winter months (1956-57) but I was able to find a job working in the potato cellars on the lower Three Mile. The first job was with a father and son team (Moody) with a big cellar on the north bank of lower Three Mile. They were big men, over six feet and 200 lbs. Once we started on a Friday afternoon about 4:00pm (after school) and worked straight through to midnight. It was a tough shift. I simply could not shovel potatoes fast enough onto the conveyor belt to the sorting table. More potatoes! More potatoes! We sorted and stacked 15 tons of potatoes in 100# sacks ready for the inspector. These potatoes were to be delivered to California. I went home to sleep and take Saturday off, but early in the morning the phone rang. Moody needed me back in the cellar!

The inspector and the truck were there first thing Saturday morning. The potatoes did not pass inspection, and the truck driver was waiting. The inspector told them to re-sort all those potatoes. When I arrived the inspector was gone and they had decided to load most of the potatoes in the truck and only re-sort the last few rows of sacks at the end of the truck. We did and called the inspector back. All the potatoes were loaded so he asked us to fetch this sack, then that sack until he was tired of opening sacks and inspecting potatoes. He finally said ok. The semi truck departed for California and we all went home.

Photo 13-08 is of my sister Patsy getting an early morning phone call during the spring of 1960. Notice the replacement radio on the bookcase at the far left, a Sears Silvertone. I completely rebuilt this radio

photo 13-08

(new wiring, capacitors and tubes) in the 1960s but it was never the same as the radio that was smoked by lightning that I describe in The Outbuildings.

I got a call from Donna Higgins on this phone toward the end of the next week after the Moody cellar job. She was in my high school class. I almost never talked on the phone, much less to a girl. What did she want? Her dad grew potatoes a little south of the Moody's. So Friday night after school - it's not what you're thinking! Duard Higgins (Donna's dad) needed some help in the cellar and I was to work sorting potatoes after school on Friday.

I arrived on time and met the crew: Duard, Mrs. Higgins (Rose), the hired man and his wife. Duard showed me what he wanted, shovel potatoes. Ok, that's easy. I did that last weekend. Mrs. Higgins and the hired man's wife worked at the sorting table and the hired man handled the sacking end. Duard? Well he was sort of everywhere and checking on everything. The ladies put on their aprons and gloves and Duard turned on the sorting table. He sorted a few minutes with the ladies, and then was back sewing up a sack with the hired man while I was shoveling potatoes.

I had the conveyor loaded full of potatoes when the table stopped. Duard jumped down where I was, grabbed me by the arm and looked me in the eye. He said "Don, slow down! I want a half fork load on each slat of the conveyor. Ok?" Yes. And the table started again. About a half hour later the table stopped again. Now what? Duard walked over to me slowly, asked me to put the fork down and asked "Did you understand what I said? Half a fork load on each slat of the conveyor! Can you remember that? If not we will not be able to continue." I could see that he meant what he said and so I was very careful to put half a fork load on each slat of the conveyor. We sorted for an hour or so very nicely and just as I was into the groove and daydreaming a little, the sorting stopped again. The ladies took their aprons off and laid their gloves aside. Now what? It didn't seem that we should be finished so soon.

The ladies were leaving the sorting area and Duard was walking toward me. Oh shit! He grabbed my arm and said let's have a cookie and some coffee. Boy, this was different than that Moody outfit. We ate a cookie and drank our coffee and the hired man smoked. It was a nice 10 minute break, then back to sorting. We finished for the evening at 8:00pm or so. We started the next morning and finished a truck load of potatoes by noon. When we stopped for our morning break the inspector came. He sat, talked, ate and drank stretching our break into 20 minutes. Finally Duard got up and the inspector said "Ok, where's the paper work?" He signed and never looked at a single potato. Mrs. Higgins left at that time too.

We went to the house for lunch and loaded the truck that afternoon and drove to Missoula were we off-loaded at the potato chip factory. The factory owner showed us all around and explained the process of making chips. He told me he would have to stop if he couldn't buy Duard's potatoes, and then gave us each a 16 oz bag of chips. We ate chips all the way back to Duard's cellar. I had a stomach ache on the way home that evening.

I helped Duard sort potatoes for most of the winter, maybe six to eight hours per week. I learned from Duard that it was better to do the job right the first time and not have to do it over. I learned that to maintain your brand you had to deliver the same top quality product every time.

Many years later I went to a Jack Welch management training class at GE to learn about his Six Sigma program. It was a hybrid program he had adapted from the Japanese and Motorola. After forty hours of flow charts, pie charts, sampling methods, math and breakout sessions I learned the same thing that Duard taught me that first night in his cellar. Protect your brand! Do it right the first time!

I graduated from high school at the end of May in 1957 and applied for a job at the Wilburn Timber Company (WTC) saw mill. WTC owned a saw mill in the mountains south of Lincoln, Montana. The widow Wilburn had two sons that I knew at school. She was a good looking woman and had recently remarried a man whose name I knew. Shortly, I was informed that I could work in their mill, so that will end this chapter and I will continue in Leaving Home.

photo 13-09

Photo 13-09 is from high school graduation night. First suit, shoes shined, fresh haircut, shirt and tie. The 1948 maroon Ford sedan cleaned inside and out. I'm ready. It is time to strike out on my own.

School Days

Social environment, teachers, friends, memories

The world beyond Stevensville and the Sunset Bench didn't intrude into my smaller world much during my years in school, 1945-1957.

The Second World War did of course affect everyone. By the time I was old enough to remember things we had rationing for some products. I don't remember all of them and we were not affected by some, such as butter and meats. As I remember sugar was rationed, as were tires. There may have been a number of other things, but we were either exempt or they didn't affect us because we produced our own. Tires and tubes did cause a problem. It meant that Dad had to patch, patch again and then re-patch.

Other items were either not available or difficult to buy. Cars, trucks and tractors were not available from 1942 till 1945, likewise for spare parts and farm machinery, as well as building supplies. There was very little discussion about any of these restrictions because Mom and Dad didn't have the money, and they were used to making do with what they had. After WWII they bought many things over the next 15 years or so. It was a big change.

I recall a camp in the Bitterroot Valley along the Eastside Highway a little north of Wood Lane. There were three or four large wooden buildings and a large yard fenced with chain-link fencing. I don't know if it was for POWs or for relocated Japanese Americans. The men of the camp were allowed to work outside the camp for farmers that would hire them. Once a Japanese worker came to our place with the threshing crew; I don't know who he was working for. He was treated just like any other member of the crew (as far as I could tell).

This link is a good source for how WWII affected Montana, and the POWs that resided in Montana camps.

http://svcalt.mt.gov/education/textbook/Chapter19/Chapter19.pdf

The information on this site confirms a camp was in the Bitterroot, and Japanese immigrants from the west coast of North and South America were kept in western Montana. They could work outside the camp for $0.80 per day. I recommend the site if you are interested in Montana history during WWII.

News about events of the outside world was not part of my world. We didn't receive a regular magazine or newspaper, and radio was for entertainment when we could listen. For example, I didn't know until much later that the atomic bomb program had exploded a number of bombs in Nevada and New Mexico.

Mom and Dad did discuss one aspect of WWII - the draft. Dad was 29 to 32 during the war and he was concerned that he might be drafted. A neighbor on the draft board kept him up-to-date on the draft guidelines. Dad entered his draft years married with two children and by the time they were drafting married with two children he had three children. He was also classified as a farmer (an additional exemption), so no war for Dad.

The Korean War came and went without much notice. Dad was too old for the draft, no rationing and very little in the way of any day to day news. I remember seeing newsreels at the movie theater, Fox Movietone News, about the Korean War. We didn't go to the movies very often, maybe two times per year.

Son Of Montana

During the mid-1950s Mom and Dad did subscribe to the local newspaper. A single sheet, sometimes with an insert, delivered once per week. It focused on local news: obituaries, arrest records, marriages and births, items for sale or wanted and potholes fixed. In the latter half of the 1950s television came to the Bitterroot Valley and the Sunset Bench. I saw my first television show in 1956, a football game. Mom and Dad did not have a TV set until after I left home in 1958.

So, not much affected us from the outside world. Local gossip and local problems dominated our conversation: who was drunk, whose horses got out and who had a wreck. This may seem like a very dull life, but we were busy because there was always something to do. I read a book if I couldn't find anything to do.

Here is an example of things that kept me away from the house and a book:

http://www.youtube.com/watch?v=WVjOQw84thc .

This is a short video of a Maytag washer engine like the one we had; I tried to attach it to my red Flyer wagon. I got the engine to run fine and it would propel the wagon downhill (smile), but not uphill. I didn't have a way to key the wheels to the driven axle.

We did have a telephone, photo 13-08 of our phone appears in the Earning Money chapter. The hand crank wall mounted phone relied on a line built and maintained by the users. There were 12-13 members on our party line, which at our house was used for business and not for gossip. I almost never talked on the phone and definitely not for socializing. No phone calls for me!

Stevensville is a small town and during my youth it could be rough. It had a grocery store, drug store, restaurant, post office, a feed mill, insurance agent, bank, garage, blacksmith, creamery, hardware store, fire station, movie theater, beauty shop, two barber shops, three major churches, four gas stations and five bars. One bar (Ken's Club) had two pool tables in the back by the lunch counter and allowed us kids to play pool. We couldn't drink beer at any of the bars, but we could usually find someone in town who would buy a six pack or two for us. Most often we sat in Smily's restaurant sipping a coke, or a 'pine float' (glass of water and toothpick) and play the pinball machine. Such was our night life!

I began first grade in the fall of 1945 riding Howard Longbottom's brand new Chevrolet school bus. This was the first year that my local school (Lower Burnt Fork) was closed and a bus route was established to transport us to Stevensville. Cousin Marion (Aunt Doris' son) attended the Lower Burnt Fork School from 1936 to 1940.

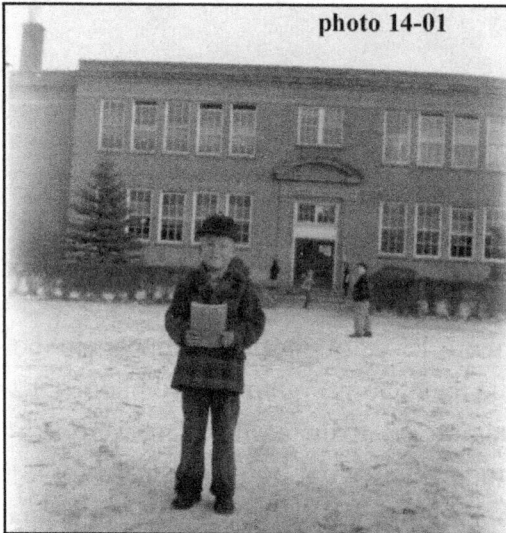

photo 14-01

Photo 14-01 is of me in second or third grade.

For 12 years I rode the same bus route with the same driver attending the same schools. Sounds boring, right! But, I saw or learned things riding the bus too. Once when the Magini girls (Darlene and Karen) were getting off I looked up through the windshield and saw a mountain sheep jump across the road. It was a big buck with a full curl of horn. Hey look! That buck stayed around the Sunset Bench for a week or so, until somebody shot him. Sad!

Son Of Montana

Mr. Longbottom was a careful driver. The bridge over Willoughby Creek once plugged up with ice and the snow melt ran over the road and froze. The road was solid ice. Mr. Longbottoom stopped and told us to sit very still in our seats while he inspected the road. He found a route over the ice and drove us safely across while we held our breaths. Not boring!

Stevensville and the surrounding area maintained a rather stable population, with a low turnover rate for the children in school. Maybe only five percent of the children in school arrived/departed each year, so most of my classmates remained the same for the first eight years.

The school building (photo 14-01) was built in the late 1920s (my guess). It had eight classrooms, four downstairs and four upstairs. There was a switchback stairs in the center entry and a pair of classrooms to the left and right on each floor, one facing the front and one on each end. An addition on the back contained a kitchen and lunch room. A heavy-oil fired boiler supplied steam for the radiators. Smoke from the chimney meant that Leo Cook (maintenance man) was on duty. The upstairs windows, opened at the top, regulated the temperature.

During my first year in school I was learning to play baseball and one day during recess was hit with the end of a bat. It hit me on the brow ridge over my right eye resulting in a deep cut. Lots of blood! I suddenly got a lot of attention from classmates and teachers, before being hustled off to the doctor near Main Street. I don't remember crying very much except when the doctor inserted the six stitches; I never will forget those stitches. Mom was called and soon I was on my way home.

Those stitches caused the hair on my right eye brow to be deformed. The tail of the eye brow curves up, resulting in a comical unbalanced appearance.

During those first years I remember playing on the football field east of the school building. The race track circled the field. A fence and railroad tracks were just beyond to the east. The train pulled by a steam engine passed by on its trip up the valley during our lunch hour. What excitement! How close we were! I remember running along the race track near the engine as it departed the station (located near the northeast corner of the football field); the engineer would wave to us and toot his whistle.

We could sometimes hear the whistle from our farm on the Sunset Bench. A few years later the steam engine was switched for a diesel engine, and a few years after that the train up/down the Bitterroot Valley was discontinued.

Mrs. Redding was our teacher in the first grade and in the fourth it was Mrs. Tamplin, wife of the high school principle. I don't remember the second and third grade teachers. I enjoyed school and learned a lot of new things, including reading, writing and arithmetic. Beginning with the fifth grade we moved upstairs, which was about the time I became more interested in my friends, games (marbles) and other distractions. Classroom learning was less important.

I began to miss school days from the age of 11 or 12 in order to help with the fall harvest and spring planting. At first it was only a day or two and only for work at home, but by the time I graduated from the eighth grade I was also helping close neighbors and missing school for days at a time. Little was ever said about the missed days except that Mom had to write a note to the teacher. School was not difficult for me and I could catch up in a week or two.

One day two friends and I missed the bell and entered our classroom late. The teacher that day was a Mrs. Metcalf, a retired teacher who often substituted when our regular teacher was absent.

Son Of Montana

Rodney was first in the door, walking full across the room in front of Mrs. Metcalf. Francis followed Rodney and I followed Francis. I didn't see what caused everyone to start giggling, but Mrs. Metcalf became very annoyed. She slapped me across the face just as I passed in front of her. That stopped the giggling! Her frustration relieved, class resumed without comment. Nothing was said about our coming in late.

We are in the seventh grade in photo 14-02. I remember Miss King, a spinster teacher who wore lace-up, half-high square heels that you've seen old ladies wear in the movies. Klik-klak, klik-klak down the hall. "Miss King is coming", time to be quiet.

One of the teachers during our last years in grade school was a young man named Louis Strand, a blonde-haired blue-eyed Norweigen from Big Timber, Montana. He was only about 10 years older than us (his students); he did not seem to have the same experience or authority as Miss King.

He lost some credibility with me when he told us to stop throwing unused paper towels in the trash can. I protested, saying that I didn't think anyone would throw unused towels in the trash. He said that he found towels in the trash that were not wet. I replied that the trash can was next to a hot radiator and the heat would dry wet towels quicky. Another time he told us we should not cut down the trees in the forest, but should conserve the forest. Again I protested because the forest provided the wood to heat our house. He asked what would we build our houses with when all the trees were gone, and I replied that the Campbell family had built their house from concrete block. Don't think he liked me very much.

photo 14-02

First row: (l-r): Dean Whitesitt, Allan Smith, David Prather, Jerry Larson, Larry Williamson, Wayne Walters, Jerry Johnston.
Second row: Floyd Wolf, Billie Waddington, Joyce Rocek, Sandra Anderson, Mary Mae Kester, Gay Lee Martin, Dixie Hubbel, Dale McHatton, Tom Rocek.
Third row: Ron Mason, Gloria Crooks, Darlene Haacke, Joan McColly, Julie Fitzgarrald, Mary Ellen Anderson, Betty Magini, Doug Miller, Don Wax.
Last row: Damian Wilcox, Howard Williams, Miss King, Don Cromwell, Gene Woolsey, Harold Campbell, Rodney Bleuchel, Francis Stang.
Missing: Donna Higgins, Mary Solomon, others?

Mr. Strand was our teacher in the eighth grade. I didn't realize what was happening, but did notice that he gave some of the girls (especially Mary Solomon) more personal attention than he gave the boys. Even today it is hard for me to believe how quickly the girls in my class developed physically. Mr. Strand eventually married another teacher and became the school principle.

Son Of Montana

My bus route was such that I rode about 50 minutes in the morning and 25 minutes in the evening, which meant that I got home from school a little after four pm. Dad often came to the house at this time, especially if he needed help. He would enter in his not very clean work shoes, really annoying Mom. I didn't understand why he did that - why annoy Mom? Now I understand that was the way he grew up. His family lived in a sod house with a dirt floor until 1936, when he was 23 years old. It was how he was raised.

Now that I'm thinking about it, Mom had her tics too. With one bathroom and three (later four) of us trying to get ready to run to the bus and Mom in the mix, she often saw us brushing our teeth. Occasionally she would tell me how disgusting it was that we rinsed and spit in the sink. Mom and Dad always rinsed and spit in the toilet. I thought "what's the difference, it all goes to the same drain". I now understand that they grew up without an indoor bath and that spitting in the washbowl was just not done.

That's me (photo 14-03) with my eight grade diploma in May 1953.

photo 14-03

I bought my first car at age 13 as did two friends. I had a 1935 Ford, Doug Miller a 1936 Oldsmobile and Francis Stang a 1934 Ford sedan. Francis and I were great pals. A couple years later I bought Doug's Oldsmobile after he traded up. We were the big shots on campus, but not for long. In high school we gained new classmates (eight?) from the Lone Rock School out on Three Mile Road.

Later at reunions we told some scary car stories, even about a few

accidents. One of the new students from Lone Rock was Philip
Lewis who had a 1938 Buick coupe. One night we were riding
around the Three Mile area and talked Philip into testing his car for
maximum speed. We were going toward Eastside Highway on
Three Mile Road and managed to hit 100 mph on the speedometer.
That was scary enough for me in an old car on a dark country road.

The high school building was north of the grade school across a
driveway. Built in 1901 with two main levels, it had high ceilings,
a basement and an attic. A later addition added more class rooms,
indoor bathrooms, a wall of lockers and a gymnasium with
dressing rooms under the bleachers. I started high school there in
1953. The biggest difference was the students changed classrooms
instead of the teachers as in grade school.

The first three years I took Vocational Agriculture class and joined
FFA (Future Farmers of America). The VoAg class was in a
separate building between the two school buildings. It had a
classroom and attached shop with entrance next to the driveway. I
finished two nice class projects in that shop.

In Vehicles & Tractors I mentioned rebuilding the floor in Dad's
red pickup. But I was most proud of designing and building 4 hog
troughs of metal during welding class.

Dad was always complaining about the pigs damaging the wooden
troughs, moving and tipping them over. The pigs chewed the wood
edge of the trough trying to get all the grain in the corners. We had
a lot of scrap metal, old machinery parts and pieces around our
shop building. I found two old water heater tanks, four rims from
wagon wheels and rod material that Dad collected from the
Willoughby Creek siphon upgrade project for the Big Ditch.

I cut the tanks and rims in half and 8 lengths of rod with the gas
welder. The tank halves would be the trough bottom, the rims

would be the legs and the rods to hold it all together. Next I cut holes on both sides along the top edge at each end of the tank halves, slid a rod through the holes and welded the rod ends to the inside of the rim halves equal distant from the ends. When finished and set right side up, we had four troughs five feet long and 15 inches in diameter suspended between 30 inch diameter arches. The rounded trough allowed the pigs to access the grain and the arch ends dug into the ground preventing them from tipping or moving the troughs.

I tried several sports during the first two years of high school: football, basketball and boxing. The school bus was the only reliable transportation for me as my car wasn't always working, or I didn't have gas, so after-school practice was intermittent at best. I soon dropped out of football and later basketball.

I continued in boxing and boxed in one of the light-weight warm-up bouts during a two school match. In the draw I learned my opponent would be a neighbor boy, Ricky Wortman. Ricky was a year younger and his family lived on the Burnt Fork. We were evenly matched until the end of the second round (three round bout) when he was able to land a solid right to my left temple causing some stars and a wobble. Some smelling salts during the break enabled me to finish the last round, but I lost.

Mom and Dad came to see me box and didn't say much on the way home after the match.

photo 14-04

Photo 14-04 is of Mom and Dad when I was in high school. Notice the pipe in one shirt pocket and tobacco can in the other.

Years later I met Ricky, my opponent, at a Creamery Picnic. I stepped up to the bar in Ken's Club, finding a place a the end, and waited for a barmaid. There were two behind the bar, one seemed to be the regular and was very busy plus a good looking helper. The regular was not getting to my end of the bar so the helper served me a short beer. We exchanged a few comments and I learned the she was Ricky Wortman's wife. I asked and she pointed out Ricky at a electronic game machine with his back to the bar.

I walked over and stood beside Ricky until he noticed and looked up at me. I said "The woman at the bar and I are leaving now to fly to Las Vegas, but she said I must tell you first". He asked which woman and I pointed to his wife. He looked back at me and said, "If you have that much money, go ahead", then returned to his game. I introduced myself and we shook hands, then had a good laugh and reminisced about the boxing match.

About 1955 a natural gas pipeline was extended up the valley. A couple of the older boys left school to work on the project. The pipeline was routed over the Sunset Bench crossing west of the Longpre barns and descending into the Willoughby west of the Big Ditch bridge and south of South Sunset Bench Road. During the first weeks of testing the line broke and created a huge blaze which burned for several hours. We could see and hear the fire just beyond the Big Ditch bridge from our house.

The last two years of high school I began working more and more - in the fall during harvests, winters in the potato cellars and springs preparing for planting. Sometimes I slept at work sites, the Warburton and McPherson dairies north of Stevensville by the river. Both of these dairies became part of the Lee Metcalf National Wildlife Refuge, a rather large refuge along the east side of the Ritterroot River.

High school like grade school was not difficult for me; I was even on the honor roll a few times. English was the most trouble for me and history the most interesting. In science classes I was studying what I had already learned while helping on the farm, like the multiplying power of a lever and the anatomy of mammals and their reproduction. I did not learn how to study, and almost never did any homework outside of school hours.

A number of students came and went during our high school years, but John Combe soon became one of the most popular. The Combe's moved from Utah in 1954 and operated a dairy north of Stevensville which they later sold to the Warburtons. John quickly became part of the "farm boy" clique. The Combe's moved back to Utah before John graduated high school.

Once Mr. Combe, John and I took a load of heifers over the Lost Trail Pass during the move back to Utah . It was a slow two day journey with Mr. Combe's farm truck and a trailer. We felt sorry for those heifers, 30+ hours without food or water.

Our senior year class trip was to the Sleeping Child Hot Springs southeast of Hamilton. We spent three fun hours in the pool and then several of us boys were playing catch on the driveway with a softball. On the last catch I slapped the ball hard (good catch) and my class ring flew into the rocks and grass beside the driveway. I heard it hit the rocks. Several other boys joined me; we searched but didn't find it. Soon the rest of our classmates were yelling at us to board the bus. Let's go!

What to do? I asked David Prather for his ring, explaining that I would throw his ring from the same place and in the same direction as happened with my ring. He agreed and I threw. With everyone watching we were sure we could find both rings. We found one immediately and handed it to David, then continued looking for the other. David yelled, "It's not mine"!

Sure enough he now had my ring! So, back to looking for the missing ring, and David was looking more and more worried. We knew where we found my ring and continued searching. Every rock and bunch of grass was searched carefully and we soon found David's ring. The fright of losing our rings was forgotten and we were on our way back.

Jerry Larson and I drove down to Utah after graduation in 1957 in my Pontiac to visit John Combe and look for work. We stopped in Rigby, Idaho to talk with a potato farmer about changing sprinkler pipe for the summer. He wasn't interested in hiring kids. We also visited a Steve Preslar who was in jail for stealing money in Montana. Steve was a year behind us in school. Sober and disappointed, we drove back to Stevensville.

Stevensville High School in 1955 (photo 14-05). The main part of this building was torn down only a few years ago (2000s). The home economics classrooms were in the attic.

photo 14-05

High school life didn't create many memorable events for me. Most of what I remember about high school was what I did away from school. I didn't join in many after school sport or social activites. It was a place to recover and rest from life outside of school.

The 'class of 57' is a close group, and most have attended at least one of our reunions. I think most of us consider our bond special and are able to reconnect easily when we meet. We have had reunions every ten years until 2002 when we changed to every 5 years. I missed the 1987 reunion when I was working in France.

Stevensville High School class of 1957 reunion (photo 14-06) in the summer of 1967.

The reunion (14-07) in summer of 1977.

Leaving Home

A factory job and union wages

After graduating from Stevensville High School in May, 1957, I got a job working at the Wilburn Timber Company (WTC) sawmill located about 16 miles east-southeast of Helmville, Montana . This could more accurately be called a lumber camp. It was an independent lumber production operation with everything needed for harvesting a tree to shipping a board ready for finishing.

There was housing for the married workers and bunkhouses for the single workers, a residence/cook house for the mill boss, cook and kitchen helpers, a separate shower/wash house and several outhouses. In addition to the sawmill building, mill pond, incinerator, machine shops, garages and storage for parts and fuel there was all the machinery needed to turn trees into lumber. I don't know when it was established at this site, but guessing from the age of the equipment it was probably pre WWII.

Most of the time I drove to work in the 1951 Pontiac that my brother and I owned together, he worked closer to home at the Longpres. It was a three hour drive from our house to the mill site: four miles of gravel road to Stevensville, 31 miles on Highway 93 to Missoula, 56 miles on Highway 12 (later I-90) to the Helmville road junction east of Drummond, 22 miles of gravel road (highway271) to Helmville and 16 miles of dirt road (highway141) going east past Nevada Lake to Dalton Mountain Road and a half mile to the mill site (still visible on Google Earth maps). Those of us who lived in the Bitterroot Valley drove to the mill on Sunday evening after supper in order to be ready for work Monday morning.

The mill started sawing logs promptly at 7:30am, stopped for an hour at noon and continued until 5:30pm Monday thru Thursday. This schedule allowed us to shut the mill down at 11:30am on Friday and head for home. Happy Friday afternoons! Every other Friday was payday, even happier Fridays. My starting pay was $1.90 ½ (one dollar ninety and one half cent) per hour, or $76.20 per 40 hours. Deductions such as meals ($10?), social security and taxes left me with about $60 a week.

Each day started with breakfast at 6:00am, and then toilet chores with most of us in the mill or on the way to jobs in the forest (logging crew) by a little after 7:00. This gave us time to prepare our work area for production to start at 7:30. At noon we had a full hour to eat and relax before resuming production. The logging crew had box lunches to eat at their work locations. After the mill shut down for the day we had time to wash up, change clothes and relax again before supper at 6:30. The food service was logging camp cuisine in every sense of the word. Lots of protein and calories and all you could eat. Only the mill pond man (we called him Doc) carried any extra weight.

My job the summer of 1957 was to stack boards off the "green chain". The green chain delivers the boards from the mill to the stacking area. There were normally three of us on the green chain, but sometimes only two and then we had to work extra hard to keep things running smoothly. The green chain area was under a shed roof about 50ft long with a floor four feet above the ground where pair of cable loops circulated on each side of a table in the middle that moved the lumber along the table. This area provided space for six stacks on each side plus space at the end for the cull boards. Two stacks became a load for a truck with wagon that hauled the lumber to the Bonner Mill east of Missoula.

The Bonner Mill facilities were built in the 1880s during the big money investments in western Montana to harvest the natural resources - gold, copper and timber. Bonner was one of the biggest milling operations in Montana, and operated for about one hundred years, before becoming an environmental cleanup site. I remember visiting the mill during a school field trip in 1955. It had its own water powered electricity, scrap wood fired steam plant, and hundreds of workers.

The last time (2000s) I saw the Bonner Mill most of the structures were gone. The dam had been removed and the creek bottom around the dam site was being cleaned and recycled. The logs are now hauled by diesel trucks to west coast ports and shipped to China then milled and made into furniture. The finished products are shipped back to the US and delivered to a store near you. I guess that's progress.

Now back to my job the WTC mill in 1957. Each pile of boards (stack) was built on "jacks" and a wood edge a few inches below floor level of the green chain. The jacks were flat wood frames that supported the stack end away from the green chain. Some skill was required to start and build a stack. To begin, first slide a half dozen wide boards down on opposite sides of where your new stack will be, jump down on the ground and raise the jack to the upright position then lift the boards onto the jack. These initial boards appear like a table with the jack supporting one end and the edge of the green chain supporting the other. Now, return to the green chain floor and continue adding boards by sliding them out onto this table to build a stack (truck load).

Each stack is about eight feet wide (divided in half) and 16ft long and four feet high (each half 4x4x16ft). The boards must be stacked straight, without spaces between the boards and with two or three spacer strips in each half of the stack. The spacers are wood strips (1x2in x4ft) needed to re-level and bind the stack halves. A loose stack could fall apart on the trip to Bonner and scatter lumber all over the road. It did happen, and the boss was not happy.

Walking out on the stack and laying down the spacers was easy; sliding the first board over the spacers required some skill. Slide the board out dropping the end beyond the first spacer and push out to the next spacer then flip the end up and push over the next spacer. The next boards can ride out onto the stack on the first board, continue stacking until this new layer is complete.

The truck that carried the lumber to Bonner had driven rollers on its bed. The driver backed the truck under the stack pushing the wooden jack to the ground then engaged the rollers to move the load onto the bed. He backed the truck up to the wagon and using the driven rollers transferred the stack to the wagon. He secured the two stacks, hitched the wagon to truck and was off to Bonner.

By the end of summer 1957 I was pretty good at building stacks off the green chain. As my skill and knowledge grew I became rather confident and would begin to let my focus wander. I could start a stack rather quickly, grab a board end with my left hand and give a quick strong pull to slide the board out onto the stack letting it slide through my right hand guiding it into position, board after board clearing the green chain.

One day I banged my left hand with the end of a board into one of the roof supporting posts and smashed my class ring on my finger. Ouch! The ring prevented some damage to my finger, but I was unable to get the ring off. Pay attention! Some cold-iron metal work and the ring came off. I still have the mostly circular ring in a drawer.

Son Of Montana

Some of us young men drove the 16 miles to Helmville after work in the evenings. There was a bar, gas station/garage and a little grocery store in town. The bar was right out of the 1890s, carved mahogany wood with a brass foot rail and spittoons. A big framed mirror hung on the wall behind the bar and out the back door were a pair of outhouses. An old couple, maybe in their 60s or 70s, ran the bar. I remember drinking a mug of beer with a shot glass of whiskey dropped in the bottom. It's beer with a whiskey chaser. Headache the next day! I was only 18 at the time.

Helmville also had movies on Wednesday night when the movie man came to town. Equipped with a projector and a couple of films, he would set up in the community center (a building I think was a barn in its previous life). He came to the bar to announce that he was ready, and to tell us the movie choices. We would shout out our first choice, which sometimes resulted in the movie man switching the reels.

We all left the bar with a beer or two in hand, some smoking cigarettes, and headed to the community center across the street. We each paid a quarter and sat on benches and a few folding chairs. The smoking and beer drinking often resulted in a rather rowdy audience. Quiet! Hang on to your beer! Whose can was that! I dropped my smoke! Put out your match! Where's my beer?

One Sunday afternoon while at home, before returning to the WTC mill, I decided to climb Saint Mary's peak. By the time I reached the top of St Mary's it was past supper time. The young couple manning the lookout tower gave me supper and suggested that it would be best to spend the night and walk back down in the morning. So I slept on the floor with an extra blanket and walked out the next morning. I arrived at the mill Monday evening, ready for work on Tuesday. I did enjoy the views, and saw a bunch of mountain goats out west of the tower.

Donald R Wax

Photo 15-01

Photo 15-01 is of Saint Mary's peak from the Wax farm driveway looking west in January 1961. The lookout tower is on the very top, just a small dot when viewed from our house.

By the end of the summer I had saved about $500. Borrowing another $500 from the bank in Stevensville (Dad was co-signer) I headed off to Montana State College in Bozeman (now University of Montana, Bozeman). I wanted to be a mechanical engineer and design farm machinery. I also had no idea what it meant to attend college, which was a complete waste of time for me at this time.

I had taken no college prep classes in high school, so I had to take them in college. One was a solid geometry class taught by an old fart with a big brushy moustache who smoked cigars all the time in his classroom. Stink! Smoke! Very little discussion and almost no learning. Another SOB taught a drafting class; he was never on time and seemed to hate coming to the class (maybe he hated teaching). One day he arrived a few minutes before the end bell rang and took roll. Everyone not present got an "F" for that day. I had left the room after waiting 30 minutes, so of course I got an "F". I also washed dishes in the mess hall a couple nights per week, and I wanted to have fun with my new friends on the weekends.

One week in February there was a lot of talk about a basketball game, so I went and saw Elgin Baylor play. What an impressive basketball player! It was clear why everyone was talking.

Son Of Montana

I left after winter quarter in March 1958, my $1000 gone. I did have some new books to bring home.

Soon I was back working in the WTC saw mill, again on the green chain. In a few weeks I was asked to operate the trim saw inside the mill building. It was more money and responsibility. The trim saw cut each board to length (12, 14 or 16ft) to get the most out of each piece cut from the log. It was fast paced and required quick judgments and constant focus.

I also was responsible for a Caterpillar (Cat) stationary diesel engine. I started it in the morning and shut it down at night. It had a small gasoline starting engine that I cranked by hand. I clutched the small engine driveshaft to crank the diesel engine for a few minutes (to lubricate and warm up) before opening the diesel's throttle. The diesel would fire up burning off the initial oil and fuel throwing out a cloud of black smoke. It then settled into a nice hum of 1500 rpm with full power to run the trim saw, green chain and scrap conveyor.

Watch a YouTube.com example with this link,

http://www.youtube.com/watch?v=xnDboHo_ctk

We had two millwrights, a father and son team. Ah yes! We did have some characters working at the mill. The father was supposed to be the expert mechanic, but he was missing parts of his fingers on both hands. The son was the grunt and the father the brains. I always wondered how smart could he be with all those missing fingers. They were responsible for keeping all the mill machinery in working order. They fueled the engines, oiled and greased all the bearings, rollers and gears and sharpened all the saw blades. The main saw blades were changed every two hours which gave us a few minutes to catch our breath and a glimpse them working together.

Another character was Doc, the mill pond man. His job was to walk around the pond pushing the logs with a long aluminum pole onto the lift chains to the saw deck. He would sometimes walk out onto the logs in the pond. Yes, he fell in once. He was a small round-faced middle-aged fellow who liked to chum around with us younger guys. He enjoyed kidding us. He owned a black Dodge van full of carpentry tools. He was a home repair handyman in his previous life. He made no secret that he was hiding from a wife and stepchildren in Washington State. He did smoke but didn't go to town with us. Don't think he ever went to town because he asked us to buy his cigarettes. Food and housing was available in this mill/lumber camp east of Helmville, Montana. It was a good place to hide.

I remember other co-workers, among them the following: Harold Campbell was in my high school class (later a math teacher), Don Wright was a year or two ahead of me in school (he became a retail shop owner), Eddie Rathbun was a few years ahead of me (a heavy equipment operator), and Gary Rhodes (?) was in the same class as Eddie Rathbun. Gary's older brother Weston has a farm southeast of Bell Crossing off the Eastside Highway. Gary's oldest brother Don used to drive by our house in his Chevrolet car with a split manifold and dual exhaust pipes, which made a very loud noise and annoyed Dad.

A little detour here to tell you about the Rhodes family dairy. They bought the place where Charlie Magini used to live and built a milking barn to the east side of Pine Hollow road. The cows were often fed and pastured west of the road, so at milking time there would be 30-40 cows crossing the road just as the road crested the bench going east and behind a blind corner going west. Time to slow down!

Among the older workers was Arlee McKinney, the sawyer and mill boss. He was in his early 60s, spending about 50 years in saw mills. He was grumpy most of time and when not grumpy he was angry. His word was the law. Nobody crossed Arlee. The Palin brothers (Ray and Ernie) worked in the forest and escaped Arlee's wrath. Steve Anderson was the widow Wilburn's new husband (WTC owners) and spent most of his time in the forest with the Palins.

Sammy Crooks came to work in the forest for a few weeks. He was sort of the Paul Bunyon character of the camp storytelling because of his reputation as a logger. His appearance - barrel chest, narrow waist, suspenders, plaid shirt and denim pants with an expansion patch at the belt line in the back to accommodate the transition from waist to belly, logging boots and hard hat - made us think he should have the blue ox at his side. His daughter Gloria was in my class. The family lived on the Middle Burn Fork Road east of Stevensville.

A large older gentleman graded the boards (summer 1958) after being cut in the trim saw (I in front and he behind the trim saw) and he sort of adopted me. If I mistrimmed a board he would hand it back to me and explain why I needed to trim it again. On breaks he would take me aside and try to teach me the basics of lumber grading and the job of a Lumber Grader. He asked several times if I wanted to be a Lumber Grader. There wasn't any desire, I had other dreams. Besides, he smoked cigars in a cigar holder like that professor in Bozeman.

One evening the two teenage girls (don't remember their names) who helped Mrs. McKinney (Arlee's wife) in the kitchen came out to have a look around the mill site and visit with us boys. They attracted a lot of attention. Soon we were down by the mill pond where Eddie Rathbun and Doc were showing them how to maneuver logs on the water. Doc was on shore and Eddie out on the logs with a short pole, both demonstrating their skills. Somehow we talked the girls in to joining Eddie out on the pond.

Yes, the girls, (one in pants and the other in a full skirt) fell into the pond! Panic! There were two girls, one chest deep and the other waist deep with that full skirt floating on the water, thrashing about in the pond before Eddie and Doc dragged them to shore. They ran to the cook house crying. It was fun while it lasted. I don't recall seeing the girls out after that episode.

I was at home on most weekends, sometimes helping Dad and neighbors usually with haying. I remember one time I was helping a neighbor named Smith, an older man whose son (Leonard Smith) also had a farm next door. We were stacking bales and he had two other young men helping. He drove the tractor with the three of us handling the bales. In midafternoon we were beginning to tire and someone asked Mr. Smith, "Why do you get to drive the tractor all the time?" Mr. Smith answered, "Because it's my tractor!" End of that discussion. It was a very brief exchange that would forever define for me the difference between socialism with communal property and free enterprise with private property.

On a few weekends I remained in camp to accompany workers who on a few occasions had to work on Saturday. Once when the logging crew was behind delivering logs to the mill I went with the logging truck driver to the forest to bring out a load of logs. I marveled at his skill driving that big AutoCar truck on those narrow logging roads. The truck was pre WWII (my guess) with a gasoline engine and three transmission shift levers (similar to truck in photo 15-02). He hooked his arm through the steering wheel and hit all three levers while double clutching in the blink of an eye. Very impressive to a 19 year old!

Another time I rode with the truck driver who took the lumber stacks to the Bonner Mill. This trip was to deliver a single stack of cull boards to someone who lived near Anaconda, so we only needed the truck without the wagon. This truck was a newer International with gas engine made for highway use. It had a big roomy cab and the driver, showing off a little, crossed his legs behind the wheel during the trip. The load was extra tall; we were top heavy so when taking a corner the truck leaned causing a surprised look on the drivers face. We finished the trip without crossed legs.

On the first Monday in September (yes, we worked on Labor Day) we awoke to see seven inches of fresh snow on the ground, even more in the forest. We heard on the radio that the mountain passes had 16-18 inches of snow and that many vacationers were stranded. We spent the day clearing snow from all work areas around the mill and putting on chains. We were back in full production on Tuesday and by Friday the snow had all melted.

By mid-September I had paid back my loan and had saved a little extra. The draft and military service obligations were on my mind. I joined the US Army and began basic training on October 2, 1958. I would return home only for vacations from this point forward.

I spent a day with Frank Hereford and Ross Prather during a vacation from the Army in January 1961 when I took these photos. They were harvesting logs from the upper Locksa near Lolo Pass on the Idaho-Montana border, on that morning it was about two hours out of Missoula. I was still looking for some type of work that could be a career for me.

This (photo 15-02) is Frank Hereford (lived on the Burnt Fork, a couple years ahead of me in school) trying to free his logging truck after sliding off the road and into the snow.

photo 15-02

I don't know what they were saying (photo 15-03), but let me guess. Looks bad! What are our options? No money if the logs stay here.

photo 15-03

This is (photo 15-04) Ross clearing a path for the logging truck, and pulling it back onto the road. The logs were finally on their way to the mill in Missoula

photo 15-04

(photo 15-05). That load is 20-30% larger than loads today because of current weight restrictions.

photo 15-05

The lumber industry might have been my life if not for- - ?

My life took a new direction during President Kennedy's Berlin stand-down crisis with Russian leader Khrushchev which resulted in a satisfying career with General Electric. I retired from General Electric as a manager of Installation Services in 1999. Another story, and more photos.

Donald R Wax

Mom and Dad

Their formative years, and as I knew them

We will meet my parents now, first Mom then Dad. Both grew up in eastern Montana in the early 1900s, graduating from high school in 1930. Both families were homestead farmers and ranchers, so they had similar experiences growing up. But they had some big differences.

Helen Margaret Zimmerman was born in Hawkins, Wisconsin, on January 3rd, 1913, and by spring 1915 moved with her newly married parents to central Montana near the town of Lewistown.

Mom's grandparents, married aunt and uncles with families, and her parents moved east to the area around Jordan in 1916. Mom's father (Mike Zimmerman) filed for a homestead about 18 miles east of Jordan on the Big Dry Creek. They spent that winter in a dugout cave near Jordan, according to Mom.

photo 16-01

Mom attended one room schools, organized by the locals near their homestead,

until she graduated from grade school. Photo 16-01 is of Mom with her siblings Donald, Florence and Pearl (right to left) on graduation day in 1926. As you can tell Mom is the oldest and grew quickly, in height and responsibitiy. And from the downward tilt of her head you can tell that she was shy and rather introverted. Notice the blanket as a backdrop and the carpet under foot.

During the 1920s the United States was a prosperous country, but not so much for struggling homesteaders in eastern Montana. By this time her father had started building their second house on their homestead.

photo 16-02

Photo 16-02 is of the initial portion of their house in 1926. It eventually grew to be a more comfortable ranch house for the Zimmermans.

The nearest high school for Mom was in Jordan, 18 miles to the west, but the school lacked a dormitory and it was too far to commute (no bus). So she went to high school in Cohagen living in their dormitory. Cohagen is 23 miles southeast of Jordan and 40+ miles by road from the Zimmerman homestead. The community of Cohagen is almost completely gone today, no more than a gas station with convience store/bar in one building.

Cohagen High School, 1927
Helen Zimmerman is 3rd left last row.
Billy Wax prbably1st left 1st row

Marie Wax is 5th left in 2nd row checked shirt & tie with letter M

photo 16-03

Photo 16-03 is of the Cohagen High School teachers and students in the fall of 1926. Mom was the tallest girl and Dad was the smallest boy in school. Billy Wax and his sister Marie were in the same class.

Mom played center on the girls basketball team and participated in other after-class activities while living in the dorm. She graduated in 1930, then attended the State Normal School in Billings in the fall. She told me that she missed her parents and siblings during these school years and was not always a good student.

The money for the State Normal School came as a loan from a Dr. Battin. Mom mentions him (16-04) several times in her diary. It was a surprise to me that he charged ten percent interest. I understood that he was the local doctor in Jordan during the 1930s.

photo 16-04

Mom started teaching grade school in the fall of 1932 and continued until 1938. Her schools were all in the Cohagen area, one of them near the Wax homestead. Her salary ranged from $30-60/month. The county issued warrants which could be cashed when the county had enough money. It seems that she signed some warrants over to Dr. Battin who then gave her some cash to spend after he cashed them.

photo 16-05

During those six years she paid off the loan and managed to save $600 which became the seed money to purchase the Bill and Helen Wax family farm on the Sunset Bench in 1939 (see The Land).

Photo 16-05 is "The last day of school, 1935". It is interesting to me because of the number of students (I counted 15) and the people I could identify in the photo. Mom is first left back row, next to Grandma Wax. My Aunt Pearl is in front of the fourth and fifth person in the back row.

photo16-06

Both of Mom's sisters, Florence and Pearl, came to live with and attend her school during their last years of grade school. Photo 16-06 is of the teacherage where Mom and her sisters lived in 1935, Pearl (left) in grade school and Florence (next) in high school in Cohagen.

Son Of Montana

At some schools Mom lived with neighbors (the Lund family) near the school as she mentions in her diary. The teacher and two girl students living in the same house. No favorites in that classroom! It was during this time that she (noted in her diary) borrowed a horse to ride back home to the Zimmerman ranch for the weekend, some 23 miles across open prairie (46 miles round trip), and the sore muscles afterwards.

In the summer of 2013 I attended my Aunt Florence's funeral in Miles City, Montana, and met a little old man named Art Pluhar who was well into his 80s. We visited some and he told me that he was a bomber pilot during WWII, and that my mother had been his teacher in grade school. He said he had fond memories of her.

I found this photo (16-07) of Arthur Pluhar in Mom's photos. The Pluhar boys are also mentioned in Mom's diary. That's Art second from left and his brother behind him.

photo 16-07

After Aunt Florence's funeral my brother Gordon and I went to get a sandwich for lunch and saw a group at the next table that also attended the funeral. I didn't get a chance to meet them at the funeral, so I stopped to say hello. We exchanged names and a few pleasantries. Then one of them asked if I was related to Billy Wax. I said I was his son. They then mentioned they had heard stories from years ago about a Billy Wax around Cohagen.

Mom kept scrapbooks and photo albums, and also a diary during her teaching years. She copied many poems and over the years added to her collection, enough to fill a three ring binder. She was always writing. Sometimes she would record purchases, perhaps a trip, or just her thoughts of the day. She also wrote many letters to family, friends and to me when I was in the Army.

Photo 16-08 is one example. This was written on a 2x4 inch piece of paper on both sides (you can see the ink bleed through), and contained some new information for me.

photo 16-08

I transribed her diary. It was leather covered and had a leather strap with brass hasp to keep it closed. A nice diary book that measured 4x5 inches organized for five years. Mom tried to make it last more than five years writing so small that I needed a magnifying glass to read the tiny lettering. Her script was very neat and small. She did **not** note the date or year, only the day of the week. Using the internet I found calendars and matched the days with the dates and year.

Mom was not always into the moment and sometimes seemed to be daydreaming. I now understand that she was organizing her thoughts and how to express them, sometimes resulting in a poem. She did not sign or date what she wrote, but I did find a poem that was published in a window and door catalog in the mid-1930s.

The Two Temples

A builder builded a temple,
He wrought it with care and skill
Pillars and groin and arches
Were fashioned to meet his will
And men said when they saw its beauty
"It shall never know decay
Great is thy skill, O builder
Thy fame shall endure for aye"

A teacher builded a temple
She wrought with skill and care
Forming each pillar with patience
Laying each stone with care
None saw the unceasing effort
None knew of the marvelous plan
For the temple the teacher builded
Was unseen by the eyes of man

Gone is the builder's temple
Crumbled into dust
Pillars and groins and arches
Food for consuming dust
But the temple the teacher builded
Shall endure while ages roll
For that beautiful unseen temple
Was a child's immortal soul

By Unknown Author

I chose this poem from her binder because I think she thought of her job as a teacher in this way. She understood that efforts on behalf of her students would have long term consequences. She was serious and resourceful in her efforts to build a legacy - the molding of her students. Meeting Art Pluhar at my Aunt Florence's funeral was one example of her success. She once told me "A teacher by his students shall be taught" which didn't mean anything to me at the time. Years later I taught operating system software classes and learned that it is through the student's questions that the teacher will be educated.

Mom was a good listener, and had several close friends. She did not join in the usual womens' clubs or other group activities except on occasion as a guest. She always made time for a visitor. She was not into the culinary arts, the basics would do. I often joke that todays' ladies have more flavors in their bath than Mom had in her kitchen. Salt and pepper, cinnamon, chocolate, vanilla and not much more. She was not into sewing, but did make some things for my sisters and also patched all our clothes. And she taught me to iron my shirts, which I have done ever since.

photo 16-09

This is Mom center, Aunt Pearl left and Aunt Florence right in 1937 (photo 16-09). Mom had red hair and brown eyes, Pearl blue green eyes and much darker brown hair. Florence had red hair and blue eyes.

Mom was very loyal and patient, and could spend hours doing

repetitive chores such as shelling garden peas or plucking chicken feathers without complaining. She spent endless hours washing, cleaning, canning and cooking for all of us. Duty was important to her. On the day she died she prepared Dad's breakfast. She loved children. Mom and Dad wanted to have 6 children, but it didn't work out that way. They had to settle for five children.

My father, Billy Wax, was born on November 19, 1913, in a covered wagon in an area southwest of Lewistown, Montana, called Judith Gap. His birth was soon after the Walter Wax family arrived in Montana, so they named him Montana William Wax, William after his grandfather. I always thought the covered wagon part of the story was Dad's exaggeration. I would later come across an affidavit swearing to the date and place of his birth signed by his father (Walter) so the state of Montana could issue a birth certificate. It was when Dad was near 60, so I assume the birthday certificate was requested by the Social Security office. I believe now that he was born in a covered wagon, or something close to it.

The Walter Wax family moved to Garfield County (from Judith Gap, Meagher County) and in 1914 Grandpa Walter filed for a homestead 17 miles southeast of Jordan, Montana. He built a home of sod and mud stucco where they lived for twenty years, until the spring of 1936. The conditions of the homestead law were satisfied in the spring of 1919 and Walter Wax received a patent for 320 acres.

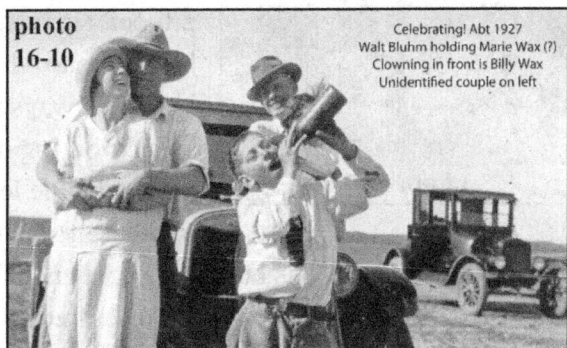

photo 16-10

Celebrating! Abt 1927 Walt Bluhm holding Marie Wax (?) Clowning in front is Billy Wax Unidentified couple on left

Dad was small for his age and slow to mature. He is 12 years old in photo 16-10, a freshman in high school. Yes, he graduated at age 16.

Dad was the baby of the family. His brother Robert, nearly 10 years older, spent most of his school years living with relatives in Iowa and Nebraska so he could attend school. Robert never really lived in Montana, only during holiday visits and summer vacations. So Dad was raised in a family with two sisters, two and four years older. During his formative years his sisters got all the attention, first from their Mom (Carrie) and Dad (Walter) and later from boyfriends. Both sisters married after high school, Aunt Doris in 1928 and Aunt Marie in 1930. Needing to make himself seen, Dad developed a lifelong habit of being a bit of a showoff or clown which was just the opposite of Mom and something I didn't always appreciate or understand.

Carry Wax, Billy Wax with pony
Abt 1928

photo 16-11

Photo 16-11 is of Dad with a pony at about age 15, perhaps getting ready to ride to high school in Cohagen six miles from their house.

After high school, Dad farmed with his father until 1934, when he got a job working on the tunnel construction for the Fort Peck dam project. He mentions this in one of his letters to Mom (see Appendix). He was always proud of the time he spent working on the project and the things that he learned. He kept a number of souvenir photos and descriptions that he was happy to show and talk about with anyone interested. So, I heard the same stories many times.

By December of 1935 it was clear that the drought and depression would force the Walter Wax family to move. Thus in the spring of

Son Of Montana

1936 Dad along with parents and divorced sister Doris with son Marion arrived in Ravalli County, settling on the Sunset Bench. Mom and her sister Pearl came for a visit in 1937, and the next year Mom and Dad married.

Photo 16-12 is inside one of the tunnels at the Fort Peck Dam project.

photo 16-12

Dad was a slightly built man, with sloping shoulders and a slim face, and weighed about 145lbs. Still he was quite agile and strong. I remember him performing one of his gymnastic tricks when I was seven years old. He would grab the broom handle with his hands spaced about 30" apart, hold it out at waist height and then jump through the opening. The broomstick was now behind his back – amazing! How did he do that? Then he jumped backwards through the opening so that the broomstick was now in front of him again. WOW! If you watch gymnasts on TV today you can see similar movements on the parallel bars.

photo 16-13

Photo 16-13 is Dad in his Stetson hat, probably in his early 20s during the time that he worked on the Fort Peck Dam project.

I have many memories of my Dad's strength that I want to tell, but first I have to describe a couple of physical characteristics, one often unnoticed and one not visible. Dad had LARGE hands for his size, and they were well developed and very muscular. Most people do not pay much attention to another person's hands. What was not seen were his forearms because he always wore a long sleeved shirt. As I think of Dad now I think of the cartoon character PopEye with outsized hands and forearms.

How did he develop such a physique? He milked cows by hand during his early years, increasing the number until 1948 when he was milking eight cows. And all of the work he did building the Wax farmstead was by hand. Everything was done by hand, so he spent hours each day (sometimes all day) gripping a teat or a tool. An ax, shovel, pick, bar, hammer, saw, post maul, nail puller, pitchfork, grain scoop, all needed to be tightly gripped and guided to be useful and efficient.

He consumed and burned a lot of calories, so he could tolerate the cold weather well. During the winter Dad cut the top from Mom's old nylon stockings, a four inch double-layered band. He wore it like a sweat band (nearly invisible) covering his ears, which allowed him to wear his favorite felt Stetson hat over it.

Neighbors who saw him doing farm chores on cold winter mornings saw the Stetson and often bare hands and couldn't understand why he was not frozen. Everyone else was in caps and mittens. I frost bit my ears, nose and toes several times trying to keep up with Dad.

Photo 16-14 is Dad feeding some heifers in the early 1940s. Note hat and bare hands.

photo 16-14

Dad began spending time visiting the bars in Stevensville in the 1950s where he gained a 'strong man' reputation. It was common for the bar patrons to test their strength wagering for beers. One test is the arm wrestle. One story has Dad arm wrestling a much bigger man who failed to pin Dad's arm to the table but lifted him off his chair instead, so other patrons held Dad in his chair to finish the contest. I don't know who won!

Another test is the handshake, gripping your opponents hand tighter and tighter until he gives up. It was rumored that Dad broke a bone in a challenger's hand. Dad was left-handed, so he wagered one handed pushups with the left hand. Never heard how many he could do, just that he did enough to win. His favorite, however, was the finger pull. Middle fingers are hooked together and pulled. Dad was often pulled sliding on the floor, so others were enlisted to hold him to keep him from sliding. Norman and I always lost the finger pull when up against Dad.

One example of Dad's strength I did not understand involved Dad using a 16lb post maul. Dad would open a hole in the ground with a post bar and I held the pointed wood post upright in the hole. Dad then stood on the edge of the wagon with 16lb post maul and drove the post into the ground 18 or more inches. As Dad swung the maul he would appear to jump off his feet. I didn't understand why. I now believe that he put so much rotational energy into each swing that the centrifugal force at about the 11 o'clock mark lifted him off the wagon an inch or two. He would land on the wagon, and guide the maul to a perfect strike on the post top. A dozen or more swings and the post was planted.

Dad's leisure activities were very physical as well. He loved to hunt big game in the mountains east of our place. I went hunting with Dad a few times, while Norman went much more often. He also hunted with friends and sometimes alone. I remember one time he went alone and didn't return that night. The next day we returned from school and found him at home. We learned that he got lost and couldn't find his pickup. He had spent the night in the mountains, before hiking out the next morning and hitchhiking home. Mom had to drive him back to fetch the pickup.

Dad loved to gather wood in the mountains with neighbors and family well into his 80s. He mentions in one of his letters to Mom in 1938 (see Appendix) harvesting poles for building our telephone circuit in the late 1930s. His fascination with the mountains began when he first arrived in the Bitterroot Valley and lasted until he died.

photo 16-15

Photo 16-15 is of Dad (notice hat and hands) in 1992 with a neighbor whom he called Whiskey Dave. Whiskey Dave died later when his pickup full of wood ran off a logging road and crashed into a tree.

Dad was also smart, and graduated from high school at age 16. He was always making improvements, looking for a better way to do things or make something work better.

He repaired the machinery, overhauling our 1948 Case tractor a couple of times. The last time I remember working on that tractor, Dad was in his 80s and becoming forgetful, not remembering where he laid a tool. But he did remember exactly what was needed to get that 50 year old tractor running again.

I mentioned before that Mom and Dad loved to play cards, and Dad used to play cribbage with us after Norman and I learned our multiplication tables. We had to be fast with the scoring, or we were soon left scrambling in the digits. He was always challenging us to calculate the score faster.

Dad's grey blue eyes could become quite intense when he became angry. I didn't have a close relationship with my father, which was unlike my close connection with Mom. We didn't always agree, but I eventually learned to do things his way. We did, of course, love and respect each other.

Two things of great value I learned from Mom and Dad. Mom made me write letters as soon as I left home and she expected to receive a letter every week or so. Once, returning to my Army post after being home on vacation, I neglected to write for several weeks. She grew tired of waiting and called the Army base where I was stationed. I was quickly in front of the First Sargent, who told me to send a letter today! Mom saved many of those letters. Dad taught me the value of honesty. To Dad your word and a handshake was as good as a written contract. If people can trust your word they will always respect you. These lessons have served me well.

I want to make a few comments on my parent's partnership, and about money, work, discipline and romance.

While Mom and Dad didn't always agree, they did have a rather smooth division of labor and responsibility. Dad handled all the outdoor work except for the garden, which he helped prepare and plant. Mom took care of the house work and the garden after planting. She harvested and canned the garden crop, and he butchered and cured meat and cut wood (see Food & Fuel).

Mom managed the check book, paying bills and the household expenses. She looked after the day to day money matters, while he made decisions about the big money items such as a new tractor or land purchase. Dad was responsible for most of the income as he produced and sold the crops. Since neither worked off the farm, except occasionally, most of our income came in the fall and was expected to last until the next after-harvest sale. I mentioned earlier that Dad did work briefly in a mine near Darby, and Mom worked some in the spring of 1950 taking the census on the Sunset Bench. My brother Gordon was 15 months old at the time.

A few more thoughts about money, noting traits that Mom and Dad shared. They both had a strong belief that money was to be conserved, saved. I remember that Dad never threw away a nail, so when pulled it was added to a gallon can for later use. Norman and I pulled many nails for that can and during new construction we straightened them for reuse. Fence wire and staples were also reused.

As kids, we wondered where Mom found those thin bath towels. After leaving home we learned that bath towels actually have cotton pile on the base netting. We began to tease Mom about her 'transparent' bath towels, which led to new towels in the closet. She also did something I have never seen anyone else do; she wiped the inside of each half of the egg shell with her finger to make sure every drop was used.

Son Of Montana

Parenting and discipline was divided as well. Mom taught us boys to be gentlemen, including how to dress and comb our hair, and helped us succeed in school. She had a tough job given what she had to work with, and she had limited success. Dad taught his sons how to work, how to drive tractors and other vehicles, and reap the satisfaction gained by completing a job. He didn't put much emphasis on school work and often reminded us that he finished school at age 16. Norman and I spent most of our time outside with Dad, watching, working and learning.

Dad provided most of the discipline which came at the end of his belt. Sometimes we protested our innocence, but that didn't change anything. Dad explained "Ok, then it's for the time you didn't get caught". Punishment didn't happen often, was probably deserved and seems not to have caused any permanent damage. Mom's attempts at corporal discipline were less successful (remember the incident when the car ran off the road?). Mom once took a broom to swat Norman and me for fighting in the house. We ducked and ran outside, getting swiped only with the bristles.

It wasn't always apparent when I was growing up, but I do believe my parents loved each other as teenage sweethearts do when they spend their lives together. They were married for more than 63 years and knew each other for 12 years before that which resulted in a long relationship as friends, lovers and partners.

It is not common to talk about romance outside of a long marriage such as Mom and Dad's, but I now believe there were other romantic interests. I suspect that in both cases, one for each, the interest was directed at them and was mostly unwelcome. I now believe a neighbor lady (frequent visitor), had a romantic interest in Dad. Another neighbor must have had a romantic interest in Mom as it caused Dad to speak and act with jealousy toward him.

photo 16-16

As a child I didn't know anything about love, or romantic feelings. I did hear words and see actions that didn't make sense at the time, but are now understandable if the result of romantic interests.

Photo 16-16 is of Mom and Dad at their 50th anniversary celebration on July 3, 1988. I missed this anniversary because I was working in Spain.

photo 16-17

Photo 16-17 is on Mother's Day 2000 in Salem, Virginia at Mac & Bob's restaurant, left to right is Dad, Aunt Florence, Aunt Nell and Uncle Don Zimmerman, and Mom.

Mom died on August 26, 2001, and Dad died on November 30, 2006. Both are buried in the Riverside Cemetery south of

Stevensville, Montana, and both funeral services were provided by Dean Whitesitt of the Whitesitt Funeral Home.

Dean Whitesitt was in my class at school. It was a comfort to me that someone I knew provided the services. Here are Dean and his wife at one of the receptions (16-18). Jim Kester assisted Dean Whitesitt during

photo 16-18

the funeral services. Potluck memorial receptions were held for Mom, and later Dad, at the Stevensville Methodist Church and each was well attended.

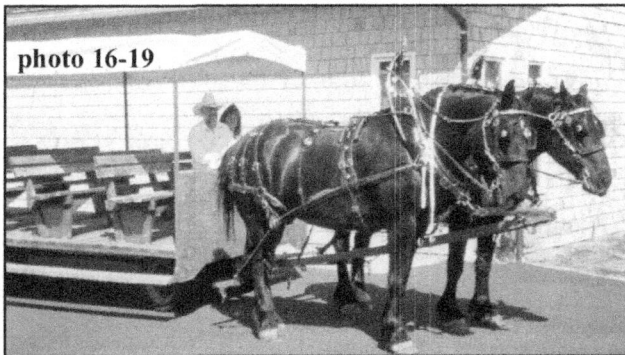

photo 16-19

Rex Griffin, a longtime friend of Mom and Dad in photo 16-19, provided a horse drawn trolley to carry us to the cemetery for Mom's burial. Here are Rex and wife with his team of Percherons.

Saying Good Bye to our parents was less painful when so many neighbors, friends and acquaintances from the Stevensville community were there to say Good Bye with us.

The Grandparents

An introduction to my roots

These are my grandparents, the Zimmermans first and then the Waxes. I knew them, but not well enough for me to describe them in detail. I will show you a few photos with some description and a few short stories.

Photo 17-01 is of Sarah Verhulst my maternal grandma (born June 15, 1893), and her brother Peter, probably about ages 12 and 14. Sarah's parents (and family) left Wisconsin to homestead in the northwest corner of North Dakota in the early 1900s. Adrian Verhulst (Sarah's father) died from a wagon accident on November 22, 1903, before his 50th birthday. Mary Verhulst (Sarah's mother) and the children returned to Wisconsin.

Sarah's father and her maternal grandfather were born in The Netherlands. I spent three weeks in The Netherlands in November 2001 researching my mother's Dutch ancestry. My brother-in-law, Bob Bowman, used much of what I discovered to document my mother's family history (the Dutch roots).

Mike Zimmerman, my maternal grandpa, was born October 1, 1889, and orphaned at age nine. He never talked much about his youth; perhaps he didn't remember or simply didn't want to remember. I found evidence of him being in a Catholic Home for Children in central Wisconsin (Eau Claire). We guessed that his parents were born in Germany.

He ran away from the Catholic Home at age 12 and worked in

photo 17-02

lumber camps near Hawkins and Lady Smith in northern Wisconsin until he married Sarah Verhulst on September 5, 1912 in Minneapolis, Minnesota.

photo 17-03

He was popular during the time he spent in the lumber camps. I have seen several photos of him with other men in their Sunday suits, and with the baseball team. He is on the right in both photos 17-02 and 17-03.

By the spring of 1915 Mike and Sarah Zimmerman my grandparents), with several others of the Verhulst family, were in central

Son Of Montana

Montana looking for a homestead of their own. My mother wrote about them living in a dugout cave during their first winter on the homestead. Grandma's younger brother (Peter Verhulst, left in photo 17-01) died in 1916 of appendicitis in the Lewistown area at the age of 21.

In late fall of 1915 Mike Zimmerman (Grandpa Z) filed for a 320 acre homestead on the Big Dry Creek 18 miles east of Jordan, Montana. Grandpa Z told me that he walked the 18 miles from Jordan to mark his homestead claim and walked back the same day (36 miles on foot).

photo 17-04

Photo 17-04 is of the Zimmerman family in late 1915: Sarah (Grandma Z), Helen (my mother) and Mike (Grandpa Z).

Those first few years in Montana were very difficult for the Zimmerman and Verhulst families. The Verhulst relatives left Montana for Oregon and Minnesota a few years after receiving their homestead patents, but Grandpa and Grandma Zimmerman remained on their homestead until they retired in June 1963.

Grandpa Z built their first home from Cottonwood trees that he cut from the Big Dry Creek bottom near their homestead. He had grown to manhood in the lumber camps of northern Wisconsin where he learned the skills needed. The house had one room and a clay roof, about 16 feet square.

photo 17-05

Photo 17-05 is the best photo I can find of that first house, here in the background with unidentified rider. I remember seeing this house after it was converted to a garage/shop (as seen here). Mom mentions in her diary sleeping in that house.

Grandpa Z began building the second house of lumber and tar paper (photo 16-02), probably in the early 1920s. In one of Mom's notes and in her diary she tells about moving a house belonging to Otto Smith, which was added onto their house in 1935. I remember visiting the Smith family (also moved to the Bitterroot Valley) near Victor, Montana, in the 1940s.

photo 17-06

Photo 17-06 is the Zimmerman house I remember from the late 1940s, when Mom and Dad sent me by train to visit.

The house did not have electricity until Grandpa Z installed a windmill charger with a rack of batteries in the basement (only for lights to replace the kerosene lanterns) in the early 1950s. In summer 1952 I traveled by bus with my brother Gordon (age three) and remember Grandpa Z showing us the components. The Rural Electrification Administration (REA) finally distributed electricity to their ranch in the mid-1950s.

They didn't have indoor plumbing until after the REA electricity was available. It was pot and outhouse until then. Before they retired Grandpa Z bought a BBQ grill and joked that they would cook outside and go to the toilet inside, just the reverse of what he was used to.

Grandpa Z continued to add land to the homestead until they owned 6 sections (3,840 acres), and were able to run about 100 cows. I once complimented him on his nice looking herd, and he agreed. He said that it was his third herd. I didn't ask him to explain, but evidently he had two previous herds that were sold because of drought and/or depression.

Photo 17-07 is cowboy Grandpa Z with grandson (Don Mike, my cousin) and his favorite horse (Glory) in the fall 1949. Glory was a sturdy and faithful horse that served Grandpa Z for many years.

photo 17-07

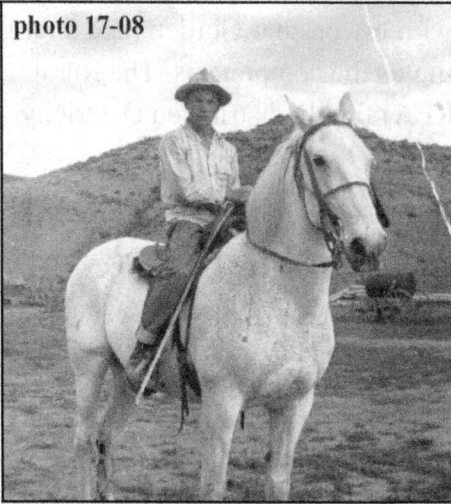
photo 17-08

I once rode Glory (17-08) while Grandpa Z rode his second horse (Traveler) to locate scattered cows in August, 1952 (a pair of cowboys). It was great fun riding the prairie with Grandpa Z; we were gone until middle of the afternoon. It was my connection to the cowboys of the 1890s from the book "We Pointed Them North" (see Additional Reading in the Appendix).

More and more ranchers today ride four-wheelers and drive pickups because the ranches in eastern Montana now extend upwards to 100 sections (640 acres/section). On a recent visit I saw cars parked at the end of ranch driveways, which can be miles long, driven by school children to meet the school bus on the highway to town.

My Dad often told me about how cold the winters were when he was growing up in eastern Montana. Dad said he had to put his thumb on the thermometer bulb to raise the mercury out of the bulb (lowest temperature marked, minus 50 degrees). It seemed to me an exaggeration.

So in January, 1961, (the last time I visited Grandpa and Grandma Z on the ranch) I asked Grandpa Z "What was the coldest winter you remember"? I was looking for verification of my Dad's story. Grandpa Z's answer surprised me.

Photo 17-09 is Grandpa Z working on a Civilian Conservation Corps (CCC) project building bridges in eastern Montana.

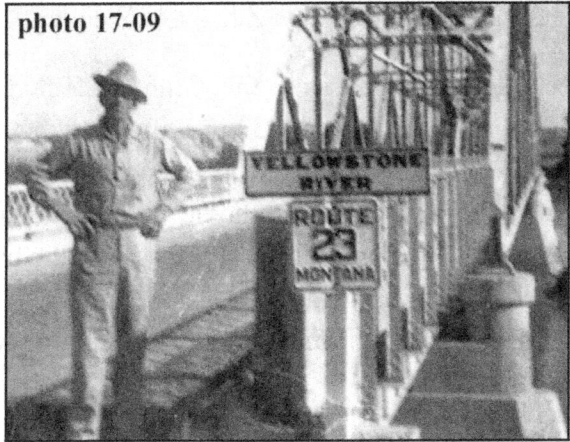

photo 17-09

Grandpa Z didn't state the year, but said it was the January he worked on a CCC bridge project. He continued, "We were camped in a tent at the work site, and decided to take a 10 day break for the Christmas and New Year holidays. I returned after the break, but none of the others were there, so I waited. I waited the entire month of January, afraid of missing work, and the temperature never rose above minus thirty degrees".

I didn't ask for more detail, but I assumed he was talking about night time temperatures. I also assumed it was the winter of 1936. I get cold just thinking about spending a month in a tent during the winter. Anywhere!

Here (17-10) are Grandpa and Grandma Z feeding cows a few years before they retired in 1963. Notice the chains on the tractor and the crutches across the

photo 17-10

steering wheel. Grandpa Z had a broken leg.

Let me tell one last story that Grandma Z told me about Grandpa Z. It was in the fall of 1952 just after they bought a new Chevrolet coupe, and they had attended an auction sale and bought a young ram. How to take the ram home? Grandpa tied the ram's legs together with some rope and placed it in the back seat. You're smiling! The ram wiggled out of the rope and charged, breaking the side window. It must have been a chore securing that lose ram in the back seat.

He was 74 and she 70 when they sold their ranch and moved to a small house in Jordan, Montana. They had lived on their homestead for 46 years.

photo 17-11

Here (photo 17-11) are the Zs spending winter months in Arizona (once) during their retirement.

Grandpa Z died on April 22, 1969; Grandma died November 30, 1971. Both are buried in the Pioneer Cemetery in Jordan, Montana. Also buried there are two daughters (Aunts Florence Burchett and Pearl Schimdt Sickles) and my great grandmother Mary Verhulst Schaap.

They were honest, determined and hardworking pioneers, good parents and valued members of their community. Grandpa Z served on the school board while Grandma Z joined the Green Trail Club (local women's club). They attended many basketball games in Jordan and at local dances they occasionally won the two-step competition.

After I retired in 1999 I began copying photos from relatives in my mother's family: Mom, aunts, uncle and cousins. I always took my computer and a scanner whenever I went on a trip, and spent time looking through photo albums, copying photos that interested me. In 2004 I assembled a collection of these photos from early 1900s to 2000s which included at least one photo of every descendant of my grandparents Mike and Sarah Zimmerman. My brother-in-law, Bob Bowman, published a Zimmerman Family Tree on CD that included photos from my collection.

Now an introduction to my Wax grandparents.

photo 17-12

Photo 17-12 is my Grandma Wax, Caroline (Carrie) C. Johnson at about age 24, in 1900. She was born Oct 7, 1876 in Page County, Iowa. I don't know much about Carrie. I think she was the firstborn in a family of poor Swedish immigrants, and had two brothers and two sisters. It is likely that she did not attend more than five or six years of school, and then began working as a housemaid for other families. I think she was still a housemaid when she married Walter Marion Wax (my grandfather) on March 18, 1903.

photo 17-13

This is (17-13) my Grandpa Wax, Walter M. Wax in 1900, at age 20. He was the seventh born (Dec 3, 1880) in a family of 10, five boys and five girls. He was closest to his brother William Allen Wax (my Dad's uncle Al), his next younger brother. Walter's grandfather (Jonathon Wax, my great-great-grandpa) came to Iowa before the Civil War from Pennsylvania by way of Ohio. Jonathon lived to be 102, or 103 depending on birth year, and was celebrated as an Iowa pioneer. Jonathon Wax's grandfather Peter Wax (my gggg-grandpa) arrived in the US from Germany before the Revolutionary War. I researched the Wax family history in Pennsylvania and Iowa, and prepared a family history book (Descendants of Peter Wax) in 2001.

I think Grandpa Wax (Walter) was also hired help when he met

Grandma Wax (Carrie). I did not find any evidence that they owned property in Iowa.

I once told Grandpa Wax about my first job making two dollars a day. He informed me his first job paid 25 cents a day. I asked what he did and learned that he walked behind a section of harrow holding the reins of a horse in soft Iowa soil from sunup to sundown. That answer shutdown the conversation; I didn't have any more to say.

photo 17-14

Photo 17-14 is of my grandparents marriage certificate (witnessed by Grandpa Wax's brother-in-law). It is a photo of the original which is large and in color, a rather elaborate certificate.

Photo 17-15 is of my grandparents Wax and children in summer 1907 while still in Iowa (Carrie, Mabel, Robert and Walter Wax). Mabel died soon after this photo was taken.

photo 17-15

Grandpa Wax and family lived in Iowa until 1913, during which time they had two more children, Doris and Marie (my aunts). Marie was not yet two years old when they moved to Montana by covered wagon, probably following the Missouri River north into Montana. My father (Billy) was born that fall (November 19, 1913) in a wagon southwest of Lewistown in an area called Judith Gap.

In 1914 Grandpa Wax and family moved east to Garfield County (from Meagher County) to file a homestead claim for 320 acres southeast of Jordan, Montana. I found evidence that Grandma Wax and the children returned to Iowa for the winter of 1914-15. I don't know what kind of accommodation Grandpa Wax had while living on his claim that winter.

Grandma Wax and the children returned to Montana in the spring. Grandpa Wax built their house from sod and mud stucco, with a clay roof (the locals call it gumbo), dirt floor and a wooden entry porch. They lived in this house for the next 20 years. The windows were broken out and the roof had collapsed when I saw this house in the fall of 1948.

photo 17-16

Here (photo 17-16) are my grandparents and family in 1923, (Doris, Grandma, Marie, Grandpa, Billy and Robert Wax) in front of their house. Notice that Robert is wearing a suit, perhaps a recent high school graduate.

I gained access to a large number of old photos after December 2012 when Cousin Marion (Doris' son) died. It seems that Doris acquired a snapshot camera in 1923 and took many photos until 1928 when she married.

Walter Wax and Doris (16) haying Abt 1924 Cohagen, Montana

photo 17-17

Could this wagon (photo 17-17) be the one my father was born in? With its wooden wheels plus a canvas cover it would look like a prairie schooner seen in western movies.

Grandpa Wax was always helping others. Here (17-18) he is moving a house with Walter Johnson, Grandma Wax's younger brother.

J. Walter Johnson (Dad's Uncle Walter) had a homestead near Grandpa Wax. I have a photo of Walter Johnson standing in the doorway of this house on his homestead. Mom mentions Walter Johnson and his new wife in her diary.

Moving a house abt 1925.
Probably Walter Wax in doorway
Nothing was left unoccupied or wasted.

photo 17-18

Aunt Doris graduated from Cohagen High School (CHS) in 1928 and married soon after; Aunt Marie and Dad graduated from CHS in 1930 with my mother.

Marie married soon after. The period from 1930 to 1940 is covered in The Beginning and The Land.

My grandparents Wax with Aunt Doris and Cousin Marion moved to Missoula in the spring of 1940 when Grandpa Wax got a job working for the railroad. He turned 60 years old in December that year and continued working until forced to quit at age 70 when there were no longer steam engines. Grandpa Wax's brother (Dad's Uncle Al) worked for the railroad for many years in Glendive, Montana.

photo 17-19

I remember Grandpa Wax taking Dad and me on a tour (mid-1940s) of the round-house and maintenance shops in Missoula. He worked at night prepping the engines (photo 17-19) for the next day, emptying the cinder box, filling oilers, cleaning boilers, filling the fuel and water tanks, and oiling and greasing where needed. He complained about some of the work being very hot.

During the time Grandpa Wax worked for the railroad he also found time to help Dad and others. He must have spent his vacations working.

Ida May (Longpre) Asbury told me recently (2012) that she remembers Grandpa Wax staying with them during haying season in the mid-1940s, and that he snored very loud. I don't think Grandpa Wax owned a car, so he rode the bus from Missoula to Stevensville when he worked for the Longpres.

Photo 17-20 is Grandpa Wax in the Longpre yard with Pine Hollow Road behind him. Notice that he is wearing tie (?).

Dad mentions in one of his letters that Fred and Ida Longpre were guests at their house in 1938.

Photo 17-21 is a card addressed to Grandpa Wax for his 89th birthday (1969) from Fred and Ida Longpre. I had no idea this friendship existed when I worked for Fred. It seems their friendship began early and lasted a long time.

photo 17-20

The two Wax families (my parents and grandparents) visited several times each year, either in Missoula or on the Sunset Bench, usually at holiday times. Aunt Doris always lived with (or next door to) her parents, so the visits always required a large table for the seven of us plus four of them. And more if other relatives were visiting.

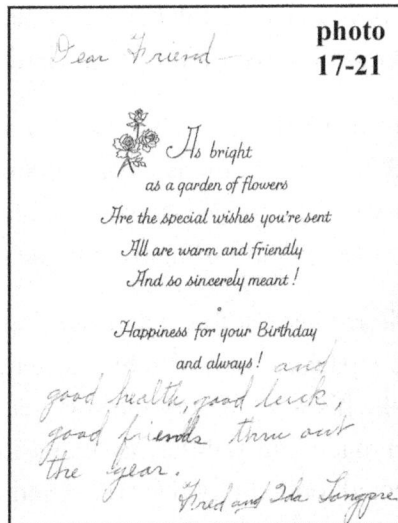
photo 17-21

It is really unfortunate that I never talked to my Grandpa Wax about his family when he was alive. We did talk, but mostly about current topics.

photo 17-22

I always liked photo 17-22. It hung on the wall in Mom and Dad's house in the sun until it was very faded. I worked on it with Adobe Photoshop to get it to this condition. It is of Grandpa Wax, Dad, me, Mom, Norman and Grandma Wax in the winter of 1943.

I visited Grandpa Wax on October 1, 1958. He had recently purchased a new Volkswagen (Beetle) and he really admired it. Before leaving to join the Army he proudly drove me around Missoula visiting the bar where he worked and introducing me to the morning barmaid he was visiting in the afternoons.

He was working at a bar early in the morning (4-9am) restocking and cleaning so the bar could open at 6:00am for breakfast. This bar was near the Missoula train station at the end of Higgins Avenue and served many travelers and railroad workers.

It didn't last. Before Thanksgiving of 1958 Grandpa Wax slid off a snow packed road with his barmaid friend, damaged his car and broke his wrist. Everyone was very upset. Aunt Doris took his keys and made him sell the car, many in the family felt that Aunt Doris reacted too harshly. He was essentially under house arrest for the last 20 years of his life depending on others for transportation. Sad for a man so active all his life.

Grandma Wax died on June 3, 1959. I saw her the last time before I joined the Army in October, 1958. Grandpa Wax would live the remaining years of his life a widower.

The last time I saw Grandpa Wax was in the spring of 1973. He was in his rocker carving a new bridge for his fiddle. He died on January 12, 1979 at age 98 and one month. Grandma and Grandpa Wax are buried in Sunset Memorial Gardens along with Uncle Jack and Aunt Doris Bohman and Cousin Marion McWilliams.

photo 17-23

Photo 17-23 is four generations of Waxes in the spring of 1973. From the left: my brother Norman, his son Spencer, my father Bill, my son William, Grandpa Walter Wax and me.

Grandpa Wax also had a great-great-grandchild before he died.

Wrap It Up

Conclusion and analysis

It's time to measure or critique what I've written. Did I accomplish what I set out to do? Did I meet any of my objectives? The following is copied from the Introduction:

Why would I want to write a memoir? One of the reasons was to help me better understand myself and to get my arms around the larger picture, why I always had a feeling that there was something different about those who were second and third generation Montanans. Why I always felt I was living on the edge of society and needed acceptance.

Let's separate "needing acceptance" from being a Montanan to look at each in a little more detail, first being from Montana.

Montana is a large state with a small population, only 675,000 in 1960. About 38% are age 19 or younger of which 7.4% are age 15-19, or 19,000, and about 80% of those graduate from high school, or 15,500. If we accept that 50% are from rural homes and 50% of these are from western Montana and 50% of these remain in Montana, then we have less than 2000 leaving Montana with a high school certificate. I was one of those young high school graduates who left Montana.

I came from a rather small tribe (<2000) scattered amongst 180 million Americans in 1960. It was not likely that I would find, work with or live amongst others my age from Montana.

Seeking acceptance is a normal human need. We do all kinds of things to gain acceptance: follow a fashion trend, join a club or political party, play a sport or engage in a hobby, buy a particular car or house. We find acceptance in groups from our tribe, such as: the graduates from our school, citizens from our state, members of our profession, the church we attend or ideology we adopt.

I found work helped me gain acceptance in many different situations during my adult years outside of Montana. I didn't feel comfortable with most other ways of gaining acceptance (finding my place) in a larger group.

During my working years it seems I was always changing my environment (location and group) and this kept alive the need for acceptance. I now better understand my need for acceptance.

I define work as "making a contribution to your group", being productive in ways that benefit yourself and others. I believe work is a necessary component of a satisfying life. I have noticed that even a dog or a horse is most happy and content when working. I think of work as something that causes moving the body, busying the hands or engaging the mind.

The young, even the very young can contribute. The young should be encouraged to work, to be responsible for making a contribution. Our educational system needs more practical/work assignments to build confidence and allow the young to feel a sense of accomplishment. I am glad I was introduced to work early in life.

Again from the Introduction:

I also want the stories to move quickly and provide a sense of involvement. Do you feel what I felt? Do you see what I saw? Do you understand what I learned? Do you now think about things differently?

I can't offer a meaningful critique for these objectives. I am satisfied that I have done my best, but it will be for you to judge. The story does slowdown in some places to cover the detail that I felt was necessary. Names of the many people that I mention may cause some confusion, but they are real people and part of what I remember.

I've included more than 150 photos, documents and drawings. Copying, selecting and preparing these 150 items took more time than writing the stories.

I thought it was worthwhile for several reasons: to preserve the item, to give my words more meaning, to interest the young and spark more discussion and to allow you to follow my process of remembering.

As I consider what I wrote in total, I realize that I not only described where I came from geographically, but also genetically. For us to grow to be productive adults requires not only a nurturing environment, but also a genetic predisposition to being nurtured in that environment. And I believe that environment can affect genetics. If you believe in evolution you should agree that environment affects genetics.

Given that environment and genetics interact causing a specie to change I am concerned that as we change our culture, traditions and environment we are not giving enough attention to the impact this will have on the future of our country and our people. For example; honesty. It seems to me that in some professions today honesty is considered a "defect". Being dishonest is considered a skill needed to get ahead. I once heard someone say that if you can fake sincerity you've got it made. Does that help make anything better?

If I view the total in relation to time I realize that I experienced life during the 20th century in person and through my parents, and a little bit of life from the 19th century through my grandparents. I am now living in the beginnings of 21st century. How things have changed!

And to close I will describe one last view from the Sunset Bench. Late in the year the changing weather sometimes caused a temperature inversion which trapped heavy fog along the river on the valley floor. We were just high enough that the view from our house was like looking out over a lake. We could see the top of the fog layer hiding all except the surrounding mountains.

Appendix

This is a map of the Sunset Bench orchard lots developed by Sunset Land Orchard Company (SLOC) beginning in 1910. It is one of nine maps that were marked up to show Sunset Irrigation

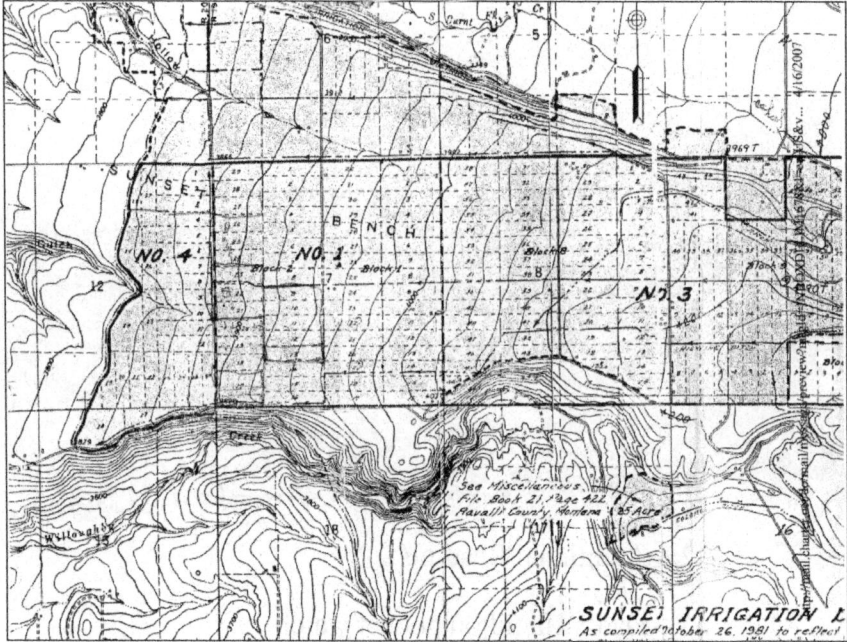

District (SID) water distribution and irrigated lands.

The map has a standard orientation here, top = north. The wiggly lines are elevation gradients, from 4200ft on the right to 3800ft on the left. The Willoughby Creek is to the south and Burnt Fork Creek to the north. The shaded areas are the SID irrigated lands.

In the bottom right quarter there is a note indicating 35 acres in the Willoughby Creek that is serviced by the Solomon ditch, which was part of the Solomon ranch and just above their house. In the middle of each section is its number (12, 7, 8, 9), for the central shaded areas. The map doesn't show any roads or lanes except those surveyed by SLOC.

This map is the western part of the previous map with the same orientation.

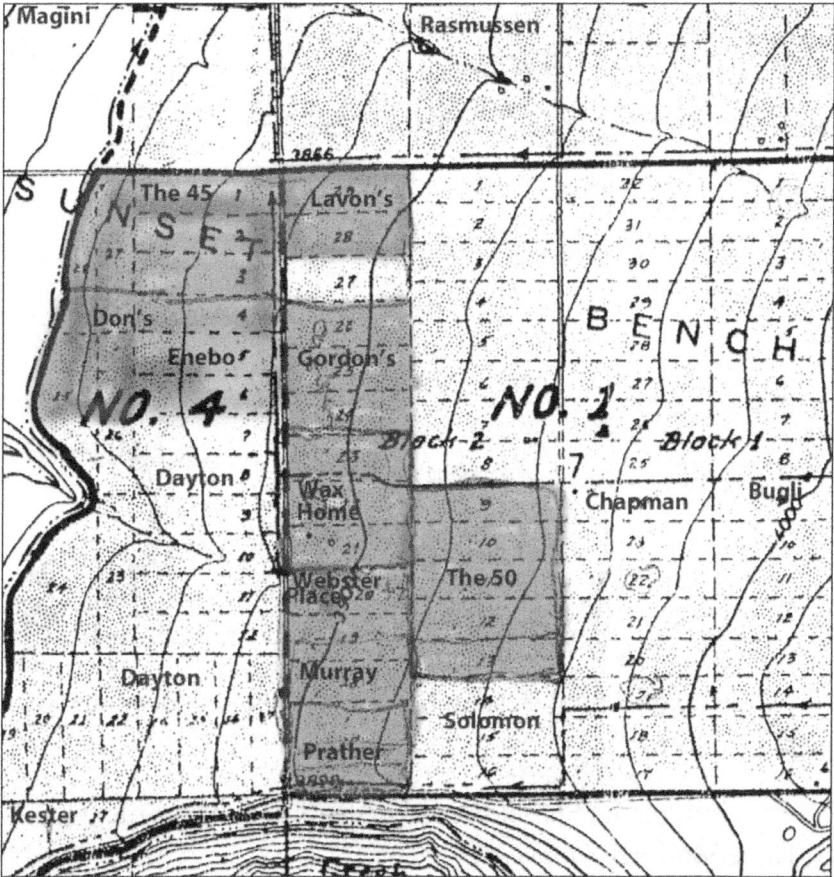

The shaded areas are lands owned and/or farmed by Bill Wax from 1936 to 1979. The names are mentioned in The Land and Our Neighbors chapters. The Magini and Kester actual locations are a short distance off the map in their respective directions. The Solomon ranch house is off the map to the bottom right corner.

This area of course looks very different today, many of the lots have homes and are hobby farms or ranches.

This is a map of central western Montana. I marked locations mentioned in various chapters, as follows:

* - Wax farm on the Sunset Bench (under S in Stevensville),

\# - Three Mile area (above S),

** - Working for Arlo Ellison (above lo in Florence),

\#\# - Working at the WTC lumber mill/camp (right of highway 141 label),

*** - Harvesting fence posts (above 2nd e in Stevensville),

\#\#\# - End of Burnt Fork bike ride (under 2nd e).

Scale: Stevensville to Corvallis = approximately 14 miles.

Son Of Montana

This is a map of central eastern Montana with standard orientation.

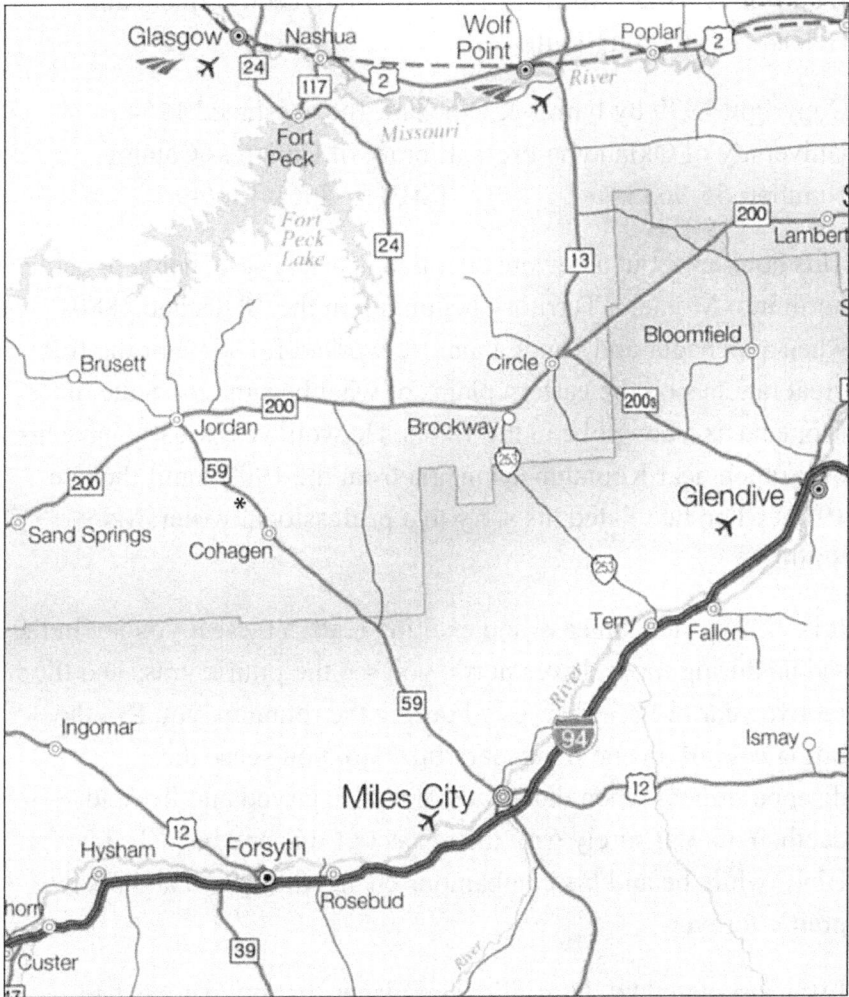

The Zimmerman homestead is between the two and zero of the highway 200 label east of Jordan and north of the road.

The Wax homestead is marked with an asterisk northwest of Cohagen and west of highway 59.

Additional Reading

We Pointed Them North by E.C. Abbott ("Teddy Blue") and
Helena Huntington Smith.

Copyright 1939 by Farrar & Rinehart, Inc. Assigned 1954 to
University of Oklahoma Press. Library of Congress Catalog
Number: 55-9632.   ISBN: 0-8061-1366-9

This book is about a cowpuncher that drove several herds of cattle
north into Montana Territory beginning in the 1870s and 1880s
when a teenager and young man. He worked for some of the first
great ranches on the eastern plains of what became the State of
Montana as a cowpoke in the 1890s. He would eventually have his
own ranch near Roundup, Montana from the 1900s until the late
1930s when he related his story to a professional writer, Ms.
Smith.

It is well written, an easy and exciting read. You feel you are in the
saddle during those drives north, you see the prairie grass and the
fat two year old beef harvested during the roundup, you feel the
biting cold of an end of January blizzard, you sense the
disappointment when thousands of cattle starved and froze to
death. You will surely gain the respect of this cowboy "Teddy
Blue" while he and his companions changed the wild and open
prairie forever.

I was fascinated by descriptions of places that my parents had
known and that I had visited, such as: the Big Dry and Little Dry
Creeks, Miles City, the Missouri Breaks, all the open prairie
between the Yellowstone and Missouri Rivers of eastern Montana.
It was an opportunity for me to get a sense of the land before my
grandparents arrived and filed for their homesteads.

A must read for anyone interested in the beginning of cattle
ranching in eastern Montana.

Son Of Montana

Montana, An Uncommon Land by K. Ross Toole

Copyright 1959 by the University of Oklahoma Press. Library of Congress Nbr F731.T65, 978.6, 59-7489. ISBN: 0-8061-0427-9.

Kenneth Ross Toole was a history professor at the University of Montana in Missoula. He was born in Missoula of parents who were early settlers in Montana. He wrote several essays and books on the history of Montana and later became an activist for environmental causes.

This book is mainly about the great natural wealth that was harvested from Montana by eastern interlopers and entrepreneurs. Some stayed to further develop Montana such as Marcus Daly, but others moved on. You gain an insight into how the boom and bust cycles affected the politics and culture.

It is a book that examines Montana history, politics and culture which gave me a better understanding of the environment of my youth. I do remember a description by Mr. Toole that I felt was so true about how the native (lived in Montana more than a year) treats the newcomer. If the newcomer arrives with a sense of class or class distinction he is quickly reminded that there are no classes or class distinctions here. He is reminded in ways subtle and in-your-face, and if he insists on keeping his class distinction he will find it more comfortable elsewhere.

This attitude helps explain how I interacted with persons in positions superior to my own, with a certain kind of irreverence that some interpreted as disrespect. I respected each for who they were, not for the title they had.

This book is a history book by an academic. It is full of facts and figures, and sometimes requires patience to get through all the words connecting them to the politics and culture.

Montana 1878, Tough Trip through Paradise by Andrew Garcia, edited by Bennett H. Stein.

Copyright 1967 by The Rock Foundation. Library of Congress Number: 66-14758. ISBN: 0-89174-008-2.

This edition published by arrangement with Houghton Mifflin Company.

The author, Andrew Garcia, was a Hispanic born in Texas who moved north to Montana. He worked as a wrangler for the army, then with savings and a loan he bought supplies to trade with the Indians in central Montana. He wrote whole boxes full after retiring from ranching near Missoula. These boxes were discovered after he died and through various transactions came into the hands of Bennett H. Stein who assembled and edited the writings for this book.

Stein did not rewrite, only edit, the words of Andrew Garcia. Garcia's native tongue was Spanish and he was not well educated, so some phrases, word meaning and sentence structure make it sometimes difficult to understand. But, what you read is the authentic life of an Indian trader in Judith Gap Montana; the place where my father was born.

Garcia married an Indian maiden. His wife told him about the battle of the Little Big Hole, and he wrote what he understood from her. This section was difficult and I did not read all of it. This is supposed to be the foundation material for the movie "Little Big Man" starring Dustin Hoffman.

It is a chance to meet the natives of Montana before the white man pushed them onto reservations, through Garcia who got to know them one on one.

Son Of Montana

Photographing Montana, 1894 – 1928 by Donna M Lucey, The life and Work of Evelyn Cameron

Copyright 1990 by Donna M Lucey. Published by Alfred A Knopf, Inc. Library of Congress Number: 770'.92-dc20, TR140.C26t.83, 89-43298.   ISBN: 0-394-55192-3

The photographs in this book were made by Evelyn Cameron and discovered by Donna Lucey some years after her death. These are first class photos made with a large plate camera and show excellent detail. Most of the photos are from the period in which my grandparents homesteaded in eastern Montana.

The Cameron ranch was near Fallon, Montana. The Cameron's travels and hunting trips took them through the area where my grandparents homesteaded. They also traded at Miles City. Evelyn Cameron earned money taking portraits and photos of celebrations as well as documenting her husband's interest in the wildlife, especially birds. So the collection of photos covers a broad spectrum of Montana life in the early 1900s.

The text provides a rather detailed time line of Evelyn Cameron's life, including her husband's death from cancer without modern medical care. It touched me. I am a cancer survivor.

I bought this book for my parents. Later I bought the book for myself and have read it several times, enjoying the photos anew each time. An expensive book, but worth it.

A decent, Orderly Lynching – The Montana Vigilantes by
Frederick Allen.

Copyright 2004 by Frederick Lewis Allen III. Published by
University of Oklahoma Press. ISBN: 0-8061-3637-5. Library og
Congress Number: HV6468.M9A55 2004, 364.1'34-dc22,
2004046069

Frederick Allen is a journalist, researcher, teacher and author from
Georgia. He spent time in Bozeman, MT while writing this book.
He details the crimes, criminals and justice of the Montana mining
camps of 1860s and 1870s. For some of the main characters he
describes their lives before arriving in Montana Territory.

A well-researched and well written book viewed through the lens
of modern ethics and morals that I felt judged the actions of the
vigilantes too harshly. It was what the settlers (vigilantes) had
available to bring justice and peace to their settlements in a time of
gold rushes, civil war and a lawless frontier. I felt his comment
about "speed limits or other boundaries on personal behavior" of
present day Montana was over-the-top and unfairly links the
responsible and law abiding citizens of Montana today to past
abuses of the vigilantes.

Justice by any means at any time is never entirely without error or
abuse. Any human process can never be perfect. Justice by honest
men imposed by the means they have available is required to
prevent chaos. I say the vigilantes of early Montana did what was
necessary and the legacy in Montana culture is a positive, not a
negative.

I recommend reading this book.

Dad's Hamilton pocket watch

I had Dad's old pocket watch repaired, and it is now working just fine. The main spring was broken. The watch repairman said that it is more and more difficult to buy replacement main springs. The total cost for repair, cleaning and service was $165. He told me that the watch is worth $150 - $300 depending on condition, and that it is the **lever set** model.

After having it at home for the last couple weeks I became curious to learn more about the watch, so I did some searching on the internet. I took the back off and noted all the information inside on the watch mechanism:

Hamilton Watch Co., Lancaster, PA, 17 Jewels, 974 Special, Double Roller.

Adjusted, 3 Positions, (serial number) 2549816.

The back lid had the following marks. Note that the guts were made by Hamilton and case was not.

*Star * Case Company, 10kt gold filled, (serial number) 2082523.*

The Hamilton serial number indicates that the watch was likely manufactured in 1934. It is the 16 size, smaller than the 18 size watch. I found a YouTube video of a watch that is the same, but manufactured in 1935.

http://www.youtube.com/watch?v=qvC8i6GzmoU.

The main difference is that it has large block letters rather than the large script letters of Dad's watch. The other thing that is important to note is the **lever set** used to set the time.

I also found a site with photos of a 974 Special that is exactly like Dad's.

http://ihc185.infopop.cc/eve/forums/a/tpc/f/1086047761/m/454390
5857.

This site is interesting because it shows a photo of a page from the 1935 Hamilton Watch Company catalog and a picture from the 1938 catalog of a 974 Special. Note that the listed price was $35.00.

Dad probably bought this watch in 1935, after working on the Ft. Peck Dam and before moving to Stevensville. It was a pretty nice watch for a young man to have who was living on a homestead in eastern Montana during the Great Depression.

I certainly remember Dad wearing this watch while I was growing up. As I recall it was attached to narrow leather strap of 8-10 inches long that had a loop for his belt. All pants in those days had a watch pocket. One of the things I remember is that Dad always wound the watch each time that he looked at it. The routine was: pull the watch from the watch pocket with the leather strap, check and announce the time, then wind the stem and return it to the watch pocket.

Now that I have the watch I understand why he wound it each time he checked the time. The main spring will last 18-24 hours. Setting the time is a hassle because you have to unscrew the bezel (face) to allow setting the time. I wound it in the morning after breakfast and before going to bed so it didn't stop. It keeps good time, off less than 1 minute per week.

This was the least expensive of the so called "Railroad Watches" made by Hamilton Watch Company. The "lever set" watches did **not** allow setting the time from the winding stem. It was thought that setting the watch with the winding stem might accidently change the time. So, there was a lever (or screw) that you needed to access to change the time. The screw set model could be changed to allow the time to be set by the stem, but not the lever set model.

This is what I learned today about Dad's old pocket watch.

Don Wax

(From letter sent to my siblings on 11/18/2011)

Donald R Wax

Dad's letter to Mom in 1938

Stevensville, Mont.

Jan. 17, 1938

Dearest Helen,

How is my old lady tonite? Better I hope. I'd sure like to visit you for a while to nite instead of writing, but beins I can't then I'll have to write. There isn't much to write about – no news that amounts to much.

I've been thinking of you Honey and the more I think about you the more lonesome I get. Did you ever get that way? I'd just give a lot to get so see you tonite. Maybe I shouldn't feel lonesome I see somebody about every day & Doris is home too, but it seems I just don't get to see the right people or right person. I think I know what's the matter. I've just been away from that little white house that sits in Pluhar's front yard to long.

I have been to two dances lately and I had a good time both times, but still there was something missing it seemed. Both times I kept thinking of you and wishing you could be with me. It won't be long now though till I'll be going over the mountains again. Just about 4 ½ or 5 months.

Last sat. nite Doris, Bill Mc, & his wife & I went to a dance at the Cerlean school house. We all had a real good time. The dance tickets cost 50c and there was a free lunch. It was something like the dances they have at the C.C. There was just a few there that we knew. Maude Brookins and her guy was there. Charley Magini & Keneth Brown was there for a while, and the two boys that threshed for us.

Son Of Montana

Yesterday McKinneys & Longpres were here for dinner. Mrs. Longpre brought a freezer full of ice cream and it was pretty good stuff too.

Dad & I have been chasing water down the ditch since Saturday. We have the cistern full once more now. All last week we had to drive our stock to water. It sure was lucky for us that we could get the water down here the way the ditch was leaking up by DeMott's place.

This winter sure has been nice so far. Some times it freezes pretty hard and storms a little but it never has been any colder than 10 above zero yet. There never was much snow but there was quite a lot of rain. Every thing is all muddy now and the roads are all cut up & slick. Its going to freeze up to night though.

Doris is going back to school saturday. I suppose things will be pretty dull around here after she leaves. I guess we will go to Hamilton some times this week to get the license for the car. And I think I'll try to get some work while I'm down there. If I don't get a job some place I'm going to be pretty short of money in the spring. I let the folks have $30 and I gave Doris $10 to get her teeth fixed with. Then I had to pay out some on that damned old car. I have been pretty saving but the money goes anyway. If things don't look any better by spring I think I'll try to get a job in the mines at Butte. How would you like to live there for a while? We could stop there on our way out here and if I can't get work there then we will go on to some place else. I think the best for us would be to work out for a while. At least till we can get caught up on the payments on our place. We could save up enough to get a few good milk cows & some hogs then I think we will make it pretty good here.

Longpres have been milking 12 cows all last year and Fred told me that he had about $1000 of cream stuffs. That is for one year. Gee Honey, if we had a bunch of cows like that we would get along fine wouldn't we?

The Federal Land man from Hamilton was here yesterday. And he still thought that we could make this farm pay out. He asked if I could make the payment for this year and I told him that I couldn't. And he says I'll just have to put out a big crop in the spring. He told me I should pull the orchard as it wouldn't make me anything any way. I think I will too. We have enough trees around the house & along the fence to keep us in apples most of the time any way.

Every one is in bed around this joint except me. So I think I will hit the hay too. Tell the folks hello, and Emil & the rest of the kids. XX Good night Sweetheart. XX

XXXXXXXXX   *With Lots of Love & X's*

                               Your old man, the Mr.

Son Of Montana

Stevensville, Mont.

June 5, 1938

Dearest Helen,

Monday we finished with our ditching and tues. I set posts where they were broken off.

Wednesday we went to the mts. and cut down about 30 telephone poles. And it took two more days to get them home. And yesterday we dug the holes.

So that is the way the week went. Its first one job and then another. Today we tore up the car to put in new piston rings and grind the valves. I suppose it will take all day tomorrow to finish the job. Then there is those god blessed telephone poles to set. I have begun to believe in that old saying – there is no rest for the wicked. Now if I could have been a St. Pat. or St. John I could be sittin in a bed of roses.Huh? Ha! The heck of it is these ifs, ands, maybes, & buts are getting me no place fast.

I'm in a heck of a picklement, and I don't know what to do or say.

The way you wrote you have decided not to go to school. Well it suits me fine and I'll be real glad to come and get my Mrs. You let me know when you want me to come and I get there some way. I counted the money in the pennie bank and there is just $15.00. That won't go very far for what we planned to use it for. But I think I can raise about $60.00 more.

I am going to Hamilton this week some time and see if I can get on that West Fork dam. That will only be 4 trips down there since the work started. In case I'm lucky enough to get on I could get some one to work in my place while I'm gone down there.

Donald R Wax

Realy Honey it looks to me like you are getting a counter fit husband. All the time broke and no income. You know I've often wished that we would have been married when you were up to Ft. Peck that time. It seems like when I was back there I always had a little money and since we came up here I can't get any ahead. All though I have been helping Doris out a little.

Maynard Layman was here for a little while. And the way he talked there wasn't any chance to get on at that dam – well I'm going to try again any way. He said he was in Butte the first of may and the day he got there - there were 600 miners layed off. It seems hard times hasn't got here yet.

Oh well, we will find some way to make a living, won't we Honey? I guess if we keep waiting for better times it might be quite a while before we start our partnership farming. Huh? So Sweet you just tell me when you want me to come. I would like to go right now, but it might be best if you set the day. What do you think?

I'll be waiting to hear from you left for school.

In case you have gone to Billings than I plan on going some time later. Heres hoping you didn't go. I wished I hadn't wrote that way last time.

Kennith, Bud & I was hunting work yesterday. Its real hard now to find anything. The big projects have all closed. The mines in Butte, the smelters, and mills have all closed all over the western part of the state. The only chance for work now is waiting for haying.

Well Honey its dinner time, and heres hoping you didn't go to school.

XXWith Lots of Love XX's

Your old Man

Son Of Montana

June 11, 1938

Hello Honey,

I have been holding this letter to find out what you have planned on in this weeks letter.

I went to town yesterday and got it so now I am sending this today.

Now if you haven't went to Billings I plan on coming some time between the 20th & the 25th of this month. As that will give me time (to) irregate and then get back for haying.

If you are home when you get this it might be a good idea to start getting ready, because there is a chance that I might come before the 20th. The way I felt yesterday I was ready to go then. But I thought there might be a chance that you had every mail day now until we have decided on when the day will be. I think some time the last of this month or first of July would be all right, but if you think it better before then it will be just fine.

Well Sweet I've got to hit the hay. XX So good nite Honey. XXX

With Lots of Love & Xs   Your old Man, the Mr.

Stevensville, Mont.

June 16, 1938

Dearest Helen,

Here I am late as usual. I didn't write last Sunday, because there was a possibility that you were in Billings. And yesterday I figured on writing, the I had to start irregating and it was about 10:30 when I got to bed. So I'm taking time to do it now. It was 10 o'clock when I came out of the field last night.

There was two nice rains this week and it looks as though it might rain some more.

Well Honey I was some what dissappointed when I got your letter. I was wishing you hadn't went to school. Its funny how I change my mind ain't it?

I got your letter saying that you weren't going so then I started making plans to go down there next week. I told the folks that I was going. They were going to help me out by lending the car – even though I never asked for it. Right now I'm not sure that I can come on the first, but I'll try. If I can that will make four days we can be together. We could go see the preacher the 2nd couldn't we? Don't you think that we could look over the rings there in Billings? I think we can get every thing we need right there. Unless you think of some different & better plan I will make arrangements for the first of July.

DeMott has asked me to irregate his hay. That will take about 10 or 12 days, so I'm going to try to get started there this sunday. Then I should get done in time to have a day to rest & get ready in.

Son Of Montana

And with a real early start in the morning of the first I should be able to get there that evening.

I took time out to look over the map. It's a little over 415 miles from here. I think I can get started on the evening of the 30th then it won't be such a drive for the 1st.

Do you have a phone at the place where you are staying? If so be sure to write out the no. in the next letter. I could call you up when I get to town (Billings), and then we could arrange for a meeting place.

If you want to pawn that ring or trade it in it would be OK.

That school business is quite a item allright – all right. How long do you have to go to get the other 9 ½ credits? We might make some arrangements later so you can finish, being you have started.

Well Honey its time to hit the hay. We can do a lot more talking & planning when we can see each other than we can on papers.

XXX Good night Darling. XXX

(a variety of X symbols)   *With Lots of Love & Xs*

Your old Man.

How is that for an assortment?

Stevensville, Mont.

July 6, 1938

Dearest Wife,

How you was tonite? I'm OK and I made it home all in one piece.

After I left Billings I picked up a hitch hiker. He rode up to Butte with me, and helped drive. I guess he must have driven half of the way. We stopped at three Forks for supper. He gave me my supper & after supper we had a glass of beer on him also. Then he showed me where to leave the car and the good (lined thru). We got to Butte about midnight. We got on the wrong road otherwise we could have been in Butte by 9:30.

After I left Butte I picked up another guy that wrote up to Missoula. Then I had another one from Missoula to Stevensville. All three were pretty nice fellow.

You find out what those cards and pictures cost and I will pay the folks. Its funny that I didn't think about it before. I thought about this morning when I left Butte.

Say Honey why didn't you take those bannas that were in the car? I could have got more along the road. I hope you will over look my absent mindedness.

I figured up my expenses, all but what we spent for meals. $25.26 for gas & oil on the round trip. Suit $19.75, tie 49c, shirt 77c, suspenders 35c, ring $7.50, license $2.00, and the preacher fee $5.00. Hotel rooms were, Billings $1.50, Hysham $1.00, Roundup 75c & Butte 50c & 50c for leaving the car at the garage.

Son Of Montana

I left home with $13.00 I my bill fold &$15.00 in the penny bank. Then you gave me $40.00 and I counted in the money in your penny bank at $5.00. That would make $73.00. What did you have in that penny bank? $4.99? Any way that leaves $7.38 that I can't account for, so we must have used that for our meals, fruit, and gum. And the candy & cigars. I didn't think we spent that much for eats. I might have made a mistake on the gas by a dollar or two, but it took $12.93 going down then & $12.55 coming home. I payed the Texaco man $4.26 when I came thru town, and bought 4 bars of candy for the folks. Now I have 20c left over from the trip. That bill at the Texaco station in Stevensville was 15c higher than I thought it was.

I figures every thing over again & there was $7.08 spent for eats. Instead of $25.26 there was $25.41 for gas and still I forgot 25c for fuses for the car and 40c for a bacon & egg breakfast in Butte, which was quite steep I thought, and 50c for dinner at Missoula for myself & the fellow that was with me. So that would be $5.93 for our eats. This fellow that I picked up at Butte didn't have any money & he hadn't had any breakfast & only a hamburger for supper. So I gave him that qt. of tomatoes for breakfast and he ate it all. Then we got to Missoula at 1 o'clock so I got a 25c dinner for both of us. That is a 25c dinner apiece, so that was 50c. Now I have those figures straight.

That boil broke at the hotel in Butte last night and it is practically well now. When it broke there was a hole in it big enough to stick the eraser end of a pencil in it and quite deep. I looked all over 4 or 5 block for a drug store that was still open to get some thing to dress it with, but they had all closed. So I went back to the garage where the car was stored & got my Listerine & a handkerchief and fixed it up with that.

Donald R Wax

I put all of your things in the little house. And in the evenings I am going to clean it up and move the bed & dresser in.

Well Honey its time to go to bed so I'll sign off.

XXXXX   With Lots of Love,

Your old Man

(More extra large Xs)

Son Of Montana

Stevensville, Mont.

July 20, 1038

Dearest Helen,

Well its time to write to the Mrs., vat you tink?

I've been rather busy lately making hay. We got thru cutting & raking Monday, and Tues. we began the stacking. After we get thru here at the home place then we will start on that 150 acres across the road from home. De has 40 acres here and it sure was thick. We figure it might run 2 ton to the acre.

You know I wrote you & said that that boil was all well. It did look that way then, but it has broke 3 or 4 times since the first time – there in Butte. I think there might be a ingrown whisker in it. If it don't quit breaking I think I'll see if Dr Nelson can fix it. It isn't bad just a mean pimple.

Sat. nite Frank & I went to town & every one I saw was asking when you were coming. I guess the news is all over the Bitter Root by now.

You know I have never written & told Doris yet, I suppose Ma has though.

I didn't have much time to write the last time so I'll look over your last letter to see if I missed any thing.

Oh yak, I all most forgot to tell you that I was out cherrie stealing last night. We got back 15 to 11 with about a gallon of cherries besides what we ate.

As I was looking over your letter I saw some writing inside & after it was tore open I found that little note. Well I'm glad that every thing was OK at the office. And it sure is the bunk that Mrs. Higgins didn't hire you, ain't it? I didn't think there was a very big chance for you, because it seems that some of these people don't care to have outsiders come in here. But we don't care Honey you have your credits & grade points so if its necessary for you to teach you won't have so much school work to do to get your diploma.

I showed DeMotts that paper clipping the other morning. They wished us luck.

Did you say that your school would be out the 11th? The creamery picnic is on the 11th. Wished you could be here to go with me. I don't suppose I'll go at all now.

Well Frank is rearin to go take a swim guess I'll go along. Honey I sure am glad we don't have to live so far from each other. Now we will be side by side. And I so glad that you are happy. I'm always going to try to keep you that way too.

Well good nite Darling. XXX

With Lots of Love & Xs

Your old Man

Bill.

Mom's Notes

Mom's Note 1

We were married July 3, 1938 at my parent's home. Stayed there that nite & on to Roundup on July 4th & to Billings July 5 where I was attending normal school. Bill continued on to Stevi where he lived with his folks. He drove their car over. I came from Billings to Stevi on Aug 11th. Paulsons, some of the Maginis (Emma Gene & Chas) Paul & Evelyn & maybe the Michaels had a chivaree for us one night a wk so later. In Sept Mrs Ralph Kramer had a misc. wedding shower for me. Myrtle Pope, Mrs. Magini, Mrs. Miller, Nell Cook, Evelyn, Ann Pope, Lorene Mc., Evelyn Magini (maybe) were some of the guests. We stayed at Ben Magini's place (Carl & Mamie's) for a month or so in Sept or Oct.

We traded a horse (old Ned) for a young black cow.

In Apr. 1939 Mrs. Magini had a baby shower for me. She & Edith (Magini) Jensen made a pretty lined & padded basket. In Aug. Mother Wax & I had a baby shower for Doris Kester. We had a boy – they had a girl. In July or Aug. Pearl came to visit for a week with Mrs. Uhl & Hirth – they only stayed and hour or less & drove on to Wash to see Helen Vannoy.

Donald R Wax

Mother's Day card to Carrie Wax, (mother-in-law) 1944.

If there's any special joy
You want to come your way,
If there's any special wish
You'd like fulfilled to-day,

If there's any special hope
You'd like to have come true - -
From the bottom of my heart,
I wish them all for you!

Signed **Bill & Helen**

How are you all? We are fine now again after our flu & colds. We are all busy. I set 4 hens last nite. Have 18 chicks so far. Bill is picking rock today. He finished irrigating yesterday. He took 12 fat hogs to Missoula a few weeks ago & got $337 for them. Has 12

more ready to go next week. Patsy walks all over now and sure gets into things. Donnie is 5 today & Normie will be 4 tomorrow. Am having a party for them tomorrow P.M. Will have Magini's two girls, Jackie Harr & 4 more neighbor kids. Would like to come up but guess we can't take a day off now unless Bill hauls the hogs up himself. You folks come down when you can.

Mom's Note 2

Never had a bathroom 'till I was 32 years old - none at home & none here after Bill & I were married until 1945. Bill & I didn't have a car, just went with his folks or used theirs until in the fall of 1939 or spring of 1940. We had an old grey Ford Gideon which we must have used until in the fall of 1940 or spring of '41 we bought a brown Chevy sedan in Hamilton & made a trip to Jordan in fall '41.

The folks had just bought Otto Smith's old house & were adding it to our house which had originally been my grandparents homestead house near Jordan & which Dad and Grandpa moved to Dick Capwell's place (which we had rented & lived on for 3 yrs).

Had that Chevy till we bought a new green '48 Chevy in Hamilton which was wrecked in Dec. 1951 at intersection of Burnt Fork & Eastside rds. Then bought a dk. Blue from Jim's Cars in Msla. Donnie was back-ended in Victor with it which caused problem with body. Then bought an aqua colored V8 Chev. Sedan. Norm wrecked it when on leave from Marines in 59 or 60. He paid $1100 to have it fixed. In '62 we bought a brown Galaxy in Ham. Skippy & Fido got shut in it one night & ripped the inside to ribbons. Sold it to Lavon & Chuck for $1. Then bought a wh. Ford Galaxy in Msla. (a'72) for $3400+. Had over 100,000+ miles when we traded it in at Bill McCall for an Br. 84 LTD. We had gone on many trips with the Galaxy – Roanoke, D.C., CA & AZ. In 89 we traded in the LTD for a Taurus (silver). Sold it in 1994 & bought a wh. Taurus (1992).

Ross McIntyre

Born Nov 19, 1907 – Died Dec 14, 2000

One of the first persons to visit us when we moved from eastern Montana to the Sunset Bench near Stevensville was Ross McIntyre. He was a friendly single fellow born and raised in the hills east of our small home willing to share his knowledge about farming logging and hunting practices of the neighborhood which Bill gladly accepted.

We married in July 1938 and Ross and Jean married in Nov 1938, and for 60 years they have remained staunch and true friends through good and bad times. Everyone was always welcomed to their home day or night with a hot cup of coffee and one of Jean's famous cookies or a piece of cake.

Ross was always "Johnny on the spot" if you needed help or to borrow any item. Ross was a role model for our three sons and probably many other boys in this county.

We spent many enjoyable times with Ross and Jean on trips, card games, etc. Bill loved their hunting trips, mountain hikes and working together. We will miss you Ross. May you rest in peace.

Note by Helen Zimmerman Wax for funeral services in December, 2000

ABOUT THE AUTHOR

The author retired in 1999 after a 30 year career with General Electric working as a technician, field engineer and manager installing control systems in steel mills. He lived in a number of different countries and traveled widely during his career and in retirement. He has many different interests but has spent more time recently writing about his family's history and preserving old photos. His first effort was a Wax family history book "Descendants of Peter Wax" which was distributed in 3-ring binders to historical societies and libraries. His second was a book of photos of his maternal grandparents and each of their descendants distributed to relatives on CD. This book "Son of Montana" is the first to be published.

Contact the author: donwax@aol.com